Detecting Wimsey

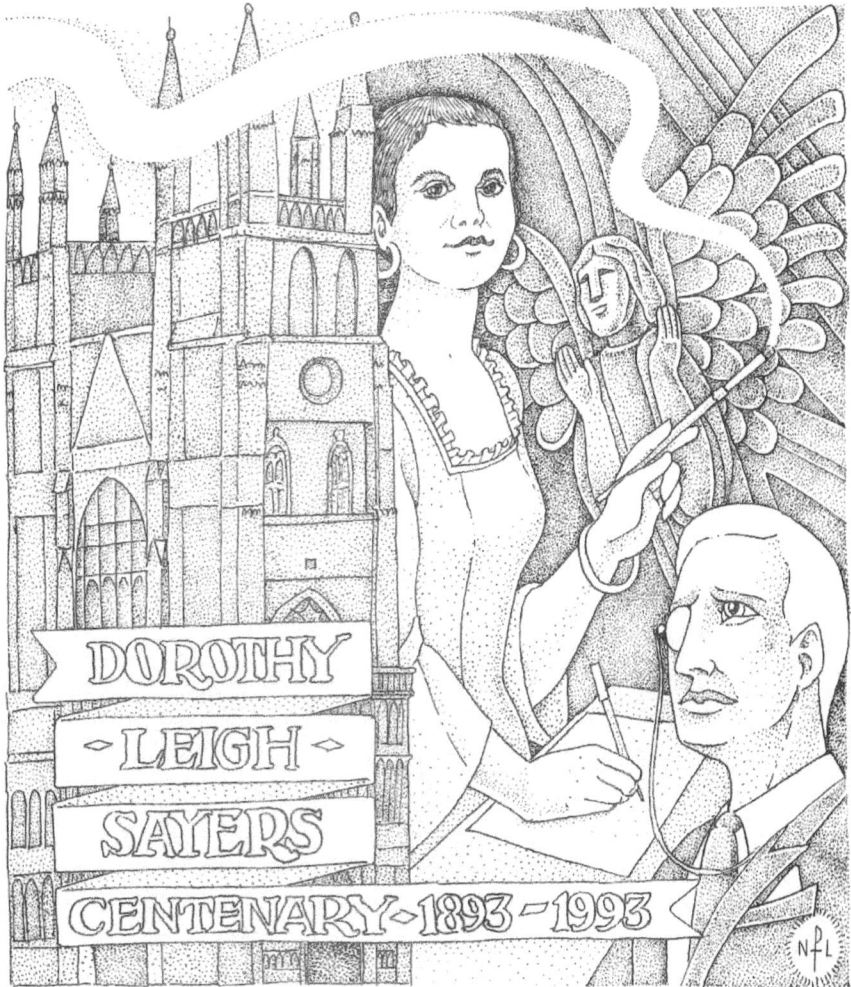

DOROTHY
· LEIGH ·
SAYERS
CENTENARY · 1893 – 1993

Detecting Wimsey
Papers on Dorothy L. Sayers's Detective Fiction

by

Nancy-Lou Patterson

Editors

Emily E. Auger

and

Janet Brennan Croft

Valleyhome Books

First Printing 2017
Second Printing with minor corrections 2020
The pronoun has been corrected to clarify Fleming's death date of 1950 (197), the publication dates for the first books of poetry published by Sayers (1916) and C.S. Lewis (1919) have been clarified (232); and *The Attenbury Emeralds* (2010) has been added to the list of books by Walsh (257).

Detecting Wimsey: Papers on Dorothy L. Sayers's Detective Fiction
Hardcover ISBN 978-1-987919-11-0
Paperback ISBN 978-1-987919-12-7
EPub ISBN 978-1-987919-13-4

Table of Contents

Abbreviations for Dorothy L. Sayers's Fiction

Detective Fiction by Dorothy L. Sayers

WB   *Whose Body?* 1923. London: Victor Gollancz, 1977.

CW   *Clouds of Witness.* 1926. London: Victor Gollancz, 1978.

UD   *Unnatural Death.* 1927. London: Victor Gollancz, 1979.

UBC   *Unpleasantness at the Bellona Club.* 1928. London: Victor Gollancz, 1975.

DC   *The Documents in the Case.* With Robert Eustace. 1930. London: Victor Gollancz, 1978. [This is the only one of Sayers's detective novels that does not feature Lord Peter Wimsey.]

SP   *Strong Poison.* London: Victor Gollancz, 1930.

FRH   *Five Red Herrings.* London: Victor Gollancz, 1931.

HHC   *Have His Carcase.* 1932. London: Victor Gollancz, 1979. [The 1976 and 1979 Victor Gollanz editions are identical.]

MMA   *Murder Must Advertise*: *A Detective Story.* 1933. London: Victor Gollancz, 1979.

NT   *The Nine Tailors: Changes Rung on An Old Theme in Two Short Touches and Two Full Peals.* 1934. London: Gollancz, 1975.

GN   *Gaudy Night.* 1935. London: Victor Gollancz, 1979.

BH   *Busman's Honeymoon: A Love Story with Detective Interruptions.* 1937. London: Victor Gollancz, 1976

MK   *The Man Born to be King: A Play-Cycle on the Life of our Lord and Saviour Jesus Christ.* Written for broadcasting by the BBC Dec. 1941–Oct. 1942. London: Victor Gollancz, 1943.

TD   Thrones, Dominations. Unpublished manuscript in the Marion E. Wade Collection, Wheaton College, Wheaton, Illinois, 37A.

Anthologies of short stories by Dorothy L. Sayers

PVB   *Lord Peter Views the Body*. 1928. London: Victor Gollancz, 1979.

A collection of 12 short stories. Those mentioned in this volume include the following:

"The Abominable History of the Man with Copper Fingers." 5-26.

"The Entertaining Episode of the Article in Question." 27-39.

"The Undignified Melodrama of The Bone of Contention." 93-159.

"The Vindictive Story of the Footsteps that Ran." 161-180.

"The Adventurous Exploit of the Cave of Ali Baba." 283-317.

HH   *Hangman's Holiday*. 1933. London: Victor Gollancz, 1971.

A collection of short stories, including four Wimsey stories:

"The Image in the Mirror." 7-46

"The Incredible Elopement of Lord Peter Wimsey." 47-86.

"The Queen's Square." 87-114.

"The Necklace of Pearls." 115-132.

LP   *Lord Peter: A Collection of All the Lord Peter Wimsey Stories*. Ed. and Introduction by James Sandoe. First edition. New York: Harper Paperbacks, 1972.

Includes "The Haunted Policeman" 408-30. The first edition includes twenty Lord Peter stories. The second edition adds "Talboys," making twenty-one stories.

SF   *Striding Folly*. London: New English Library, 1972.

An anthology including Janet Hitchman's "Introduction: Lord Peter Wimsey and His Creator," and the three final Wimsey stories, "Striding Folly," "The Haunted Policeman," and "Talboys" 92-123.

Introduction: Nancy-Lou Patterson's Wimsical Scholarship

Nancy-Lou Patterson's scholarly interests in literature were almost exclusively centered on mythopoeic fantasy. She wrote essays and reviews of secondary literature on C.S. Lewis's adult and juvenile fiction, Charles Williams's supernatural thrillers, J.R.R. Tolkien's high fantasies about Middle-earth, works by George MacDonald, Lloyd Alexander, Madeleine L'Engle, and other fantasy authors. So why was she interested in a series of relatively realistic detective novels—interested enough that her scholarship fills a fairly hefty volume, even without her many reviews of secondary and scholarly literature on Sayers (which will be collected in a later volume in this series)?

Patterson found that many of the same themes she looked for and studied in fantasy literature abounded in Sayers's Wimsey novels, and that is what she wrote about: patterns of reference to literature, to Greek and other mythologies, and to the Bible and Anglican theology; developmental and interpersonal motifs that invited Jungian interpretation; mystical aspects of the novels that resonated with her interests in shamanism, the hero's journey, and women's spiritual issues. She also viewed Sayers's mysteries in the context of her life's body of work—her earlier poetry, her later apologetics, liturgical dramas, and Dante translations—and found similar motifs and concerns throughout.

While Sayers did not consciously create myth in the sense Tolkien or Lewis did, she used archetypes and mythic resonances to both drive and demonstrate the transformations of her characters, and had similar opinions on "continuity [with earlier literature] as an essential attribute of the creative process"[1] and on creativity and sub-creation more generally. Sayers was a close friend of several of the Inklings, the other authors Patterson primarily studied (though not a member of that exclusively male group itself), and this would have made her interesting even if she hadn't been a writer of considerable talent and merit on her own. In the terms Diana Pavlac Glyer (2007) uses in her studies of the Inklings as a writing group, Sayers's frequent thoughtful correspondence with Williams and Lewis makes her an important *Resonator* for these two writers; she and Lewis were often *Editors* of each other's work; Williams was a major *Influence* on her Dante scholarship and translation; as an active member of the Socratic Club she very likely served as an *Opponent* in debates with several of the Inklings; and she was a *Collaborator* with Lewis on his volume *Essays Presented to Charles Williams*, contributing a Dante essay.[2]

Additionally, and perhaps most importantly, both Patterson and Sayers interpreted and defended the mystery novel genre as both mythopoeic and as a Mystery, capital M. To quote extensively from one of Patterson's *Mythlore* review essays:

> Although Sayers is not mentioned in Eric S. Rabkin's study of *The Fantastic in Literature* (1976), detective fiction is. And it is discussed in the context, and as a part of, fantasy; so eminent a writer as W.H. Auden is quoted to point out that the underlying myth of detective fiction is the Garden of Eden. Detective fiction in fact grew out of the same garden as other nineteenth-century fantasy: that plantation of post-romantic forms which includes the gothic novel, the thriller, and the tale of horror, as well as the mythopoeic fantasies of George MacDonald and the medievalizing tales of William Morris, both of which directly influenced Lewis and Tolkien. Charles Williams's works can scarcely be understood without reference to the former tradition: they are detective/thriller/mythopoeia all at the same time, beginning with the corpse in *War in Heaven*. […]
>
> On such a basis, discussion of Sayers's works belongs in *Mythlore* […]. Her qualifications, however, surpass her association with the Mythopoeic Triumvirate. […]
>
> If I may skirt blasphemy, I am reminded of Jung's joy when he perceived that the Dogma of the Assumption of the Virgin Mary raised the Feminine Principle to convert the Trinity into a quadripartite whole. What reads as richly masculine in Tolkien, Lewis, and Williams, reads as richly feminine in Sayers, without the slightest waver of orthodoxy or power.[3]

The arrangement of the first section of this volume, "Transformations and Transgressions," provides an overview of Lord Peter Wimsey's character arc in a (mostly) chronological consideration of the novels and stories Patterson felt were most important and resonated most strongly with the themes that interested her. "'All Nerves and Nose'" outlines the way in which Peter can be read as a "wounded healer" throughout the sequence, providing a solid basis for discussions of *Strong Poison, Have His Carcase, Murder Must Advertise, The Nine Tailors, and Busman's Honeymoon*. His courtship of and eventual marriage to Harriet Vane is of course essential to his development, and Harriet's own growth and transformation is not neglected. In "Eve's Sharp Apple," the "transgressing women" of the series—the villainesses in their varying degrees of sinfulness—are examined. The final essay in this sequence, on love and marriage in the unfinished *Thrones, Dominations*, synthesizes the whole, and is particularly interesting as it was written well before Jill Paton Walsh's attempt to complete and finish the novel.

The second section, "Reflections," addresses broader issues in Sayers's writing: how her upbringing, education, and romantic entanglements influenced her mysteries; problematic issues of anti-Semitism and racism in her writing; her spirituality; and her place in her time and in the literary movements of contemporary England and Oxford. In this section in particular we find that Nancy-Lou Patterson was not blind to Sayers's faults and did not shy from addressing them critically; the contradictions between her somewhat Bohemian youth and her moral beliefs are considered in both "'A Bloomsbury Blue-Stocking'" and "'Cat o' Mary,'" and her problematic usage of racial stereotypes in "Images of Judaism and Anti-Semitism."

Overall, Patterson is an astute critic of Dorothy L. Sayers, with a similar tidiness of mind and a fine attunement to character, spiritual and psychological systems of symbolism, and women's issues and spirituality. Her clear, direct, and fair-minded writing style and mastery of a broad range of scholarly reference are a fine match for her subject.

——Janet Brennan Croft

Notes

[1] Diana Pavlac Glyer, *The Company They Keep: C.S. Lewis and J.R.R. Tolkien as Writers in Community* (Kent OH: Kent State UP, 2007) 222.

[2] Glyer, throughout but especially p. 23n21.

[3] Nancy-Lou Patterson, "Sayers's Best Pieces of Theology," "Rev. of Gaillard, Dawson, *Dorothy L. Sayers,* and Panek, Leroy Lad, *Watteau's Shepherds: The Detective Novel in Britain 1914–1940,*" *Mythlore* 9.4 (#34) (1983): 44. "Why We Honor the Centenary of Dorothy L. Sayers (1893-1957)," pages 231-236 in this volume, covers many of the same points and more.

Editorial Notes

This anthology includes all of Nancy-Lou Patterson's papers on Dorothy L. Sayers's Lord Peter Wimsey novels and stories that we have located. We have collected her numerous reviews on books related to Sayers and her work under a separate cover. Patterson cites all of the books that she reviewed about Sayers, except Jane Chance, ed., *Medievalism: Inklings and Others* (Studies in Medievalism 3:3/4) 1991. Publication information for these reviews has been added to the bibliography citations of this volume. Patterson's review of *Medievalism: Inklings and Others* may be found in *Mythlore* 19.2 (#72) (1993): 36-37.

The epigraphs are from the original papers, but the abstracts and credit paragraphs at the beginning of each paper are additions. A few minor editorial changes and deletions were made to improve the uniformity of the scholarly authorial "voice" of some of the papers. The other changes or corrections were of a technical nature. The citations to the novels have been adjusted so that, wherever possible, they refer to the Victor Gollancz editions. Where possible, quotations and sources have been checked and corrected as needed. Bibles, dictionaries, and the Thrones, Dominations manuscript citations have been left as Patterson gave them. In the instances where corrections to other citations and sources were required and editions were in doubt, the edition has been updated or citations added to those that were available for checking.

By way of acknowledgements, I want to thank my co-editor Janet Brennan Croft, editor of *Mythlore*: without her interest in Patterson's work and generous contributions (introduction, index, and appendix, and a large part of the source-checking research) this collection would simply never have come to publication. E Palmer Patterson and his daughters Fanny, Melanie, and Samantha have also been very supportive and generous with their time and interest. Laura Schmidt, of the Marion E. Wade Center of Wheaton College, Illinois, was happy to resolve a proofing issue involving Sayers's unfinished Thrones, Dominations manuscript. The Special Collections Librarians at the University of Waterloo provided access to the relevant papers. All of the librarians with whom I came in contact at the Universities of Guelph, Waterloo, and Sir Wilfrid Laurier were extraordinarily helpful and interested in supporting this project.

Transformations and Transgressions

Nancy-Lou Patterson. "Shamanic Descents of Lord Peter Wimsey" and
"Shamanic Ascents of Lord Peter Wimsey."
Mythlore 14.4 (Summer 1988): 14 and 15. Further reproduction prohibited.

1. "All Nerves and Nose": Lord Peter Wimsey as Wounded Healer in the Novels of Dorothy L. Sayers

"Fifteen of us, marching across a prickly desert, and we were all chained together [...] I saw the bones of my own feet, and they were black, because we had been hanged in chains a long time ago."

——Lord Peter Wimsey in *Busman's Honeymoon*

In "All Nerves and Nose" Patterson examines the character and biography of Lord Peter Wimsey in Sayers's novels with special attention to his turn to detective work as a way to overcome and heal himself from the psychological damage he suffered during the war, particularly from being buried alive. She draws comparisons with elements of shamanism, including flight, birds, and the cosmic tree, and then considers the influence his war experiences have on his attraction to and relationship with Harriet Vane.

"All Nerves and Nose" was first published in Mythlore *14.4 (Summer 1988): 13-16.*

Dorothy L. Sayers's first detective novel, *Whose Body?* (1923), opens with the words, "Oh, Damn!" (WB 17; ch. 1) spoken by Lord Peter Wimsey. The jauntiness, affectiveness, and whimsicality of his personality dominate the first half of the novel, but in Chapter VIII, Lord Peter awakens his valet Bunter "in the small hours" with a "hoarse whisper": he raves, "Listen! Oh, my God! I can't hear—I can't hear anything for the noise of the guns. Can't they stop the guns?" (WB 198-99; ch. 8). Bunter responds, "It's all right, Major," and gradually restores his dreaming master to normal sleep. For those who first read the novel within five years of the war's end, this striking scene was a touch of sharp realism in a work that is otherwise relatively light in tone despite its macabre subject matter. But there is more to this motif than realism.

I would suggest that the key to Lord Peter's detective career is his burial alive and rescue in World War I. He has returned, as it were, from the dead. After a period of complete breakdown, he finds a way of recovery through detective investigation. This factor is introduced in *Whose Body?*, and in nearly every other of the eleven novels in which he appears, a central or major clue is revealed in a scene in which his special *bona fides* as a "wounded healer," one familiar with death, is invoked.

The phrase "wounded healer" is borrowed from the language of shamanism, the oldest of human religious systems. Its structure is deeply rooted in the human psyche: through the many phases and variations of religious history its permutations continue to express themselves, not least in Christianity. The concept of the "suffering servant," enshrined in Isaiah 53, is understood by Christians as an Old Testament prefiguration of the role of Christ as one whose sufferings enable the healing of others. When Lord Peter, as an *alter Christus*, becomes an agent of justice, he does so in an exchange of pain and both sinned-against and sinning.

Joan Halifax (1981) describes "the inner journey shamans take during a life crisis and the ways in which they order the chaos and confusion of the voyage into Cosmos."[1] Like the "great detectives," shamans have power through a knowledge deeper and higher than that of other people. This knowledge is awakened in a series of stages. First, "the call to power necessitates a separation from the mundane world."[2] In the case of Lord Peter, this separation takes him from aristocratic England to the muddy trenches of France.

Lord Peter has made "the descent to the Realm of Death"; he has undergone the requisite "trial by fire,"—gunfire—and he has been submitted to the "assimilation of the elemental forces,"[3] specifically, to burial alive in the earth. There is a sexual element in this downward way, a "sacred marriage with the untamed spirit of the opposite sex."[4] This marriage sequence begins for Lord Peter with the moment when he conceives an instant attraction for a girl who is accused of murder—Harriet Vane—in the novel *Strong Poison* (1930), and ends with their marriage in the final novel, *Busman's Honeymoon* (1937). The theme of Lord Peter's shell-shock experience is gradually woven together with this developing love during intervening novels, and in the concluding novel, the final healing of Lord Peter himself is experienced in Harriet's arms.

In the "sacred way of the wounded healer" which Lord Peter follows, "the map of the hidden cosmos is revealed. The paths to and from the realm of death are repeatedly traversed."[5] In particular, "It is through dreams and visions that the purely sacred is often attained."[6] Both the first novel, *Whose Body?,* and the last novel, *Busman's Honeymoon,* contain significant dreams. In the latter, Harriet greets her husband as they waken in their honeymoon cottage: "Peter, what were you dreaming about early this morning? It sounded pretty awful" (BH 363; ch. 19) and he replies, "Fifteen of us, marching across a prickly desert, and we were all chained together [...] I saw the bones of my own feet, and they were black, because we had been hanged in chains a long time ago." He explains: "It was only the old responsibility-dream" (BH 364; ch. 19).

The specific contents of this dream are directly related to vital clues in the solution of the murder, specifically the "prickly desert," and the chain that binds the marchers. But Sayers links the broader imagery to the state of spiritual as well as physical death. For Lord Peter, it was the responsibility that broke him during the war. The Dowager Duchess explains it to Harriet: "He doesn't like responsibility, you know," she says, "and the War and one thing and another was bad for people that way. [...] I suppose if you've been giving orders for nearly four years to people to go and get blown to pieces it gives you a—what does on call it nowadays?—an inhibition" (BH 426-27; Epithalamion, part 2). But it has been his detective work, with all its inherent responsibility, which has healed him. His uncle's biographical account of him says that he is "all nerves and nose," and this exactly sums him up: "nerves" is the most common term used in the novels for Lord Peter's condition, and his "nose," poked curiously into so many hidden places, forms the cutting edge, as it were, of his detectival procedure.

Halifax explains: "The psyche that is emotionally saturated organizes itself by means of mythological conceptions that form an explanatory system which gives significance and direction to human suffering."[7] In the shamanic sphere the mythological conceptions are expressed in the shaman's downward paths, embodying the immanent and the transcendent ways. There are two examples of the downward path in the novels. Most obvious is the experience in France, recalled in *Gaudy Night* (1934) when Lord Peter meets the door-keeper of Harriet's Oxford college, who unexpectedly greets him: "Good night, Major Wimsey, sir!" (GN 370; ch. 17). Peter replies, "Last time I saw you, I was being carried away on a stretcher." "That's right, sir,"

Padgett agrees: "I 'ad the pleasure of 'elping to dig you out." Peter answers ruefully, "Unpleasant sensation, being buried alive."

This experience is reiterated in *Clouds of Witness* (1926) as Lord Peter scours heaven and hell—overworld and underworld—to save his brother from the gallows. As Lord Peter and Bunter walk across the moors, a fog comes up: "How long that nightmare lasted neither of them could have said" (CW 224; ch. 11). The relationship of this sequence to their war experiences is made clear by the shriek of a horse: "They remembered having heard horses scream like that. There had been a burning stable near Poperinghe—" (CW 224; ch. 11); and at this moment, Peter stumbles into a bog. Bunter saves his master from this plight with the help of farmer Grimethorpe: "To Lord Peter the memory of his entry that night into the farmhouse at Grider's Hole always brought with it a sensation of nightmare" (CW 229; ch. 12). Nightmare again, you see. In the morning, Peter arises and finds the detectival clue—in that very bedroom—which will save his brother's life.

The shaman's upward path, which leads to the heavens, is also followed by Lord Peter in *Clouds of Witness*. In shamanic tradition, this can take two forms: flight, symbolized by association with birds, and climbing the cosmic tree, which is the analogue of the vertical structure of the cosmos. It is flight which figures powerfully in the concluding chapters of *Clouds of Witness*: the "bird" is an airplane, in which Lord Peter and an intrepid aviator cross the Atlantic with a final piece of evidence, a year before such a trip was actually taken for the first time by Charles Lindburgh.

The motif of the shamanic ascent is given its most forceful expression in *The Nine Tailors* (1934) when at the climactic moment of the novel, Lord Peter climbs the bell tower of Fenchurch St. Paul, to receive his terrible revelation of how the victim in the novel met his death. Peter exits the bell chamber "Staggering, feeling as though his bones were turned to water, and with blood running from his nose and ears" (NT 344; ch. 4 part 2) and "as he flung the door to behind him, the demonic clamour sank back into the pit." Bones, blood, demons, the pit: this is the very constellation of shamanic imagery of the initiatory ordeal. Lord Peter's agony is not gratuitous: as a bell-ringer, he himself has been an unknowing agent of death. The note of responsibility, sounded again and again in the novels, emerges here with all its ironic implications.

One can follow the responsibility motif throughout the series: it becomes a central feature in the third novel, *Unnatural Death* (1927). Here, Peter is looking for his detectival assistant, Miss Alexandra Climpson, and his search brings him to her parish church, St. Onesimus. Seated with the rector, Mr. Tredgold, in the churchyard, on a recumbent slab which covers a dead body, Lord Peter asks about the culpability of a murderer who has given "a little push off, so to speak" (UD 228; ch. 19), to a dying woman. Mr. Tredgold, who like all Sayers's clergy is fit to tread golden streets of Heaven, replies that "Sin is in the intention, not the deed" (UD 229; ch. 19).

Peter's deeper concern now emerges—there has been a second murder because he has pursued the murderer for the first, but Mr. Tredgold advises him to "Leave the consequences to God. And try to think charitably, even of wicked people" (UD 229-30; ch. 19). The rector "watched him as he trotted away between the graves. 'Dear, dear,' he said, 'how nice they are [...] And much more nervous and sensitive than people think'" (UD 230; ch. 19). The graves with their hint of death and burial are combined with a recognition of Lord Peter's nerves. We learn later that Miss Climpson, as Lord Peter's surrogate, has in fact received a revelation of the murderer's identity on her visit to St. Onesimus Church. Curiously, in the light of Halifax's statement that the shamanic "journey's mythic end is the sun,"[8] *Unnatural Death* concludes with an eclipse of the sun. Lord Peter's distress has not yet been erased; that awaits the moment of sunrise with which the final novel, *Busman's Honeymoon*, concludes.

Lord Peter continues to suffer remorse for the events in *Unnatural Death* in *Gaudy Night*, when, chatting about his investigations in the common room of Shrewsbury College, he speaks about "my own victims," those killed by the murderer he had pursued in the previous case (GN 355; ch. 17). Later in the same conversation, Miss de Vine tells a story of one of her own "victims" of interference, thus revealing an essential clue to the mystery of the College's Poison Pen. The common theme of these conversations is the nightmare of responsibility, the dark side of Lord Peter's self-cure through detective investigation. As Paul Delagardie is made to say in his biographical note: "You cannot get murderers hanged for your private entertainment. Peter's intellect pulled him one way and his nerves another, till I began to be afraid they would pull him to pieces. At the end of every case we had the old nightmares and shell-shock over again" (WB 10).

The fourth novel, which follows *Unnatural Death* in the series, is the *Unpleasantness at the Bellona Club* (1928). Here shell-shock arises from reiterated motif to central theme, embodied in Captain George Fentiman. The first chapter of this novel closes with the discovery of the dead body of George Fentiman's ninety-year-old grandfather, lying in repose before the fire-place. In a grotesque response to this event, George is led out screaming, "We're all dead and we never noticed it!" (UBC 19; ch. 1). In contrast with the shock of the elderly club members, "The younger men felt no sense of outrage; they knew too much" (UBC 20; ch. 2). Eventually, George suffers a major breakdown; he wanders away from home, enters a police station, and gives himself up as the murderer. The police surgeon sums it up: "Nervous shock with well-marked delusions" (UBC 271; ch. 21). At this moment the central clue to the real murderer is revealed.

With the next Wimsey novel, *Strong Poison* (1930), a new element is introduced: Harriet Vane. Lord Peter's distress now becomes focused on her. He loves her because, under threat of death herself, she alone can understand him—if only she will. But of course his importunate proposal of marriage, made in the prison interview room, thrusts her away; she cannot accept him under these circumstances.

In his investigation of the case, the word "nightmare" signals his distress: he "was accustomed to say, when he was an old man and more talkative even than usual, that the recollection of that Christmas at Duke's Denver had haunted him in nightmares, every night regularly, for the following twenty years" (SP 146; ch. 12).[9] The Christmas at Denver is thus, not unexpectedly, an occasion for the revelation of an important clue. The novel concludes, after a sleepless night of meditation by Wimsey, with, first, the rising of the sun—"the reluctant winter dawn struggled wanly over the piled roofs of London," and second, the solution to the murder.

In the six novels following this pivotal book, the shell-shock motif is increasingly interwoven with the love theme. The process begins with a diffusion of affect, in which the symbolic elements are displaced or projected to other characters. In *The Five Red Herrings* (1931), the various elements—military memories, shock, and

"Nerves" (FRH 256; ch. 22) as well as an apology to the accused, are present, but only the last of these is experienced by Lord Peter.

The primary investigator in *Have His Carcase* (1932) is Harriet, who has also gone on holiday—a "solitary walking-tour" (HHC 7; ch. 1), where on "a solitary rock" she discovers a solitary corpse. After reporting it, she checks into a resort hotel, where she is surprised to encounter Lord Peter when she descends to the dining room for breakfast. In the next to the last chapter there is a striking reference to Lord Peter's war: "Ever seen a horse that has suddenly had fresh blood splashed all over it? Not pretty. Definitely not" (HHC 437; ch. 33).[10] This reminiscence immediately precedes a vital revelation about the murder victim.

Lord Peter is on his own again in *Murder Must Advertise* (1933), fulfilling the shaman's role as shape-shifter in three disguises: he assumes the role of Mr. Death Bredon, a mild-mannered copywriter, the role of his own fictitious cousin, a dangerous dope-dealer, and the role—most appropriately—of Harlequin. Sayers writes, "From this abominable impersonation he could now free himself, since at the sound of his name or the sight of his unmasked face, all the doors in that other dream-city—the city of dreadful night—would be closed to him" (MMA 188; ch. 11). As might be expected, there is a clue in this hell: "One other piece of information Dian had indeed given him, but at that moment he could not interpret it" (MMA 189; ch. 11).

By contrast in *Gaudy Night* Harriet is very much the central figure. She is invited to her Oxford college to investigate an escalating series of incidents, and this time, Lord Peter having learned his lesson, she goes alone. Finally, well into the novel, she looks up and there he is. The themes of love and death now come together, and as the novel concludes, they are engaged.

Finally, in *Busman's Honeymoon*, they are married. When the "detective interruptions" are concluded, they drive to Lord Peter's ancestral home, where the dowager duchess describes in detail the course of his original breakdown. The novel concludes with the night before the execution of the murderer. Lord Peter has been out driving, and then sitting in the kitchen, shivering, while Harriet waits to see if he will come to her of his own accord. He finds his peace at last, while "Through the eastern side of the casement, the sky grew pale with the forerunners of dawn" (BH 445; Epithalamion, part 3). In an echo of his first words in the first novel, "Quite suddenly, he said, 'Oh, damn!' and began to cry— […] so she held him, crouched at her knees, against her breast" (BH 446; Epithalamion, part 3). Thus these two familiars of death find healing in one another's arms.

Notes
[1] Joan Halifax, *Shaman: The Wounded Healer* (London: Thames and Hudson, 1981) 5.
[2] Halifax 6.
[3] Halifax 7.
[4] Halifax 7.
[5] Halifax 16.
[6] Halifax 16.
[7] Halifax 19.
[8] Halifax 24.
[9] Advancing age is a central motif in this novel: see also "'Changing, Fearfully Changing': Polarization and Transformation in Dorothy L. Sayers's *Strong Poison*" (1985).
[10] See Philip L. Scowcroft, "Wimsey's War," *Sidelights on Sayers* 1 (July 1981): 16-21 (Witham, Essex, England: The Dorothy L. Sayers Historical and Literary Society, 1981), for a discussion of Lord Peter's war.

2.   "Changing, Fearfully Changing": Polarization and Transformation in Dorothy L. Sayers's *Strong Poison*

"To my wife, who can make an Omelette."

——Atherton Fleming, *Gourmet's Book of Food and Drink* (1933)[1]

Patterson analyzes the structural aspects of Strong Poison, *specifically life and death, not as oppositions only, but as a set in which one aspect may become the other. She considers such apparent opposites as good and ill, fresh and spoiled (or poisoned), truth and lie, and real and fake in such varied contexts as omelette making, séances, thievery, the consumption of food and drink, and Harriet's relationship to Peter. In all of these examples, she shows that the element of change may transform any falsity to truth.*

Patterson also addresses the theme of falseness transforming into truth in "'Bloody Farce': Irony, Farce, and Mortality in Dorothy L. Sayers's* Have His Carcase" *and in the conclusions to* "'A Comedy of Masks': Lord Peter as Harlequin in* Murder Must Advertise" *and* "'A Ring of Good Bells': Providence and Judgment in Dorothy L. Sayers's* The Nine Tailors." *She applies a structural approach to the analysis of fiction in several of the papers anthologized in* Ransoming the Waste Land Volumes I and II.

"Changing, Fearfully Changing" was first published in the University of Waterloo Courier *(Sept. 1985): 11-17.*

Strong Poison is the sixth of Dorothy L. Sayers twelve detective novels. Harriet D. Vane, a detective novelist, is on trial for the murder of her lover, Philip Boyes. The plot is bracketed by two courtroom scenes, of which the first has two parts, one in which the judge describes the circumstances of the crime in detail, followed by one in which the jury cannot reach a verdict. In the second courtroom scene, Harriet is found innocent, due to the efforts of Lord Peter, who, having both fallen in love with her and intuited her innocence, has discovered (with a great deal of help) the true murderer.

Most commentators on Dorothy L. Sayers treat the sixth of her twelve detective novels, *Strong Poison*, in terms of its love interest.[2]

Sayers admitted to an "infanticidal" intention—she hoped to have done with her creation by marrying him off—but the interest of the novel for most critics is its introduction of Harriet and the consequences not only for the three more novels in which she appears, but for the changes in all the six novels that follow it, as Sayers moved toward what has been called "a novel of manners." Contrary to usual practice, I intend to discuss not the love theme as such, but—since the reader in 1930 knew nothing of the books to come—the novel itself in its own terms. I do this not *contra* other commentators (upon whose insights I have relied) but as an exercise in applying the techniques of structuralism to a novel which presents its structural elements very clearly.

Strong Poison concerns, for one of the few times in Lord Peter's experience, a truly life-and-death situation. In most cases, when someone has died—and he, by finding the murderer, brings about the killer's death too—it is a life-or-death situation for them but not for him. In *Strong Poison*, however, the woman he loves will die if he does not find the true murderer. The novel is, structurally, *about* the opposed pair LIFE/DEATH. As a novel is already "about" *time*, however, there is the forward-moving, time-factored element in which *change* becomes significant: the binary set must be either *LIFE becoming DEATH* or *DEATH becoming LIFE.*

"Please don't alter yourself"

In this novel, Lord Peter becomes aware of his own mortality, perhaps because the mortality of someone he loves has been so vividly demonstrated to him. This theme—of his own capacity for change, and the possibility that mutability equals mortality—is first hinted in Lord Peter's initial interview with Harriet. When he proposes, he asks her if he can make "Any minor alterations" in himself to please her.

> "Don't," said Miss Vane, "please don't alter yourself in any particular."
> "You really meant that? Wimsey flushed a little. (SP 56; ch. 4)

The significance of this exchange becomes apparent later, when Marjorie Phelps, his friend in Bloomsbury, intuiting his anxiety, exclaims:

"Peter—do please be happy. I mean, you've always been the comfortable sort of person that nothing could touch. Don't alter, will you?"

That was the second time Wimsey had been asked not to alter himself; the first time, the request had exalted him; this time, it terrified him. As the taxi lurched along the rainy Embankment, he felt for the first time the dull and angry helplessness which is the first warning stroke of the triumph of mutability. Like the poisoned Athulf in the *Fool's Tragedy*, he could have cried, "Oh, I am changing, changing, fearfully changing." (SP 103-104; ch. 8)

As Dawson Gaillard (1981) has commented, this theme is reiterated in the subsequent novels, and includes references to the culture in which Lord Peter lives as well as to the life he is leading.[3] In fact, however, not only are the novels still alive, Lord Peter himself is still with us, if his prediction in *Strong Poison*, and his personal time-frame (he was born in 1890) are applied: he remarks to Marjorie,

"Give me good food and a little air to breathe and I will caper, goat-like, to a dishonourable old age. People will point me out, as I creep, bald and yellow and supported by discreet corsetry, into the night-clubs of my great-grand-children, and they'll say, 'Look, darling! that's the wicked Lord Peter, celebrated for never having spoken a reasonable word for the last ninety-six years.'" (SP 104; ch. 8)

Lord Peter will reach the age of 96 in 1986, and it is likely that readers then will still find him delightful. The theme of mutability is reiterated in a description of Cremorna Garden's room. She is the old aunt of Philip Boyes, whose will and trust fund (the one falsified, and the other squandered by the murderer) have provided the motive for the killing:

It was the room of a woman [...] to whom the fact of possession had become the one steadfast reality in a world of loss and change. (SP 235; ch. 18)

Detectival Procedures: Intuition and Stealth

The detectival procedures of the novel turn more upon the "why?" and the "how?" than upon the "whom?" Several commentators have noted that the murderer is identified about mid-way through the novel.[4] In fact, he is proposed as the guilty party several times before that, and is first considered as a suspect by Lord Peter himself:

> "Who might have an insurable interest? His father, his cousin (possibly), other relations (if any), his children (if any), and—I suppose—Miss Vane." (SP 62; ch. 5)

In these musings he also comes upon an approximate version of the motive:

> "Dash it all, his cousin's a solicitor. Suppose he has been embezzling trust deeds or something, and Boyes was threatening to split on him? [...] Urquhart drops some arsenic into his soup and—ah! There's the snag. He puts arsenic into the soup and eats it himself. That's awkward." (SP 64; ch. 5)

After a second interview with Harriet, in which Lord Peter suggests to her the only scenario he can imagine that could implicate her, and satisfies himself logically, he muses:

> "How about this fellow Urquhart? He looked all right in court, but you never can tell. I think I'd better pop round and see him." (SP 85; ch. 7)

While preparing for this interview, which is delayed because Urquhart is away, Lord Peter sends out two agents—his valet Bunter to Urquhart's house, and someone from Miss Climpson's apparent employment and covert detective agency (which he sponsors) to Urquhart's office.

As Lord Peter continues his own investigations, a plain accusation of Urquhart's villainy is made by two of Harriet Vane's friends:

> "Have you seen the cousin yet—the Urquhart creature?"
>
> "Got an appointment with him for to-morrow. Why?"
>
> "Sylvia's theory is that he did it," said Eiluned.
>
> "That's interesting. Why?"
>
> "Female intuition," said Eiluned, bluntly. "She doesn't like the way he does his hair." (SP 106; ch. 8)

The crime is solved, in fact, by a combination of intuition—Lord Peter's that Harriet is innocent—and feminine stealth. The moment when

Lord Peter himself consciously suspects Urquhart occurs when for the second time he has noted, mechanically, the idiosyncrasies of a typewriter used by the solicitor for the purposes of forgery:

> For the first time, in this annoying case, he felt the vague stirring of the waters as a living idea emerged slowly and darkly from the inmost deeps of his mind. (SP 145; ch. 11)

The use of intuition and of feminine agents reinforces the importance of Lord Peter's intuitive relationship with Harriet, which is in its earliest and most inchoate stage in this novel, as it was in the mind of their creator, Sayers.

The fundamental dichotomy LIFE/DEATH and the possible transformation of one and the other, to produce change, loss, and gain, forms the central theme of *Strong Poison*, and figures in the basic situation—an innocent woman accused, and a guilty man discovered, and in the detectival methods employed. Lord Peter's contribution is a series of interviews: his aides include men (Bunter and Chief Inspector Parker) and a remarkable series of women. These women can be analyzed as figures for Harriet: they are all unmarried, career women.[5] But in addition, they employ false or illusory or illegal or (seemingly) occult or otherwise negative means to bring about a positive end. If we create a four-part diagram for the novel's structure we find this:

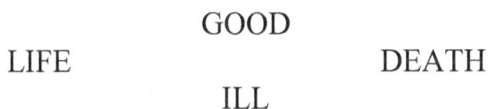

GOOD

LIFE   DEATH

ILL

In other terms, LIFE is to DEATH as GOOD is to ILL. In the novel a transformation takes place following this rule, as death yields to life, and ill to good. The discovery of the murderer gives life to Harriet (and hence to Lord Peter's hopes), and the ill means yield good ends. I have avoided the word "evil," preferring ill with its clear sense of goodness *manqué*.

The Structural Transformation of the Egg

Sayers has included a charming symbolic code for this structure in the details of the murder and the process of its detecting which will appear in the following analysis. Harriet Vane is accused of having killed her lover, Philip Boyes, by giving him a cup of coffee poisoned with arsenic. As Lord Peter intuits, the coffee was in fact harmless. The actual act of murder, the giving of an egg full of arsenic by Norman Urquhart to his cousin Philip Boyes, is described by the judge in Chapter 1:[6]

> "The final course was a sweet omelette, which was made at the table in a chafing-dish by Philip Boyes himself. Both Mr. Urquhart and his cousin were very particular about eating an omelette the moment it came from the pan—and a very good rule it is, and I advise you all to treat omelettes in the same way and never allow them to stand, or they will get tough. Four eggs were brought to the table in their shells, and Mr. Urquhart broke them one by one into a bowl, adding sugar with a sifter." (SP 18; ch. 1)

At this point Boyes is invited by Urquhart to take over; the eggs and sugar are beaten together, cooked in a chafing-dish, filled with hot jam, and shared by Boyes and Urquhart alone. Even the judge notes the fact that the omelette was, of that meal, "the only dish which did not go out to the kitchen" (SP 19; ch. 1) to be finished by the cook and the maid. Nothing of it was preserved for future analysis. It is customary in England to smash eggshells and dispose of them: Venetia Newall (1971), the British folklorist, records that "My husband, born in 1930, remembers being taught as a child to put his spoon through an empty egg-shell."[7]

When the judge completes his charge to the jury, they retire, and Lord Peter waits in an agony of anticipation for their return. He learns that Miss Climpson, an old acquaintance and associate, is delaying the jury's decision by refusing to find Harriet guilty:

> "Good egg," said Wimsey "Oh, excellent, excellent egg! She has a fearfully tough conscience—she may stick it out yet." (SP 42; ch. 3)

This is the first mention of eggs to follow their introduction into the plot in the form of an omelette: eggs are, in Wimsey's use of the conventional phrase, something good, even excellent. But the eggs for the omelette have been, of necessity, broken: this aspect of the preparation of omelettes and of the egg motif appears in a conversation between Sir Impey Biggs and Lord Peter:

16

"You'll be careful," said Sir Impey. "Anything we can discover will come in much more effectively if the prosecution don't know of it beforehand."

"I'll walk as on egg-shells." (SP 49; ch. 4)

This reply by Lord Peter refers to the fragility of eggs rather than to the necessity of breaking them, but the motif is there.

In a scene in which Bunter expresses his own intuition of Lord Peter's love for Harriet (and his fear of consequent changes in the household of which he is a central feature), Lord Peter has been praising him in the process of asking him to help carry out the investigation: "morning by morning, my coffee is brought, my bath is prepared, my razor laid out, my ties and sock sorted, and my bacon and eggs brought to me in a lordly dish" (SP 89; ch. 8). Coffee and eggs are, respectively, the suspected but innocent "agent of death" and the unsuspected but actual agent of death in *Strong Poison*. Both motifs recur in the text. Eggs figure again in the same chapter: when Lord Peter seeks aid from Marjorie Phelps in interviewing the Bohemian friends of Harriet, he muses that "A telephone call at 10 a.m. would probably catch her scrambling eggs over her own gas-stove" (SP 93; ch. 8). Eggs are equated in these passages with well-being, kindliness and loving service, as is coffee.

When the interviews in Bloomsbury take place, Lord Peter is praised by Eiluned for taking his coffee black: "I thought all men liked to make their coffee into syrup" (SP 107; ch. 8), to which he replies, "Yes, but I am very unusual." This passage, seemingly so slight, is to be echoed in the denouement of the novel, as will be seen below.

Eggs naturally form a subject of Bunter's investigations: Mrs. Pettican, the cook of Urquhart's household, speaks of

"[…] a omelette, wot could be lighter and better? Not but there's people as can't relish eggs in any form, my own mother was just the same, give her so much as a cake what had bin made with a egg in it and she'd be that sick and come out all over spots like nettle-rash you'd be surprised. But Mr. Boyes was a great gentleman for eggs, and omelettes was his particular favourite." (SP 114; ch. 9)

A slightly negative association of eggs is both suggested and dismissed in this passage. Urquhart is shown to have been interested in eggs too; Mrs. Pettican continues,

> "[...] Mr. Urquhart asked particular after the eggs, was they new-laid, and I reminded him they was some he had brought in himself that afternoon from that shop on the corner of Lamb's Conduit Street where they always have them fresh from the farm, and I reminded him that one of them was a little cracked and he'd said, 'We'll use that in the omelette tonight, Hannah,' and I brought out a clean bowl from the kitchen and put them straight in—the cracked one and three more besides, and never touched them again till I brought them to table." (SP 114-115; ch.)

Here, another negative association of eggs—that they can be unfresh and thus spoiled or rotten—is introduced, and like the possibility of allergy, dismissed. We do learn that one egg was cracked (a motif introduced by Lord Peter's "egg-shells") but the subject is immediately set aside, like Mrs. Pettican's bowl. North American readers might remember that the eggs would not be put in a refrigerator, but simply set upon a shelf.

The egg as a symbol of value (and of creativity) is mentioned at the painful Christmas house-party endured by an anxious Lord Peter at his ancestral home, Duke's Denver. The guests are discussing the increase in sales of Harriet's detective novel, *Death in the Pot*, due to her trial:

> "[...] it looks like a case of hanging the goose that lays the golden eggs this time," said Captain Bates, with a loud laugh. "Unless Wimsey means to pull off one of his conjuring tricks." (SP 148; ch. 12)

The motif of occultism, sleight of hand, and conjuration appears here in the context of a remark about eggs: conjuring tricks in fact prove to be an essential part of the detecting process, though it is Miss Climpson who uses them.

The egg motif is expressed in the boldest possible way in Chapter XIII: Miss Murchison, who is about to be interviewed by Lord Peter, thinks over the disaster which befell her previous employer, a "brilliant financier who juggled with so many spectacular under-takings" that he was finally "juggling for his life."

> As the pace grew faster, he added egg after egg to those which were already spinning in the air. There is a limit to the number of eggs which can be spun by human hands. One day an egg slipped and smashed—then another—then a whole omelette of eggs. (SP 157; ch. 13)

Here the motive (a disastrous investment by the treasonous clerk Ur-quhart of his client's fund), the means (death by a poisoned omelette), and the symbol of the smashing of life by a broken egg, are brought together in a single arresting passage.

The Consumption of Coffee and Omelette

The coffee motif is reiterated when Miss Climpson drinks cup after cup in a series of tea shops, hoping to waylay the nurse of Ur-quhart's elderly client and aunt, Cremorna Garden. In Ye Cosye Cor-ner, she orders "a cup of coffee and a plate of digestive biscuits" (SP 199; ch. 16) and in the Central she orders "another cup of coffee and a roll and butter" (SP 199; ch. 16). At her third stop, the Oriental, she manages to "consume her fourth cup of coffee" (SP 200; ch. 16). These coffees are "false" in that Miss Climpson drinks them to pro-vide an excuse for her vigil, rather than to refresh herself. But like the coffee served by Harriet to her former lover, they are innocent.

Both coffee and egg recur in this chapter: on a second visit to the Oriental, where the long-sought nurse is now seated, Miss Climp-son approaches "a couple of girls consuming coffee and cakes" (SP 204; ch. 16) to ask if they have dropped a parcel. Again, it is a false parcel, which she has in fact purchased herself. The contents of the bag are reviewed: "That's eggs and that's bacon and—what's this, Ger-tie? Is that the mouse-trap?" (SP 205; ch 16). In fact the mouse is trapped, for Miss Climpson manages to strike up a conversation with nurse Booth by means of the false parcel.

Before the final confrontation with the murderer, we hear one last mention, first of "the omelette, so ostentatiously prepared at table by the hands of the victim" (SP 259; ch. 20), and then of the fact that "when they had finished the omelette, Urquhart said something about coffee" (SP 261; ch. 20), thus neatly placing the opposed motifs—coffee (benign) and eggs (lethal)—in one sentence.

Coffee, alluded to by Eiluned above as both sugar-filled and black, reappears when Urquhart visits Lord Peter: Turkish coffee, "that curiously syrupy brew, so offensive to the average Occidental," is partaken by Urquhart, while "Wimsey, with an austere smile, took a few sips of strong black coffee without sugar or milk" (SP 275; ch. 22). Coffee plays a role in distinguishing the personalities of murderer and sleuth, but not in the actual killing.

The eggs, however, finally come to the center of the scene. Lord Peter reminds Urquhart of his own testimony:

> And now there remains only the omelette. A most admirable thing when well made and eaten—that is so important—eaten immediately. A charming idea to have eggs and sugar brought to the table and prepared and cooked on the spot." (SP 278; ch. 22)

And of course, the whole omelette was consumed on the spot as well. And, Lord Peter adds, "Er—I believe I am right in saying that one of the eggs was cracked when it came to the table?" To Urquhart's muttered acknowledgement, Lord Peter describes how the cracked egg was set aside for the omelette: "In fact, you yourself laid it in the bowl for that purpose" (SP 278-79; ch. 22). To his uneasy quarry, Wimsey then explains that "It is not very difficult to introduce powdered arsenic into a cracked egg" (SP 279; ch. 22). He describes his own experiments, his use of a tube or funnels, the number of grains and the solubility of white powdered arsenic. Urquhart inquires whether "one particular poisoned egg was somehow kept miraculously separated from the rest […] ?" (SP 279; ch. 22) and says scornfully: "There seem to be some flaws in your theory, as well as in the egg" (SP 279; ch. 22).

It is his final shot, however, for Lord Peter traps him by means of an entirely different food motif—Turkish Delight—which he has (he says) smothered in powdered white arsenic instead of sugar so that only a man who made himself immune to the poison by small doses administered over a long period—as Urquhart has done—could share an arsenical omelette with his victim. This was the means used by Mithridates to overcome his enemies, as Lord Peter, pondering the means, remembered. One may note that, as Lord Peter lay asleep at his table with the tell-tale book, *A Shropshire Lad*, containing the poem by A. E. Houseman which describes the method of Mithridates, Bunter brought him a cup of coffee (SP 269; ch. 20).

The constant reiteration of the egg motif includes its use in at least one aphorism—by Urquhart, who compares a flawed theory with a flawed (cracked) egg. The egg is a profoundly resonant and ambivalent symbol in human culture and lends itself very well to images of change and counter-change. The folklorist Robert Wildhaber (1931) meditates upon the egg:

> on the one hand it is pure and sacred and the bearer of radiant new life; on the other hand there is the secret inside, out of which anything may come to life: good and joyful, or bad and filled with hatred. [8]

In its most positive sense, an egg is a beginning—the "original germ from which all life proceeds."[9] In this sense, when an egg changes, it becomes a living creature, a new being. But in its negative sense it is equally powerful. Everyone is familiar with the pervasive offensiveness of a rotten egg, of something which ought to be good turning bad: this motif appears in C.S. Lewis's Narnia tale, *The Voyage of the Dawn Treader*, in a context of time and change:

> "But that would be putting the clock back," gasped the governor. "Have you no idea of progress, of development?"
> "I have seen them both in an egg," said Caspian. "We call it 'Going bad' in Narnia. [...]"[10]

As a matter of fact, there is a conjuring procedure in which the fortune-teller secretly introduces a hair or other unexpected matter into an egg, and when the client opens it, interprets the find as an omen, usually malignant. A life not appropriate to the usual contents of an egg has grown there unexpectedly: the egg is "full of hatred," like the egg used by Urquhart to murder his cousin.

Séances and Thievery

The use of trickery, illicit knowledge, and false clairvoyance is a central feature of *Strong Poison*. Both Miss Climpson and Miss Murchison, sent by her agency, work as agents of Lord Peter by using illicit or false means to pursue their investigations. Miss Climpson uses a falsified séance to gain entry to the household of the aged Cremorna Garden, the aunt of Urquhart and Boyes, and also gains knowledge of the house's contents, including her will. Miss Murchison uses a lock pick to open a box belonging to her employer, Urquhart, and discovers his secret compartment with its record of his unwise investments of Cremorna Garden's trust funds. Stealth, falsification, theft of information: these are the means. The treacherous arts used by the two women were learned from men: Miss Climpson was taught by a member of the "Psychical Research Society" how to practice the false devices of mediums;[11] Miss Murchison is introduced to the reformed thief Bill Rumm, who teaches her how to pick a lock. Both of these figures—the scientist and the safe-cracker—can be interpreted as *animus* figures, male helpers, who represent special knowledge on the part of the women, by which they are able to obtain secret information. In both cases, the women carry out their stealthy work by night. They, like the idea of Lord Peter, move "slowly and darkly from the inmost deeps of his mind" (SP 145; ch. 11).

These activities, seemingly evil or ill, in fact bring about a happy conclusion: as Lord Peter says to Miss Murchison, "Who wills the end, wills the means" (SP 266; ch. 20). The reader may even call to mind the parallel aphorism: "If you want to have an omelette, you have to break eggs." Miss Climpson, whose Anglo-Catholic conscience is especially sensitive, has pondered this matter when she hears of the medium, Miss Craig, upon whom nurse Booth has become dependent: "This person is *quite* as great a *charlatan* as I AM!!!—and without my *altruistic* motives!" (SP 246; ch. 19). One may see these lines as a reversal of the cry of Thomas in T. S. Eliot's *Murder in the Cathedral* (1935):

> The last temptation is the greatest treason:
> To do the right deed for the wrong reason.[12]

In the case of Miss Climpson, it is a matter of doing the wrong thing for the right reason.

The scenes of Miss Climpson's séances and Miss Murchison's lock-picking are the most suspenseful in the novel. We are not admitted to Harriet's suspenseful agony in prison where she awaits the verdict, but Lord Peter's female agents provide substitutes for her experience. She waits, they act. She has been passive in allowing Boyes to trap her into co-habitation without marriage; she undergoes a purgatory of passivity as the true murderer is tracked and exposed. The presence of the active women in the story prevents it from merely presenting an image of passive femininity—Harriet—and active masculinity—Lord Peter. In fact, Lord Peter makes very extensive use of agents, even including the manicurist Mabel, whom he sends to procure fingernails and hair from Urquhart, after assuring her that he has no occult intentions. His own activity consists of intuition and interviews until, in the final scene with Urquhart, by his own act of falsification, he traps his man.

Harriet's "False" Relationship to Peter

These falsifications parallel Harriet's concern that she is in a "false" situation in her relationship to Lord Peter. That is, Sayers recognized that "when I looked at the situation I saw that it was in every respect false and degrading; and the puppets had somehow got just so much flesh and blood in them that I could not force them to accept it without shocking myself."[13] Numerous commentators, led by Sayers herself, have explored the way in which she carried out her plan to put this situation right, during the subsequent six novels. But *Strong Poison* presents the theme in terms of its dichotomies and their resolution: FALSITY *produces* TRUTH. The false séance of the supposed medium, the false actions of the supposed secretary, yield the truth about Urquhart's motive. The false *food* served by Lord Peter (which is not really poisoned) proves the truth about the truly poisoned food served by the murderer.

Eric Rabkin (1976) includes the detective novel as a species of fantasy; specifically, as a form of escape. By this he means that they carry the reader away to a world which, Rabkin implies, is not like ours. He divides the escape into two forms: escape to a world where there are puzzles which can be solved, and escape to a world where justice is done.[14] Without going into the metaphysical question of whether puzzles can be solved in our world (scientists, including forensic scientists, tend to act as if they can), and into the theological question of whether justice can be done (judges act as if it can, and Christians and Jews believe that our world is ruled by a just God), Rabkin's thesis is exhibited in *Strong Poison*. The puzzle is there and it is solved in terms that supply a symbolic structure embodying justice. One could say that in every detective story, evil is, by justice, converted into good. Lord Peter says, when defending Harriet to his sister-in-law Helen,

> "in detective stories virtue is always triumphant. They're the purest literature we have" (SP 148; ch. 12).

In *Strong Poison*, the opposites—GOOD and EVIL—are reconciled by change, by process, by the structure—EVIL into GOOD is as DEATH into LIFE. The egg is broken, and an omelette is made of it.

Notes

[1] Trevor H. Hall, "Atherton Fleming: A Literary Puzzle," *Dorothy L. Sayers: Nine Literary Studies* (London: Duckworth, 1980) 51-52.
[2] See James Brabazon, *Dorothy L. Sayers, The Life of a Courageous Woman* (London: Victor Gollancz, 1981) 132, 148; Mary Brian Durkin, *Dorothy L. Sayers* (Boston: Twayne Publishers, 1980) 20; Margaret P. Hannay, "Harriet's Influence on the Characterization of Lord Peter Wimsey," *As Her Whimsey Took Her*, ed. Margaret P. Hannay (Kent, OH: Kent State UP, 1979) passim [essay 36-50]; and Ralph E. Hone, *Dorothy L. Sayers, A Literary Biography* (Kent, OH: Kent State UP, 1979) 63.
[3] Dawson Gaillard, *Dorothy L. Sayers* (New York: Frederick Ungar, 1981) 98. She quotes Lord Peter in *Gaudy Night*: "Our kind of show is dead and done for." The theme of time in itself is suggested by Alizana Stone Dale, "Fossils in Cloud-Cuckoo Land," *The Sayers Review* III, 2 (December 1978): 5. She divides the novels into two groups and begins "the second series [with] the really 'time-and-place-ridden' works," the first of which is *Strong Poison*.
[4] Gaillard says "The murderer emerges about halfway through the book" (52), and Durkin states that "How the murder was effected is the mystery that creates suspense" (54).
[5] See Nancy Tischler, *Dorothy L. Sayers: A Pilgrim Soul* (Atlanta, GA: John Knox Press, 1980): "Those who dared to reject the path of matrimony because of their ambitions" (61); and Hannay regarding "a woman's need for her *own* work" (xxii).
[6] R.B. Reaves describes the judge as "pure caricature" and part of an indictment by Sayers of the process of justice in "Crime and Punish-

Notes

ment in the Detective Fiction of Dorothy L. Sayers," *As Her Whimsey Took Her*, ed. Margaret P. Hannay (Kent, OH: Kent State UP, 1979) 9-10.

[7] Venetia Newall, *An Egg at Easter: A Folklore Study* (London: Routledge and Kegan Paul, 1971): "No one ever told him why, and he went on doing it, from force of habit, until he was a grown man" (84). The practice is based on an old belief that witches can make themselves boats from the half-shells of eggs.

[8] Robert Wildhaber, "Foreword," Venetia Newal's *An Egg at Easter: A Folklore Study* (London: Routledge and Kegan Paul, 1971) xv.

[9] Alan W. Watts, *Easter: Its Story and Meaning* (New York: Henry Scuman, 1950) 10, 29-30.

[10] C.S. Lewis, *The Voyage of the Dawn Treader* (1952), Collector's Edition with Illustrations by Pauline Baynes (New York: Harper Collins, 2010) 61; ch. 4.

[11] Trevor H. Hall says that the four chapters on Miss Climpson's séances tell "us all we need to know […] about her [Sayers's] attitude towards spiritualism and the supposed possibility of communication with the dead." "Dorothy L. Sayers and Psychical Research," *Dorothy L. Sayers: Nine Literary Studies*. London: Duckworth, 1980) 119. He suggests that "our first clue to Miss Sayers' opinion of believers in spiritualism" comes in her description of Nurse Booth's eyes, which present "some emotional instability" (121). It is Hall's conclusion that Sayers, who "knew a great deal about spiritualism" (123), regarded it as a fraudulent performance capable of being reproduced by anyone with a knowledge of a medium's tricks. For both the plot and the symbolic structure of *Strong Poison*, the falsity of the séances is their most important feature, whatever Sayers thought about psychical research and/or phenomena.

[12] T.S. Eliot, *Murder in the Cathedral* (1935; New York: Harvest Book, Harcourt Brace & Co, 1963) 44.

[13] Dorothy L. Sayers, "Gaudy Night," *Titles to Fame*, ed. Denys Kilham Roberts (London: Thomas Nelson and Sons, 1937) 79.

[14] Eric S. Rabkin, *The Fantastic in Literature* (Princeton, NJ: Princeton UP, 1976) 66.

3.   "Bloody Farce": Irony, Farce, and Mortality in
      Dorothy L. Sayers's *Have His Carcase*

"King Death hath asses' ears."

——T.L. Beddoes, *Death's Jest Book* (1850)

In "Bloody Farce," Patterson argues that Sayers's much maligned detective novel Have His Carcase *is, as her paper title declares, an example of the ironic and farcical treatment of the subject of mortality. After establishing definitions of farce and irony with reference to Northrop Frye, she analyzes the novel chapter-by-chapter in three sections titled "The Bloody Farce" I, II, and III, and appropriately subtitled and focused on the murder weapon—"An open, cut-throat razor," the murderer—"The only son of his mother," and the corpse—"We've got the body." Her observations about Sayers's use of the masque and masquerade in this farce are also relevant to her discussion of Sayers's next novel,* Murder Must Advertise, *which is the subject of the next paper in this anthology.*

Other dichotomies and themes that Patterson examines here and in other papers on Sayers's novels include the natural / artificial, falseness (relating to identity, disguise, and nobility), the development of Harriet's relationship with Lord Peter, racism and prejudice, and finally, the transformation of life into death. Specifically, Patterson addresses the theme of anti-semitism in "Images of Judaism and Anti-Semitism in the Novels of Dorothy L. Sayers," and that of falseness transforming into truth in "'Changing, Fearfully Changing': Polarization and Transformation in Dorothy L. Sayers's Strong Poison," *and in the conclusions to "'A Comedy of Masks': Lord Peter as Harlequin in* Murder Must Advertise," *and "'A Ring of Good Bells': Providence and Judgment in Dorothy L. Sayers's* The Nine Tailors."

Patterson had 150 copies of "Bloody Farce" printed in 1999, but none seem to have made their way into any libraries or archival collections except one owned by the Wade at Wheaton. The copy used for this paper, which was one of only two that we found for sale, was presented to Barbara Reynolds.

———————

Introduction

Have His Carcase is Dorothy L. Sayers's least appreciated novel. Commentators generally discuss it because it is the second in the Wimsey/Vane quartet, and thus shows a stage in that developing relationship. Margaret Hannay (1979) calls it "the weakest of the Wimsey stories";[1] Ralph E. Hone (1979) reports that its "intricacy of plot development becomes oppressive";[2] James Brabazon (1981) says it "is not by any means Dorothy's best";[3] Catherine Kenney (1990) deems it "flawed" and "unwieldy,"[4] as well as "bulky" and "brooding";[5] Philip Scowcroft (1992) declares it to be "weak in its characterisation";[6] and Sharyn McCrumb (1993) concludes that it is "a puzzle mystery that has not worn well."[7]

I would have agreed with these judgments when I first read *Have His Carcase* some thirty years ago. But a recent re-reading has convinced me that Kenney expresses precisely the quality which not only disturbs readers to the point of active dislike, but makes the book a major work in a very particular genre. She writes: "At the beginning of *Have His Carcase* [...] Harriet studies minutely the blood-soaked corpse; later, she cannot take her eyes off the pitiful, lost old woman at the ironically named Hotel Resplendent [...] Harriet's preoccupation with images of mortality become ours [...]"[8]

Have His Carcase takes us, following Harriet, "on a solitary walking tour" (HHC 7; ch.1) through what Sayers told Harold Bell, in a letter dated 12 March 1933, was a "Nephelocorcygia [sic]," that is, a Cloud Cuckooland.[9] From this isolating prologue to the long novel's final page, we experience what Lord Peter declares to be "a damned awful, bitter, bloody farce" (HHC 448; ch. 34). It is my thesis that *Have His Carcase* is the supreme example in Sayers's *oeuvre* of irony and farce in the literary treatment of mortality, and is thus, in its distinctively distressing way, a masterpiece.

Farce

Northrop Frye defines farce as "a non-mimetic form of comedy," which "has a natural place in the masque."[10] In "the ideal masque," he says, "its natural place is that of a rigorously controlled interlude." Indeed, "The archetypal masque [...] tends to detach its settings from time and space, but instead of the Arcadias of the ideal masque, we find ourselves frequently in a sinister limbo."[11] Harriet's solitary journey and her subsequent stay, shared at a separate hotel from hers, by Lord Peter, in the minor seaside resort at the edge of England during a year which Sayers deliberately disguised by altering the dates of its "tides,"[12] and in a place which she calls a "locality […] invented to fit the plot" (HHC 4; Note)—all fit the peculiar requirements of interlude, isolation, and detachment from and in time and space.

Frye further observes that "Ritual analogies are most easily seen, not in the drama of the educated audience and the settled theatre, but […] in the folk play, the puppet show, the pantomime, the farce, the pageant, and their descendants in masque, comic opera, commercial movie, and revue."[13] This may account for the frequently cited artificiality of the characters in *Have His Carcase,* accurately summed up by Scowcroft: "Leila Garland is no more than a sketch, her boyfriend da Soto is a caricature, the many theatrical characters […] are unconvincing [… and] the Darley yokels are lay figures."[14]

"The classical critics," Frye tells us, "were puzzled to understand why a disorganized ribald farce like the satyr-play should be the source of tragedy," and notes the presence in Medieval drama of such figures. The devils of the Harrowing of Hell "are the Christian forms of figures very like the Greek satyrs,"[15] and in fact one devil in "The Deliverance of Souls," the twenty-seventh play in the Wakefield Mystery Plays, is named Ribald. In his first speech he laments,

> "My joys begin to fade, my wit waxes thin,
> No longer be we glad, these souls we cannot win!
> How, Beelzebub! Bind these boys, such harrow was never heard in hell!"[16]

In the play, these "boys," including Adam, Isaiah, Symeon, John the Baptist, and Moses, are, along with Eve, rescued when Jesus descends into Hell between his death and resurrection. The descent of the lost body of Paul Alexis, the absence of which is asserted by the title, *Have His Carcase* (a play upon *habeas corpus),* into a watery underworld, only to be raised in time to aid in the discovery of his killers, is the central symbol of this novel.

Irony

The satyrs' dances and loveless couplings performed by the sad denizens of Wilvercombe's hotels, which in the novel lead toward death, can be compared to the medieval *danse macabre,* where, Frye says, "the simple equality of death is set against the complex inequalities of life."[17] He calls this *danse macabre* an "ironic reversal."[18] Frye defines the Ironic as "a mode of literature in which the characters exhibit a power of action inferior to the one assumed to be normal in the reader."[19] One mode of such literature is surely the mystery novel, whose very name betrays its intention. In the late twentieth century; readers experience an uneasy sense that in *Have His Carcase* they have been invited to go slumming, an activity no longer deemed to be politically correct.

The relationship between Paul Alexis and his would-be bride Mrs. Weldon presents a series of ironic reversals of the relationship between Lord Peter and Harriet Vane. Paul Alexis, who thinks he will become Tsar, is not a member of the nobility, and he does not want to marry Mrs. Weldon, who pursues him although she cannot meet him on equal terms (as regards age, wealth, or social status) and in fact is a major cause of his death. Lord Peter is a member of the nobility, and he does want to marry Harriet, who resists him because she cannot (at least at the beginning of the novel) meet him on equal terms, since he has saved her from death, a debt which she cannot (she thinks) repay. This quartet of interlocked and mismatched characters perfectly presents what Frye calls "the ironic human situation."[20]

Lest I be accused of engaging in "a conscious ecstasy of enigma hunting,"[21] as Sayers so trenchantly puts it in *The Mind of the Maker* (1941), I offer her own comments upon the plot of *Have His Carcase.* In a letter of 22 January 1931 to her publisher, Victor Gollancz, having discussed *Five Red Herrings* as a "pure-puzzle"[22] story, she promises:

> I will return to a less rigidly intellectual formula in
> HAVE-HIS-CARCASE
> which will turn on an alibi and a point of medicine, but will, I trust, contain a certain amount of human interest and a more or less obvious murderer. But I haven't made up the plot yet ...[23]

She refers twice to the difficulty of that plot when writing to her cousin Ivy Shrimpton. On 3 June 1931 she reports, "I am struggling with another book—horribly complicated! But it must be done, under contract, so there's nothing for it but to wire in and work it out."[24] On

12 June 1931, she adds, "I am now struggling with chapter II of my gentleman with the cut throat. He will not come right, curse him!"[25]

In comparison with these exasperated contemporaneous remarks about the murder plot, Sayers's attitude toward her inclusion of Harriet and Peter must be inferred from statements she made in retrospect. In her essay "Gaudy Night," she states that after introducing Peter to Harriet in *Strong Poison,* she "chipped away at his internal mechanism through three longish books."[26] As for Harriet, "Her inferiority complex was making her steadily more brutal to him and his newly developed psychology was making him steadily more sensitive to her inhibitions."[27] In fact there are four detective novels between *Strong Poison* (1930) where Harriet and Peter meet, and *Gaudy Night* (1935) where they agree to marry; these are *Five Red Herrings* (1931), *Have His Carcase* (1932), *Murder Must Advertise* (1933), and *The Nine Tailors* (1934). All four show Peter's internal mechanism being picked away, but only one shows Harriet's inferiority complex making her brutal to him. That one is *Have His Carcase.*

In that book we indeed see Harriet's inferiority complex, her brutality to Peter (most particularly in her repeated refusals to his repeated proposals of marriage), and her inhibitions, not only displayed but to a degree assuaged by Peter's developing psychology and sensitivity. They engage in this process while they work together to solve the mystery of Paul Alexis's murder. In a fundamental irony, the false love that leads Alexis to his death provides the context in which Harriet and Peter's true love comes to life.

Mortality

Sayers, as was her custom, provided each chapter of *Have His Carcase* with an epigraph; these were all chosen from the verse play, *Death's Jest Book* (1850) by T. L. Beddoes (1798-1850). The quotation for its final chapter, which ends with the line, "King Death hath asses' ears," cited by Lord Peter on the last page of *Have His Carcase,* exactly expresses the thesis of my essay, and hence forms my epigraph, above.[28]

In the following chapter-by-chapter analysis of the text, which forms the bulk of my essay, and which details at great length the mortality of the victim who has been murdered before the story begins, I have divided the novel into three sections. Section I opens with the discovery of the body, and takes its subtitle from the murder weapon. Section II continues the narrative with the appearance of the murderer as himself, using his own name, and is titled in such a way as to imply his motive for murder. Section III carries the action from the redis- covery of the body (absent from the narrative since the first chapter) to the discovery of the murderer in the final chapter, a discovery based upon information about that body and its innate traits. The voiceless razor and the voiceless body, taken together, reveal the truth that the killer and his mentor have labored, unsuccessfully, to conceal.

The three elements involved in the murder victim's death—the murder weapon, the murderer, and the victim's psychological and physical flaws all manifest his (and our) mortality, which is always, in a murder mystery, the central theme.

The "Bloody Farce" I: "An open, cut-throat razor"

The context of *Have His Carcase* is precisely foreshadowed in Chapter I, "The Evidence of the Corpse," as Harriet Vane decides to walk alone toward "Wilvercombe, with its seasonal population of old ladies and invalids and its subdued attempts at the gay life" (HHC 8; ch. 1). Mrs. Weldon is indeed an old lady, and Paul Alexis is in many ways an invalid; their lives conform to Webster's definition, "Given to social pleasures or indulgences; hence, loose; licentious, as, a *gay* life." To reach this goal, Harriet chooses a road overlooking "a long yellow stretch of the beach," notices "a couple of horses out at grass," and sees "a fishing-boat" (HHC 8; ch. 1). These few deft strokes pre- sent the murder site. In contrast with this idyllic seaward vision, soon to be revealed as profoundly ironic because its beauty will be found to have been marred by death, she encounters a "tradesman's van," a "di- lapidated Morris," and "the white smoke from a distant railway en- gine" (HHC 8; ch. 1), all forms of vehicle which will play roles in the detection process.

Below, as she trudges doggedly toward her encounter with the dead, she sees that "the wet beach shimmered golden and silvery in the lazy noonlight" (HHC 9; ch. 1). "Noonlight"—spelled with an "n," in reference to noonday, offers an ironic play on "moonlight," since the harsh light of day is about to expose the outcome of the victim's moondusted illusions. Gold, according to J.E. Cirlot (1962), "is sym- bolic of all that is superior," because of its association with the sun,[29] and is "the essential element in the symbol of the hidden or elusive treasure."[30] A gold and silver beach suggests references to the golden dreams of Paul Alexis, as well as to the gold coins actually in his possession as, not yet known to Harriet, he lies dead.

Harriet descends to this alluring beach, and, after a picnic lunch—the first of many picnics and lunches in this novel—she falls asleep, rather like Alice, when "the hot day made her feel very sleepy and stupid" at the beginning of *Alice's Adventures in Wonderland* (1865) before the sight of the White Rabbit leads her toward her descent. At length, a "shout or cry" (HHC 10; ch. 1) awakens Harriet. Now conscious, she feels "an irresistible impulse" to "make footprints" on "the virgin sand" and walks along in this childlike mood, thinking about neaps and springs—the lowest monthly tidal fall and highest monthly tidal rise—which are to play a part in the detection process, not least in carrying away the evidence she is about to encounter.

Rounding "the point of the cliff," she sees for the first time "a good sized rock" which is "roughly triangular in shape, standing about ten feet out of the water," and "crowned"—fateful word for a man who would be King—"with a curious lump of black seaweed" (HHC 11; ch. 1). This curious lump—one can almost hear Alice cry "Curiouser and curiouser!" as she does in the first line of Chapter II, "The Pool of Tears"—is the body, the very "carcase" of the book's title. Even from afar, Harriet sees that "It looks almost more like a man lying down" (HHC 11; ch. 1), as, when she approaches him, proves to be the case. He wears a "dark blue suit" (HHC 12; ch. 1), and "pale mauve socks" (HHC 13; ch. 1), and when she investigates closely, she sees the truth: "it *was* a corpse" (HHC 13; ch. 1), from which "a frightful stream, bright red and glistening, was running over the surface of the rock" (HHC 14; ch. 1).

In this passage there are echoes of a long theme in Christian symbolism. Julian of Norwich recounts that in this vision he "saw the reed bloud rynnyng downe from under the garlande, hote and freyshely, plentuously and liuely,"[31] and a hymn for Good Friday in the Book of Common Prayer of the Church of England includes the line, "Lifeless lies the pierced body, / Resting on its rocky bed." The profound symbolism of both blood and rock—"the red trickle that dripped down the face of the rock into the clear water" (HHC 14; ch. 1)—powerfully colors the rest of the novel.

The phrase "bloody farce" uttered by Lord Peter thus becomes the key to the human comedy portrayed in *Have His Carcase*. Whether taken as a form of emphasis or of obscenity, in Lord Peter's outcry the word "bloody" aptly fits this very bloody murder, which is both extreme and lacking in decency. Frye speaks of "the tragedy of a youthful life cut off,"[32] and of "the fall of the hero through hybris."[33] The dead man who lies bleeding on the rock has indeed died young, and has indeed been brought down by "hybris," by having been tempted to reach above himself; he has gone to his death believing that he is to lead a revolution that will place him on the throne of Russia. He has become the *Pharmakos,* whom Frye calls "The character in an ironic fiction who has the role of scapegoat or arbitrarily chosen victim."[34]

As a scapegoat or victim, he is also a sacrifice. Blood makes its first appearance in the Bible when God says to Cain, "the voice of thy brother's blood crieth unto me from the ground" (Genesis 4.10-11). It recurs in the New Testament when Judas confesses, "I have sinned in that I have betrayed the innocent blood" (Matthew 27.4). The author of Hebrews points out that "almost all things are by the law purged with blood; and without shedding of blood there is no remission" (Hebrews 9.22). For reasons like these, Cirlot states that "In spilt blood we have the perfect image of sacrifice."[35]

Equally important in the symbolism of this chapter is the great rock on which the corpse lies bleeding. "A solitary rock is always attractive," the authorial voice tells us in *Have His Carcase*; "All right-minded people feel an overwhelming desire to scale and sit upon it" (HHC 11; ch. 1). This statement, made as Harriet looks at the great rock from a distance, is certainly ironic, because Harriet (who is right-minded) will in fact find a dead body on top of this attractive rock, and the victim himself has indeed felt an overwhelming desire to scale and sit upon it too, going to it as one going to his coronation.

The dead man's position on the rock places him in the role of Prometheus, who as C.G. Jung says, "was chained to the rocks."[36] In this situation, the rock, upthrust from the earth, signifies an upsurge of the chthonic, that which Jung identifies with the unconscious. Rock "is held in many traditions to be the dwelling-place of a god,"[37] and in some traditions is seen as the source of human life. Prometheus is chained to the rock because, "like a good culture hero," he stole fire "from heaven where it can be seen in sun and stars,"[38] in order to bring it down to humankind, of whom he was the creator.[39] This over-reaching act has been punished by Zeus, who sends a vulture to feed each day upon the liver of Prometheus, a very bloody fate even for an immortal. The mortal Paul Alexis has also overreached himself, and his punishment, which in his case inevitably leads to death, is exceedingly bloody too. Zeus eventually frees Prometheus; that role in the novel is played by the tide, which takes Alexis's body down into the sea, there to lie hidden, ironically, by means of the heavy gold he has attached to his own body. Jung says that the sacrificed "hero" is associated with a descent (as we have seen in Jesus's descent into hell),[40] where he gains the wisdom which "dwells in the depths, the wisdom of the mother."[41] We do not hear from the author about Paul Alexis's posthumous encounter with wisdom; in this novel, no aspect of the afterlife is directly addressed.

Harriet accurately detects from the lack of rigor—stiffness in the corpse—that the death cannot have taken place more than four to ten hours before (which is indeed the case, and the only accurate estimate as to the time of death in the novel until the last chapter). Searching, she finds the instrument of death—"an open, cut-throat razor" (HHC 18; ch. 1). The bloody condition of the corpse prevents her from discovering the gold coins (because she is loath to examine the ensanguinated body), thus concealing their presence from the reader. Gathering up "the shoe, hat, razor, cigarette case and handkerchief" of the victim, she notes that the "fishing-boat was almost out of sight," checks the time—"just after half-past two" (HHC 21; ch. 1)—observes "a line of little swirls and eddies [...] as though breaking above the top of hidden rocks" (HHC 20; ch. 1), —the place where the dead man's "Carcase" will be concealed—and departs.

Each of the chapters in this novel concerns evidence: the above has been "The Evidence of the Corpse," which, after Harriet's departure, sinks into the deep until the last line of chapter XX: "Good evening, my lord. We've got the body!" (HHC 268; ch. 20). With the exception of that corpse, Harriet meets nobody else in Chapter 1, although the name of Lord Peter Wimsey has been mentioned on its first page.

In Chapter II, "The Evidence of the Road," her self-isolation ends, and she begins a desperate effort to inform somebody in authority about her terrible discovery. In the process, the author sketches humans (including the murderer) into her landscape, filling it with the "lay figures" to whom Scowcroft refers. It is my thesis that these essentially symbolic figures, so characteristic of the masque form, are images of bucolic innocence (with one notable exception) who are intended to contrast with the decadent persons at the seaside resort in the chapter that follows. Harriet meets a seventeen-year-old girl, a woman, an aged man, a farmer and his assistant, and "a hiker, like herself" (HHC 27; ch. 2). This hiker is the blameless Mr. Perkins; in his company, she meets a camper with a petrol-tin, dressed in flannel slacks and khaki shirt. Harriet "noticed a snake tattooed in red and blue upon his forearm, and wondered whether he might perhaps have been a sailor" (HHC 31; ch. 2). In an extraordinary example of obfuscation, this nautical motif allows the murderer to be hidden neatly in plain sight from the unsuspecting reader.

Eventually Harriet and Perkins find a small grocery beside "the little green" (HHC 32; ch. 2) of a village; there she undertakes to call "the Wilvercombe police-station," while Perkins takes himself away. Note all the imagery of this chapter is devoted to populating a rural environment: men haying, a farmer's wife, fisherfolk, the crossing-keeper, a boy with a cart-horse, an amiable grocer. The countryside itself is also brushed in with a few deft touches: "Cottages had begun to appear, small, sturdy buildings, surrounded by little patches of gay garden [...] and at length a little green, with a smithy at one corner and children playing cricket in the grass [...] an ancient elm, with a seat round it and an ancient man basking in the sunshine [...]" (HHC 32; ch. 2); in short, the archetypal English village.

Chapter III, "The Evidence of the Hotel," gives us Harriet at work. She reports the corpse to the police by telephone; she calls London to notify the press of her discovery, partly for self-advertisement, because she is a detective novelist. This self-reflexive element recurs throughout the novel, both in Harriet's thoughts and in her conversations, after he appears, with Lord Peter. Not only Harriet's fictional detective, but many of the fictional detectives of Sayers's fellow mystery writers are discussed. Kenney says that *Have His*

Carcase is "Sayers's way of examining the conventions and limitations of detective fiction in the form she understood best, a story."[42]

This chapter presents in forceful terms a central symbol of *Have His Carcase*: "one of those monster seaside palaces which look as though they have been designed by a German manufacturer of children's cardboard toys" (HHC 40; ch. 3). The natural, earth-and-sea-based countryside is contrasted with the "cardboard" world of the hotel. Sayers speaks in *The Mind of the Maker* (1941) of the "two 'cardboard' worlds" in *Murder Must Advertise* (1933), the novel which follows *Have His Carcase* in order of publication.[43] Her two acknowledged masterpieces which were to follow these—*The Nine Tailors* (1934) and *Gaudy Night* (1935)—took her away from such cardboard settings into worlds which she knew profoundly from personal experience and which she regarded as profoundly real and good: the country church and its rectory, and Oxford University. Continuing her theme of artificiality in contrast with authenticity, Sayers says of the hotel's interior: "Its glass porch was crowded with hothouse plants" (HHC 40; ch. 3), instead of plants in country gardens; "and the lofty dome of its reception-hall was supported on gilt pilasters" (HHC 40; ch. 3), contrasting with the sky of Harriet's walk along the cliffs in Chapter I, which "arched up to an immense dome of blue, just fretted here and there with faint white clouds" (HHC 8; ch. 3). Again, the indoor dome's pilasters are described as "rising out of an ocean of blue plush" (HHC 40; ch. 3), rather than from "the seaward horizon" (HHC 8; ch. 1) of the Atlantic Ocean where Harriet had sighted a fishing boat as she walked.

Settled in the hotel, she begins to think again (as she did in the first paragraph of the first chapter) of Lord Peter. Making her way "into a kind of large lounge" (HHC 43; ch. 3), a setting already contrasted with the natural rural life of the land and the pure, fresh air of the sea, she sees:

> a pair of obviously professional dancers, giving an exhibition waltz. The man was tall and fair, with sleek hair plastered closely to his head, and a queer, unhealthy face with a wide, melancholy mouth. The girl, in an exaggerated gown of petunia satin [...] exhibited a mask of Victorian coyness as she revolved languidly in her partner's arms [...] (HHC 43; ch. 3)

Epithets of artificiality—"exhibition," "exaggerated," "mask"—abound in this passage, as they do in the lines completing this sequence, in words such as "mock-modesty" and "a game" (HHC 44; ch.3).

This contrast between reality as life and artificiality as death culminates in Harriet's first sight of Mrs. Weldon, the mother of the murderer and herself ultimately responsible for the death of the man whose body Harriet has discovered: "a lean woman, pathetically made-up, dressed in an exaggeration of the fashion [...] difficult for a girl of nineteen to carry off successfully" (HHC 45; ch. 3). She bears "a look of radiant, almost bridal exaltation," and Harriet surmises correctly that she is "waiting for her gigolo" (HHC 45; ch. 3). Neither Harriet nor the woman know that this prospective bride will wait in vain, because this particular gigolo is dead. By the end of the chapter, all the ingredients of the mystery have been laid forth: the victim, the weapon, and the motive. The victim is the gigolo, killed with a razor in order to prevent him from marrying the waiting woman. Certainly Sayers has played fairly with her reader. All that is lacking is Lord Peter.

With Chapter IV, "The Evidence of the Razor," he enters. The vast majority of published commentary upon *Have His Carcase* is directed toward the relationship of Harriet and Peter as they detect their first case together. The detectival efforts of these two characters are almost equally shared, and some of the wrinkles in their relationship are indeed shaken out in the process. This progress in their lives is heralded by a striking bit of symbolism, as Harriet lays out the crime scene upon a hotel breakfast table:

> "This line of salt is the beach. And this piece of bread is a rock at low-water level."
> "And this salt-spoon," [Peter ...] said [...] "can be the body." (HHC 49; ch. 4).

The symbolism of bread and salt as the basic components of hospitality suggests the two prospective lovers' developing rapport, and provides a potent contrast with the vision of the old woman awaiting her dead gigolo.

The reference to bread, in a context where blood has been spilled, must also be noted. In the Christian sacrifice, both body (symbolized by bread) mentioned by Peter—and blood (the spilling of which has brought Harriet and Peter together) as symbolized by wine, are important components. This spilled blood is the central clue of the novel, but the detecting couple do not yet know why. They are joined by Inspector Umpelty, who identifies the dead man as a "russian" who is "Said to have escaped from Russia at the Revolution" (HHC 54; ch. 4), facts which will in the end explain everything. Umpelty also reports that "the body will have been washed off the Flat-Iron" (HHC 54; ch. 4) and will likely "have got carried out and caught up in the Grinders" (HHC 55; ch. 4); that is, to the near-shore reef Harriet has seen but not identified by name. The term "Grinders" applied to a reef implies the capacity of this stony underwater outcropping to grind up the hulls of foundered ships, but in the context of bread and body, we are reminded of the giant who ground up the bones of the dead to make his bread.

The conversation moves on to the central subject of the chapter: the razor. Peter volunteers to check its origin, and Umpelty agrees. The razor, identified by the hyper-observant Lord Peter, comes from "One of the most exclusive hairdressers in the West End" (HHC 60; ch. 4). His further comments end with one of the series of unsuccessful marriage proposals he makes to Harriet in this novel, as well as with the chapter's conclusion, as Harriet is "accosted" by "the 'predatory hag' whom she had already seen the evening before in the dance-lounge of the Resplendent" (HHC 63; ch. 4). The juxtaposition of this woman with the subject of the razor is of course no coincidence.

Mrs. Weldon, as she is identified in Chapter V, "The Evidence of the Betrothed," is an example of the archetypal "Terrible Mother," who has unconsciously (and literally, since he is eventually executed) destroyed her son's life. The irony of this situation is that every mother who gives birth condemns (as part of the bargain) her child to eventual death. It may be that a depiction of a crone as appalling as the one in this novel comes from deep anxieties in Sayers's life at this time; as it happens, she concluded the writing of the book with illness so severe that she was unable to correct its proofs. Whether or not there is any psychological element to Mrs. Weldon's description, there is no doubt that she is treated very sharply in the narrative. Harriet, detecting alone in this chapter, tells her of finding "Mr. Alexis" dead:

"His throat was cut, Mrs. Weldon."

(Brutal Saxon monosyllables.)

"Oh!" Mrs. Weldon seemed to shrink into a mere set of eyes and bones. (HHC 65-66; ch. 5)

That is, her face becomes a "mere" skull, a symbol of death. As her grief subsides, she removes her grotesque makeup with Harriet's aid, and becomes "a sallow-faced woman of between fifty and sixty, infinitely more dignified in her natural complexion" (HHC 67; ch. 5). Here again the contrast between the artificial and the natural is emphasized, placing it in the context of the contrast between death and life.

"I have lived for my emotions," Mrs. Weldon explains (HHC 67; ch. 5) and continues in the vein of self-revelation, not to say self-incrimination, "my son has been a sad disappointment to me" (HHC 68; ch 5). And immediately she details the situation; she and the young victim Paul Alexis were engaged to be married. "He was really a prince, you know—but he never liked to say too much about that" (HHC 69; ch. 5). As the novel turns upon his supposed possession of royal blood, this is one more case of the author's honest dealing. Mrs. Weldon, of course, is in error when she reports that Alexis was "all eagerness and excitement" (HHC 69; ch. 5) because he was anticipating marriage to her. In fact, he was eager and excited because he expected exaltation to royal status. Ironically, indeed, they were both mortally mistaken. Harriet finds Mrs. Weldon's statements "dreadful [...] grotesquely comic and worse than tragic" (HHC 70; ch. 5), as is indeed the case. With these juxtapositions of the words "comic and [...] tragic," my case for the symbolism of the bloody farce is made explicit.

Chapter VI, "The Evidence of the First Barber," offers an exquisite portrait of the blameless Mr. Endicott, the "old barber" (HHC 81; ch. 6) for whom the prospective murder weapon, a very specific razor, was made for the most innocent of purposes. The sweetness and charm of this chapter reflects Sayers's sunny view of Lord Peter's world and class, and offers a bright picture of authenticity in contrast to the falsity of the Resplendent and its denizens. This chapter goes beyond the identification of the instrument to a portrait not only of an honorable craft, but of an elegant and well-made artifact whose role depends entirely upon the hand that wields it. Eventually the blade will betray its evil wielder as truly as if it had been able to cry out.

This capacity of artifacts to be active participants has been remarked upon by anthropologist Joan Vastokas (1994), who points out that in human culture, "the artifact is not an inert, passive object, but an interactive agent in sociocultural life and cognition."[44] It can be an actor in events, in "its performative, 'gestural' patterns of behavior in relation to space, time, and society."[45] Thus, its "signification" is not limited to its internal structure and formal characteristics, but is also expressed "when it interacts dialogically with other phenomena."[46] A razor can be an actor (even in its absence), as in Judges 13.5 where "the angel of the Lord" tells Samson's mother that she is to bear a child and that "no razor shall come upon his head," as well as a metaphor, whether negative, as in Psalm 52.2, "Thy tongue deviseth mischief, like a sharp razor, working deceitfully," or positive, when assigned the task of discernment, as in the concept of "Occam's Razor," or *"The Razor's Edge."*

The razor in *Have His Carcase* indeed functions as a symbol of discernment. It has been acquired deceitfully by a character not yet in view in this chapter, Morecambe—who will first appear as Bright—in order that it might be used, malignantly, by the murderer, and its background, role, and use must be traced and understood by the detectives (both professional and amateur). This razor performs, gestures, behaves, interacts, and signifies, in its long and delightfully detailed history as an instrument used for shaving, in its enforcedly perverse role as a murder weapon, and in its interactive agency in solving the mystery.

The sweet-hearted mood of Lord Peter's interview with Mr. Endicott is absent in Chapter VII, "The Evidence of the Gigolo," when Harriet interviews M. Antoine, "the fair-haired gigolo" (HHC 83; ch. 7). He is, as the authorial narrator unattractively puts it, "neither Jew nor South-American dago, nor central European mongrel, but French," a category of which Sayers herself very heartily approved. The word "Jew" is not qualified with an offensive epithet, but the others are. "Dago" is a generalized term derived from the name "Diego," for men who speak Spanish, Portuguese, Italian, or other southern European languages, and is not a term of approval. A "mongrel" is, at its best, a "cross between types and persons" in its dictionary definition, and, in descending order, pertains to "an impure or mixed breed or race." The analogy is to dogs. To call a man a mongrel implies that he is of mixed genetic origins, a trait not desired by those interested in the breeding of dogs. The fact that all dogs belong to a single genus and species, *Canis familiaris,* and cannot truly be "mixed" in the genetic sense—a trait they share with *Homo sapiens*—*clearly* plays no part in this profoundly irrational point of view. We learn from this passage, at the least, that Harriet shares the prejudices of her culture and period.

M. Antoine affirms the victim's engagement to "the English lady," Mrs. Weldon, as do "Doris the blonde and Charis the brunette," female dancers whom Harriet treats to a late supper, "seated on a red plush settee beneath a row of gilded mirrors" (HHC 85; ch. 7). "From the earliest times, the mirror has been thought of as ambivalent,"[47] and in this scene the mirror may be an allusion to "the mirror of Venus," an astrological sign now frequently used as a feminist symbol, which stands not only for the goddess Venus but for the female in general,[48] and hence for a gathering of three women (Harriet, Doris and Charis), an appropriate number, as the goddess figure is frequently manifested in threes ranging in implication from the Three Graces of classical culture to the three witches in *Macbeth.*

Charis says frankly that Alexis "couldn't very well *like* the idea of marrying that dreadful old woman" (HHC 86; ch. 7). Antoine, with the author's imputed French rightmindedness, says "I am sorry for her" (HHC 87; ch. 7), but Charis presses on—"all that rubbish about his noble birth and fallen fortunes—" (HHC 87; ch. 7) and the conversation soon turns to Alexis's fear "of pricking his little finger" and reluctance to "go to the dentist" (HHC 88; ch. 7) and eventually to his refusal to shave, all clues to the "point of medicine,"[49] Hæmophilia, from which Paul Alexis suffered, a fact not established until the last chapter of *Have His Carcase.* Shaving (or rather, not shaving) reiterates the role of the razor; in a touch of irony, a man who does not shave has been killed with a razor.

The above two chapters, united by the razor motif, contrast a valid or "real" occupation, that of barber, with an invalid or "false" occupation, that of hired dancing partner. The red-plush settee and gilded mirrors emphasize the theme of falsity in the sale of sexual companionship, an element implicit in the profession of gigolo.

In Chapter VIII, "The Evidence of the Second Barber," we find Lord Peter, "sleek with breakfast, sunshine, and sentiment," interviewing Colonel Belfridge about the razor, which he has at one time owned (in accordance with Mr. Endicott's testimony), but has given to his gardener, Summers, who in turn passed it on to "his sister's husband, who kept a hairdressing establishment in Seahampton" (HHC 95; ch. 8). Rejoicing, Lord Peter departs, meditating upon the "beautiful town [...] bathed in the mellow afternoon sunshine," which "seemed to him the loveliest jewel in the English Crown" (HHC 96; ch. 8), in an image vividly expressing his status as well as his mood. This imagery of benignity is subjected to ironic reversal when Peter searches out Summers's brother-in-law and finds that he has passed the razor on to "a little rat of a fellow. Sandy-haired and too smooth in his manners by half" (HHC 97; ch. 8). Here the author gives us our first picture of the man who has plotted the murder, though his true identity is quite other than the one presented in this chapter. He is given the ironic name of Bright; his plan for the murder was a clever (bright) one, but it was defeated by an unknown fact; he was indeed "a rat," and no brightly shining example of human behavior.

Having pursued their investigations separately, Peter and Harriet join forces in Chapter IX, "The Evidence of the Flat-Iron." As they sit on the beach, "a basket of food lay between the pair, not yet unpacked" (HHC 100; ch. 9), a symbol of their capacity to share not only a picnic but other forms of common cause. Their visit to the murder site takes place in this holiday atmosphere, recalling Harriet's mood before she made her discovery.

She relives that experience, and recalls the boat she had seen, but her mind is also on Lord Peter; they prepare to swim, and she notes that "he strips better than I would have expected" (HHC 106; ch. 9), and takes inventory of his exposed anatomy. Such frankness about women's appreciation of men's bodies was not a common feature of detective stories of Sayers's period, but this passage expresses accurately what women actually think. The analysis of the murder site is equally detailed, and concludes as Peter says, "Why should we give up our picnic for any number of murderers?" (HHC 114; ch. 9). In this mood of cheerful distraction, the couple explore the idea that Mr. Perkins (Harriet's brief companion after she discovered the body) is

Mr. Bright in disguise. The possibility of disguise is thus introduced, but Mr. Perkins is in fact blameless.

Lord Peter meets with Inspector Umpelty in Chapter X, "The Evidence of the Police-Inspector," and learns of Paul Alexis's reading habits (novels and works in Russian) and recently emptied bank account. Umpelty reports that Alexis's former girlfriend, "Leila Garland—a hard-boiled little piece if ever there was one" (HHC 117; ch. 10), has taken up with another "Sort of dago fellow [...] all la-di-dah and snake-skin shoes"—da Soto—and adds that there is "Nothing wrong with him, though, as far as that goes" (HHC 117; ch. 10), which proves to be true. This is probably the passage of which Scowcroft says that "Leila Garland is no more than a sketch" and that "her boy friend da Soto is a caricature." It is characteristic of Sayers that people she describes in standard epithets regarding ethnicity or religion seldom (if ever) turn out to be villains. It is certainly the case that broad (as well as frankly racist) figures like the golliwog are still to be seen in British children's Christmas magazines, and in that more primordial of their popular forms, the Christmas pantomime, and it is such traditions as these that are operative in Sayers's lavish use of popular epithets of her day in her novels.

The motif introduced by Mr. da Soto's snake-skin shoes reflects the camper whom Harriet met in Chapter II; she identifies him to Umpelty as "a gentleman of the country sort" (HHC 123; ch. 10), not mentioning the snake tattoo she had seen. Umpelty responds ironically that "Mr. Martin isn't much good to us" (HHC 124; ch. 10), not knowing that he is the murderer under an assumed name, but Lord Peter suggests accurately that "He might have been a valuable witness" (HHC 124; ch. 10). When Umpelty continues—"We've absolutely nothing against this fellow Martin" (HHC 125; ch. 10)—Lord Peter retorts that "There are points about him which seem to be suggestive, as Sherlock Holmes would say" (HHC 125; ch. 10). Perhaps Peter is thinking also of Holmes's famous dictum, repeated in *The Sign of Four,* "The Beryl Coronet," "The Priory School," and "The Blanched Solder," that "when you have eliminated the impossible, whatever remains, however improbable, must be the truth." (I am indebted to Christopher Redmond for this insight's *tour-de-force* of sources). Nobody can say that Lord Peter (through his creator, the author) has not warned us, but as there are twenty-four more chapters in the book, we are not likely to take the "points" that are offered to us here.

The motif of gold, foreshadowed in the golden beach where Paul Alexis died, now shows itself in Chapter XI, "The Evidence of the Fisherman." The Inspector has "found out what he did with it" (HHC 127; ch. 11), "it" being the three hundred pounds Alexis has drawn from his bank account. He has changed it into gold, telling the bank attendant that he wanted "to buy a diamond from a foreign rajah who didn't understand bank-notes" (HHC 129; ch. 11), a story so fabulous that Wimsey remarks, "He got that out of a book, I expect" (HHC 130; ch. 11). Besides its hint of the British raj, this imagery also suggests the fatal effect of turning a thing into gold, as in the Greek tale of King Midas. The Inspector agrees: "Where are you going to find a rajah who doesn't understand Bank of England notes? The n——s aren't savages, not by any means. Why, lots of them have been to Oxford" (HHC 130; ch. 11) [my elision]. Wimsey suggests correctly that "Alexis was contemplating a flitting to some place where Bank of England notes wouldn't pass current" (HHC 131; ch. 11). The rest of the chapter presents an interview with the old fisherman whose boat had stood off the Flat-Iron's beach near the Grinders, the place where Alexis's body, weighed down by the gold, actually lies hidden. It concludes with Lord Peter giving an interview about the case to the press. He, like Harriet, must pay his dues as a celebrity.

The "Bloody Farce" II: "The only son of his mother"

Having appeared briefly in disguise as Mr. Martin in Chapter II, the murderer now shows himself openly in Chapter XII, "The Evidence of the Bride's Son." This chapter begins with a "lame [railroad track] gate-keeper who knew the mysterious Mr. Martin by sight" (HHC 141; ch. 12). The gate-keeper's "little daughter Rosie," who had been "playing Bluebeard," had "seen him in the village the day before and his horrid black glasses had frightened her" (HHC 141; ch. 12). This macabre touch of the pantomime tradition (no girl who has heard the story of Bluebeard and his murdered wives ever forgets it) reiterates the fantasy element of the previous chapter. The gate-keeper and his daughter open the way toward the truth about the murderer, a truly "horrid" man.

Wimsey's turn to be distressed comes when he learns that Mr. Martin had consumed a thoroughly disgusting meal of "roast mutton and cabbage on a red-hot June day" (HHC 143; ch. 12). He eventually learns, through Mr. Goodrich, who is eating a thoroughly acceptable tea of "bread and cakes and honey and Devonshire cream," that Mr. Martin "had asked straight out permission to camp in Hinks's lane" where campers were welcomed and could use "gramaphones or concertinas or ukuleles" as they pleased (HHC 146; ch. 12). Mr. Goodrich testifies at home near Darley, where Scowcroft's "Darley yokels" live; they had been, the narrator says ironically, in hopes "that they might be found to have entertained an angel of darkness unawares" (HHC 144; ch. 12).

Sayers does not tell the reader that this long section of the chapter concerns the character identified in its title, "The Evidence of the Bride's Son," but it does; the next section presents Harriet dining at the Resplendent with "Mrs. Weldon and her son" (HHC 149; ch. 12), and hence herself entertaining the angel of darkness unawares. Peter meditates upon the news of this encounter and upon "the son":

> Was he perhaps a new factor in the problem? He was the only son of his mother and she a rich widow. Here at last was a person to whom the removal of Paul Alexis might appear in the light of a god-send. (HHC 149; ch. 12)

The term god-send echoes ironically with the "angel of darkness," suggesting the role of the Adversary sent by God to test Job.

This sequence resonates with ironic reversals and contradictions, not least in the concept of the "widow's son," hinted at in the title—"The Bride's Son"—and made explicit in the phrase "the only son of his mother and she a rich widow." The "widow's son" is a term in Masonic symbolism, which refers to Hiram, the architect of the Temple of Israel.[50] As "Hiram Abiff," he is the victim in the central narrative of the Masonic ritual of initiation to the Third Degree, that of Master Mason. He is both a blameless and a tragic figure and thus is the very opposite of Mrs. Weldon's son.

Furthermore, every male born of a married woman can be called a "bride's son" in one sense, but a previously-married woman who becomes a bride when she already has a son must be either a divorcee or a widow. The relationship of these dilemmas to Mary, who became pregnant while she was betrothed but still a virgin, and who later became, according to tradition, a widow, so that Jesus could be regarded as the infinitely blameless "widow's son," adds extreme irony to Weldon's situation. Had he not been his mother's son, he would not have felt obliged to kill her prospective bridegroom to protect his inheritance. But, in his role as "Bride's son" and "the only son of his mother and she a rich widow" (HHC 149; ch. 12), this murderer of his widowed mother's fiancé is as far as one could imagine from being a victim.

Henry Weldon, we learn, "was a good, sturdy specimen of his type […] a strongly built, heavyish man with a brick-red all-weather face" (HHC 150; ch. 12). When Harriet joins him at table with his mother, Mrs. Weldon tells her that when Henry "was a little boy he had the dearest golden curls—just like mine. But he loves sport and out-door life […]" (HHC 151; ch. 12), thus summing up in a couple of sentences his failure to be what she wanted him to be; the operative word of condemnation is "But." At the bar with Wimsey, meanwhile, her son is also commenting: he doesn't "like these Popoffsky blighters" (that is to say, Russians), and he feels "a bit of a fool" that "his mother proposes to give him a twenty-year-old lounge lizard for a step-papa" (HHC 152; ch. 12). The conversation descends from this already debased level to insulting remarks about Lord Peter's brother, the Duke of Denver, who is, the author is telling us, a truly responsible and valid landowner whose "income was not derived from the Devon estate" (HHC 155; ch. 12), in comparison with Henry Weldon, the "gentleman farmer, who was not quite a gentleman and not much of a farmer" (HHC 150; ch. 12).

Later, Peter and Harriet, while dancing, compare notes on the egregious Henry Weldon. In her thoughts, Harriet realizes that in the "epoch-making moment" when Peter holds her in his arms for the first time, he has his mind "concentrated upon the dull personality of an East Anglian farmer" (HHC 157; ch. 12). Ironically, the fact is in fact not ironic; she and he are dancing because Lord Peter has come to join her in detecting the murderer, and that murderer is Henry Weldon. It is Weldon who has brought her into Peter's arms. In a long sequence of alternate quotes of which only the first and second are identified as being spoken by, first, Harriet, and second, Peter, the latter concludes with the final sentence, "I don't think Henry has the brains to have murdered Paul Alexis" (HHC 160; ch. 12). The reader, who does not yet know that somebody else has provided "the brains," while Henry has provided the brawn, must read on for nearly thirty more chapters before understanding what Lord Peter means.

The farcical elements of artificiality, surface appearances, false identities, and apparent misreadings reach a climax in the aptly-named Chapter XIII, "Evidence of Trouble Somewhere," which contains that favorite mystery-writer's device, the "double-entry" list, which Harriet attributes to "Michael Finsbury [...] as in *The Wrong Box*" (HHC 163; ch. 13). Lord Peter suggests they use the version favored by "your Robert Templeton" (HHC 163; ch. 13), who is Harriet's own fictional detective, and Harriet's effort to comply with this suggestion takes up nearly ten pages, the same amount of space as that devoted to the famous and much-discussed decipherment sequence in Chapter XXVIII, "The Evidence of the Cipher." The people listed are Paul Alexis (the victim), Mrs. Weldon, Henry Weldon (the murderer, not yet recognized as such), Esdras Pollock—whose name is also the name of a species of fish, appropriately for a fisherman—Mr. Perkins, Haviland Martin (who is really Henry Weldon), and Harriet Vane herself, since she knows the police can't help wondering about her because she was tried for murder herself in a previous novel. The ironic result of Harriet's endeavor is a quarrel between Lord Peter and herself.

William Bright (Henry Weldon's evil mentor) appears in Chapter XIV; "The Evidence of the Third Barber." He "possesses the sandy hair, the small stature, the indefinite crookedness of shoulder" (HHC 179; ch. 14) attributed to him by his former employer in Seahampton. He looks nervous, as well he might, but carries out his masquerade with care. His former business has "all been pulled down now" (HHC 180-81; ch. 14) he has no "War record" but he can say that he "tried to get work in Seahampton." In Leston Hoe, he had used the name "Walters"—indeed, has used "alias after alias"—many of which Peter does not yet know (HHC 181; ch. 14). In the midst of his long recital of woes, he describes himself as saying, "Chuck it up, Bill Simpson" (HHC 182; ch. 14) as a conveniently arranged high tide tempts him into contemplating suicide: "There was the sea, and there was the razor," he says, reiterating the scene of Paul Alexis's murder, along with the instrument used to kill him.

Speaking of the razor (as well as of the murder victim), he declares that he gave his razor to a "young fellow" (HHC 183; ch. 14) in evening dress calling himself a Russian, who, as Wimsey says, "Sounds like Paul Alexis" (HHC 184; ch. 14) which is what he is supposed to think. This sequence of lies and disguises has contained very little information indeed except for another false name for the man whose "crookedness" is not only physical but symbolic. Lord Peter's concentration, however, is upon the man's description of the tide during the supposed suicidal episode. At the reported time, Wimsey realizes, the tide was not in fact "lapping against the Esplanade," but at the "extreme bottom of the ebb" (HHC 186; ch. 14). From this point on, Bright's tide begins to run out too.

Disguise is again the theme in Chapter XV; "The Evidence of the Ladylove and the Landlady." Harriet interviews M. Antoine, of whom the author approves so much that she allows him to quote in French from a sixteenth century poet, along with Leila Garland and Luis da Soto, of whom she does not have so high an opinion. She calls them "the perfect platinum blonde and the perfect lounge-lizard" (HHC 190; ch. 15). Leila mentions the frequent letters her former boyfriend Alexis received, which always resulted in his spending time with "his door locked" (HHC 194; ch. 15). Behind this door, he deciphers these letters, and later on, Peter and Harriet too will decipher one such letter and find the verbal key to the mystery of his death. Harriet, unaware of this, spends the interview thinking of Leila's current escort, da Soto, as one of "those slinky people of confused nationality," and Leila Garland as "a regular little gold-digger and as vain as a monkey" (HHC 195; ch. 15). This reiterated litany of epithets has exactly the quality to which Scowcroft quite rightly objects.

As this interview ends, Harriet visits "Paul Alexis's landlady, Mrs. Lefranc," colorfully described as "an ample personage with brazen hair, who was dressed in a pink wrapper, much-laddered artificial silk stockings and green velvet mules, and wore about her heavily powdered neck a string of synthetic amber beads like pigeon's eggs" (HHC 196; ch. 15), in another compendium of motifs of the artificial and synthetic whose inclusion is so characteristic of this novel. Deliciously, Mrs. Lefranc is revealed to have been "a trapeze-artist" (HHC 198; ch. 15), a very high flyer indeed. This caricature is not intended to be read as a realistic depiction of the trapeze artist's life, but as a richly imagined image of exuberant artifice capable of being recognized even from the cheap seats.

Thus escorted, Harriet visits the dead man's room, described in approving terms which culminate in "a very beautiful little ikon hung at the head of the bed" (HHC 198; ch. 15). Mrs. Lefranc agrees with Harriet's estimation of Miss Garland and Mr. da Soto; she characterizes them as "that little cat" and "that dago of hers" (HHC 200; ch. 15). Paul Alexis received one of his "foreign" letters and "was shut up hours and hours with it" (HHC 201; ch. 15). Afterwards he spent the night "burning his papers" (HHC 202; ch. 15), paid her his bill in the morning, and went off to his death. He "was a foreigner, when all's said and done they aren't like us, are they?" (HHC 203; ch. 15).

Lord Peter, meeting Harriet in Chapter XVI, "The Evidence of the Sands," evidently agrees. When told about the possibility that Alexis has received "cipher letters," he exclaims, "He seems to have been surrounded by a bunch of curiously unpleasant people—liars and half-wits and prostitutes and dagoes" (HHC 204; ch. 16). It would be hard to find anybody in this novel who does not use the last of these unpleasant epithets. Peter, like Harriet, makes an exception for M. Antoine: "He seems a modest, sensible fellow" (HHC 204; ch. 16). These ruminations are interrupted as Lord Peter looks out to sea, toward the Grinders. "Fishers of men" (HHC 205; ch. 16), he says, "grimly," quoting Matthew 4.19 in this macabre context, because the boatmen are dragging for the missing corpse. The author presents the proceedings through an ironically comical conversation between Harriet and Peter, again referring to "Holy writ," specifically to "The Song of Songs" (HHC 208; ch. 16), presumably to emphasize their growing rapport as prospective lovers.

Walking away along the beach as the police continue their search, Peter makes a discovery of his own. It is a horseshoe, the sign of "good luck" (HHC 209; ch. 16). He deduces the size and other traits of the horse that threw it; questioned, he reveals that "I was expecting the horse, but the shoe is a piece of pure, gorgeous luck" (HHC 211; ch. 16), thus reiterating the theme of luck. The horse, too, plays a symbolic role. Harriet suddenly realizes of Peter "that there was, after all, something godlike about him. He could control a horse" (HHC 211; ch. 16). She imagines him "very sleek, very smart," and herself "at his side, amid the respectful admiration of the assembled nobility and gentry" (HHC 211-12; ch. 16). Though Harriet "laughed at this snobbish picture" (HHC 212; ch. 16), there is here a clear implication of the contrast between Lord Peter's real, and Alexis's false, nobility.

Now, almost halfway through the novel, "At the top of Hinks's lane they got out and walked down to the camping-place" (HHC 212; ch. 16), the camping place, that is, of the murderer, whom Harriet had met all unknowing in Chapter II. This time, she and Peter meet the horse, the very animal the killer rode across the sand on his way to cut the throat of the deluded Alexis; indeed, the only witness to the crime, as Peter will later realize. This animal has been provided with a "new shoe" to replace the one she lost on the beach.

Peter reconstructs the crime, correctly as regards all but time. "He rides along through the edge of the water, so as to leave no marks. He tethers the mare to the ring that he has driven into the rock; he kills Alexis and rides back," the mare casting a shoe in "crossing the rough pebbles" (HHC 215; ch. 16). So pondering, Harriet and Peter walk on to find "the village smithy" (HHC 218; ch. 16) conveniently placed for them to interview; this is not surprising since horses obviously still played a role in the local economy, not having been completely replaced in either agriculture or commerce.[51] After an endearingly rural interview, the smithy has "confirmed Wimsey's deductions" (HHC 220; ch. 16) about the horse and the shoe.

In order to cut Henry Weldon loose from "his mother's apron strings" (HHC 222; ch. 17) long enough to interview Mrs. Weldon, Harriet retires with that lady to the Resplendent's Turkish bath in Chapter XVII, "The Evidence of the Money." There, "In the mood of relaxation and confidence that follows on being parboiled," Mrs. Weldon is revealed as a woman whose father ("a wealthy brewer") has "left her with a very considerable fortune in her own right" (HHC 222; ch. 17). In a dreadful sense, Mrs. Weldon's only value to anybody is her money, for which Paul Alexis and Henry Weldon are rivals; the love she offers both is of no value to either of them. "The Money," in fact, destroys all three of these people, because Mrs. Weldon's fiancé is killed, her son is eventually executed, and she ends up with the money but loses her lover and her son, a fate for which she herself must take a considerable part of the blame.

Her story is told sympathetically, however, and is one of the few "realistic" elements in the novel, in that while it depicts stock characters, there is a genuine psychological realism in the combination of Mrs. Weldon's restrictive childhood and her own repetition of those traits as an adult. She has, as so often happens, "become what she beheld." She married at eighteen to escape a "strict nonconformist aunt" who raised her after she was orphaned. "That rigid lady" (HHC 222; ch. 17) had tied up the prospective Mrs. Weldon's money so that "Weldon could not touch the capital." His only fault is "a certain lack of imagination in matrimonial matters" (HHC 223; ch. 17), the intimate details of which Mrs. Weldon has revealed to Harriet. The young Henry "was inclined to run after girls and race-meetings, leaving his work to be done by his father and his farmhands" (HHC 223; ch. 17). When the father died, the son inherited "the farm and all his own savings" (HHC 223; ch. 17). Mrs. Weldon, having clearly "learnt something from the Noncomformist aunt" (HHC 224; ch. 17), made Henry numerous loans, but "steadily refused to make over any of her capital to him" (HHC 224; ch. 17). Upon her marriage, she planned to "make him a free gift of everything that [she] had lent him, and make a will, giving him the life-interest in £30,000, the capital of which was to go to Henry's children, if he had any. If he hadn't any, then the money was to come back to Paul, if Paul outlived Henry […]." She had planned to settle everything else on Paul, but he objected, so, as she tells Harriet, she "was going to settle £30,000 on Paul when we were married […] at my death […] Paul would have had all the rest, which would have been about £100,000 altogether, including his own £30,000" (HHC; ch. 17), but she had not yet done so! The temptation to dispose of Paul before she rectifies this oversight (if it was an oversight) has proved irresistible.

Lord Peter, meanwhile, has investigated the incompetent career of Mr. Bright, the bogus barber. Wimsey concludes correctly that "whatever part Bright had played in the tragedy, it was not that of First Murderer" (HHC 229; ch. 17) and the Inspector concludes that "he may be Simpson as he says" (HHC 230; ch. 17). He is, of course, Simpson, but only as one of the many disguises of Morecambe. Finally, Lord Peter dispatches Bunter to Huntingdonshire, to "find out all about Mr. Henry Weldon, who owns a farm there" (HHC 233; ch. 17). The entire mood of this chapter on "The Money" is expressed in Lord

Peter's whimsical reference to "Here we go round the mulberry-bush" (HHC 233; ch. 17), a category of rhyme devoted to "group play,"[52] and specifically identified as a "counting-out rhyme"[53] in which children hold hands and dance in a circle. Since the money is indeed the motive for the murder, all the clues center upon it; ironically, Wimsey does not know that the missing body itself has been kept hidden by the money in the form of gold.

With perhaps the most audacious symbolic motif in this symbol fraught novel, Chapter XVIII concerns "The Evidence of the Snake." The snake in Mrs. Weldon's imagined Eden is the tattoo which marks the arm of her murderous son (the same fate of a visible mark befell Eve's son Cain). Harriet has agreed to meet Henry Weldon, and has "selected a slinky garment [...] which outlined her figure," (We have become accustomed to the word "slinky" as a pejorative term), along with an "oversized hat," set upon her "black ringlets skillfully curled into position," and "high-heeled beige shoes and sheer silk stockings" (HHC 235; ch. 18). This is a potent parody of what a seductress would wear in a film of the period. The conversation is notably poisonous: "Henry was really too easy" (HHC 240; ch. 18), Harriet thinks. Finally, in the context of a shared picnic, he makes his move.

As he attempts to kiss her, Harriet gives "a scream which was no mockery," and explains "I saw a snake!" (HHC 241; ch. 18), thus scaring Weldon and freeing herself from his clutches. Escaping, she tells Peter accurately, "I believe I've been kissed by a murderer" (HHC 242; ch. 18). She identifies this murderer as "Haviland Martin," and states correctly that "Haviland Martin is Henry Weldon" (HHC 243; ch. 18). She "saw a snake tattooed all the way up his arm—just as it was up Martin's" (HHC 243; ch. 18), when she noted it in Chapter I. And, she "*saw* Alexis with his throat cut and the blood running all over the place" (HHC 244; ch. 18) in her mind when she recognized the serpent. Surely the snake image is the most overt sign of Cain that could be imagined.

Would Harriet really resort to this odious masquerade? Would Henry Weldon be so clumsily seduced? Is this a coarse parody or a clumsy drama? In the reading I am attempting, this scene is not a mere melodrama but a morality play, where Harriet enacts the role of Vanity, and Henry performs the role of Lust. It is farce, pure farce;

hence the snake, the figure of betrayal and false values, as seen in that raw, earthy and heart-rending comedy of human error which in Genesis follows hard upon the sublime Creation narratives.

Weldon, as himself, is interviewed by Lord Peter in Chapter XIX, "The Evidence of the Disguised Motorist." Peter's brother-in-law, Chief Inspector Parker, suggests correctly that Martin/Weldon "may be leading a double life" (HHC 246; ch. 19). Confronted by Wimsey with this doubleness, "Henry turned an ugly colour" (HHC 247; ch. 19). Doubleness is the heart of irony; we speak of "double-dealing"; of "double-trouble"; of one person being another's "double." Duplication is often seen as a sign of inferiority produced by the weakening of value through repetition. Peter refers to the tattoo, and Weldon, never the gentleman, replies, "So that's what the little hussy meant when she said she'd seen a snake" (HHC 248; ch. 19). Threatened with having his teeth pushed in for this inauspicious remark, he admits that he "came down here in another name" (HHC 248; ch. 19), in order to buy Alexis off, or, as Peter says, he engaged in "a qualified form of blackmail" (HHC 249; ch. 19). Even his car has been a disguise, since it is rented.

In fact, he admits "I had another name and address ready to slip into" (HHC 245; ch. 19), where he keeps a "nice little woman" (HHC 250; ch. 19), the couple thus living under the names of Mr. and Mrs. Haviland Martin. He also admits that he did indeed "camp in Hinks's Lane" (HHC 251; ch. 19), but when Peter asks if he has "rambled as far as the Flat-Iron" (HHC 253; ch. 19), he denies it. Instead he spins an elaborate tale of having gone to Wilvercombe to attend a concert at the Winter Gardens, where "the Eroica Symphony" (HHC 255; ch. 19) was being played. In this manner he accounts for the entire morning of the day Alexis died. Lord Peter lets him go, muttering "water-tight—damned suspiciously water-tight!" (HHC 258; ch. 19).

This glib alibi has indeed robbed its giver's "latest masquerade of half its significance" (HHC 259; ch. 19), as the Superintendent and the Inspector agree in Chapter XX, "The Evidence of the Lady in the Car." The word "masquerade," of course, exactly characterizes this novel. The chapter is devoted to checking Weldon's "elaborate and fishy" alibi (HHC 261; ch. 20), which he had prepared to cover his presence in the morning at the murder site; his insistence upon it looks fishy because the still-bleeding corpse has been interpreted by all investigators as having been killed in the afternoon; the operative irony of the detective situation in this novel.

A lady who says she gave Weldon a ride is located, and asked to identify him; she does so, but "Weldon gave quite a convulsive start" (HHC 265; ch. 20) at the sight of her, as well he might, since she is "Mrs. Morecambe," the wife of the man who planned the murder which Weldon committed. Forced to meet, they carry off this game of recognitions, pretending to be people who have met only slightly. Sayers, though she had yet to translate Dante, obviously knew the symbolic significance of a lady in a car, and had Beatrice ironically in mind when she made Mrs. Morecambe (herself a conspirator) act as the precursor of the return of the dead, as this chapter concludes.

The "Bloody Farce" III: "We've got the body"

Chapter XX ends with Umpelty, who "surged in, damp and triumphant," rather like an allegorical figure of Neptune in a triumphal procession or a masquerade ball, exclaiming, "Good evening, my Lord, we've got the body!" (HHC 268; ch. 20). The recovered body of Paul Alexis is the center of Chapter XXI, "The Evidence of the Inquest." This "real, solid—or comparatively solid—body" (HHC 269; ch. 21), clearly resembling the "too, too solid flesh" of the meditating Hamlet, is examined for clues, which include most notably "£300 in gold. (Sensation.)" (HHC 270; ch. 21).

The additional items are a passport "visa'd for France," "the mounted photograph of a very beautiful girl of Russian type," in a pearl head-dress, "a handsome leather note-case," and a small sheet of paper written upon in code (HHC 270; ch. 21). The victim, who had clearly prepared for a departure, though not for death, was a walking compendium of clues. The face of the dead man has, we are told, been "all eaten away," his visual identity thus stripped from him, so that he is reduced to an inventory of his belongings.

Harriet repeats her previous detailed reports to the police; the police surgeon describes the "evidence of acute haemorrhage, coupled with the severance of the respiratory canal" (HHC 274-75; ch. 21), and adds the telling evidence (for the plot) that "the body was completely drained of blood" (HHC 275; ch. 21).

Chapter 3

This chapter is the most businesslike of the book; its contents combine the utmost propriety of expression with a few touches of irony: "Wimsey grinned at Umpelty over [the coroner's] convenient summary, with its useful suppressions and assumptions" (HHC 281; ch. 21), and the jury for its part insists that "police regulations about foreigners did ought to be tightened up, like," even though they are assured that "Deceased was a naturalized Englishman" (HHC 282; ch. 21).

Afterwards, Weldon, who as the murderer takes an intense interest in the proceedings, recklessly tries to persuade Lord Peter that Harriet's evidence is unreliable, and that the blood cannot still have been flowing at 2:00 pm. All his efforts have been devoted to proving he was not at the site when he in fact killed Alexis, and in this chapter Lord Peter begins to recognize this desperate effort to establish an alibi as being, precisely, a desperate effort to establish an alibi.

In Chapter XXII, "The Evidence of the Mannequin," Harriet visits Paul Alexis's empty apartment and becomes familiar with his romantic taste in fiction, wherein "young men of lithe and alluring beauty […] turned out to be the heirs to monarchies" (HHC 291; ch. 22), succinctly presenting Alexis's hopes for himself. Lord Peter meanwhile is reading Bunter's report on Henry Weldon / Haviland Martin, along with a letter from a young woman named Olga Kohn, the "mannequin"—professional model—of the chapter's title, stating that the photograph found on Alexis's body is a picture of herself

Peter and Umpelty proceed to Regent Square, where they interview Miss Kohn. Wimsey has already assumed that she is "a Russian Jewess" (HHC 296; ch. 22), and she is accompanied by "a dark haired young man of Semitic appearance" (HHC 297; ch. 22), as her fiancé, just in case the reader has missed this point. In one of his whimsical moods, Lord Peter assures Miss Kohn that he believes her when she says she has never met Alexis, and, "now merrily launched on a flight of fantasy," declares that "a case founded on stark unreason I have never met before" (HHC 300; ch. 22). Not fully reassured, Miss Kohn asks Peter if he really does believe her:

> "I do," replied Wimsey. "But you see, I can believe a thing without understanding it. It's all a matter of training." (HHC 301; ch. 22)

The reader may be reminded of the White Queen's statement in Lewis Carroll's *Through The Looking Glass* (1872): "Why, sometimes I've believed as many as six impossible things before breakfast."

Following Miss Kohn's testimony, in Chapter XXIII, "The Evidence of the Theatrical Agent," Wimsey and Umpelty interview Mr. Isaac J. Sullivan, who, after the efforts of his secretary to protect him have failed, greets Lord Peter with joy, mistaking him for an actor applying to play the part of a nobleman. As all Sayers's readers know, Peter does, in his detecting, play upon his nobility as if it were a role, partly, perhaps, to disguise his capabilities, and partly to hide his vulnerabilities. Mr. Sullivan chortles, "Carries his clothes well, eh?" (HHC 305; ch. 23). Peter, happily playing the part, escorts Sullivan and his partner Rosencrantz into their inner office, declaring himself (not inaccurately) to be the "Picadilly Sleuth, hot on the trail of Murder" (HHC 305; ch. 23), thus hiding in plain sight his actual intentions and role.

The stage-clown figure of a Jew with an Irish surname, playing Guildenstern to "Rosencrantz" in a sly reference to the blameless and hapless fellow students of Hamlet, presents these theatrical personages in the role of music hall comedians, in accordance with real conventions of the period. This scenario gradually becomes serious as the men (not, after all, clowns) identity a visitor "who said he wanted Russian types for the provinces" (HHC 307; ch. 23). That is, he wanted actors whose impersonations would convince an unsophisticated audience. "Russian types" of this period were stereotypes too, usually of expatriots and escapees from the Russian Revolution, often depicted as pretending to be royalty. The visitor who made this request is identified as Maurice Vavasour, who is Alfred Morecambe in disguise again. He has been given a selection of theatrical photographs, including that of Miss Kohn.

The author uses this carefully crafted theatrical setting to describe the conspirators by specifically comparing them to Shakespeare's *Richard III*. Mr. Sullivan comments upon the character of Richard in this play:

> "Too slimy at the beginning and too tough at the end. It ain't nature [...] he's made Richard two men in one [...] One of 'em's a wormy, plotting sort of fellow, and the other's a

bold, bustling sort of chap who chops people's heads off."
(HHC 308-309; ch. 23)

These perceptive characterizations suggest both Morecambe (the
wormy plotter), and Weldon (the bustling murderer); Peter remarks
that Shakespeare's Richard is "one of those men who are always deliberately acting a part" (HHC 309; ch. 23), which is certainly the case
with Alfred Morecambe/William Bright/Maurice Vavasouri/William
Simpson, as well as with Henry Weldon/Haviland Martin.

The funeral of Paul Alexis opens Chapter XXIV; "The Evidence of the L.C.C. Teacher"; this event includes "a floral emblem in
the shape of a saxophone," thus introducing farce into a situation
which also includes Mrs. Weldon "being theatrically overcome and
carried away in hysterics" (HHC 311; ch. 24). Henry Weldon, who
has good reason for wishing to leave, tries vainly to persuade his
mother to depart; William Bright is more successful, and is reported
to have "started a trek northwards" (HHC 312; ch. 24).

Meanwhile another suspect, the innocent Mr. Julian Perkins, is
extensively interviewed by a policeman, who learns mostly that Perkins is "not a very courageous person" (HHC 314; ch. 24), as the man
himself confesses. The interview does lead to information, however,
about "a gentleman that was camping in a tent" (HHC 316; ch. 24).
This "gentleman" (Weldon/Martin) has unkindly kicked Mr. Perkins
"from behind" (HHC 317; ch. 24); an event considered comical in
some circles. In telling this, Mr. Perkins also reveals that he sat alone
on the beach "about fifty yards from the lane" (HHC 318; ch. 24) for
the better part of an hour, and saw no one between "two o'clock and
three" (HHC 319; ch. 24), that is, during the time that everybody (except the killer and his mentor) thinks the murder has taken place.

In Chapter XXV, "The Evidence of the Dictionary," the young
constable who conducted this interview considers its impact: "Either
Perkins was a liar, or Weldon had deliberately deceived him" (HHC
320; ch. 25). Weldon is indeed a deceiver, as we have seen, though
his deceptions are ironically aimed in another direction, that is, toward another time. Much checking of clocks and times follows, reinforcing the extreme focus upon true and false time in this novel. Numerous other witnesses are consulted, some of whom corroborate
Perkins's and Harriet's accounts. The combination of time and tide in
Have His Carcase is not accidental, let alone incidental. The tidal ebb

and flow, from low tide to high tide, is expressed in physical terms, that is, in space, moving back and forth (in and out) horizontally and up and down vertically, while at the same time marking the time through this series of repeated movements which coincide with the motion of earth and moon in space, thus exactly embodying the fact that, historically and symbolically, "both time and space are the outcome of the same principle."[54] Time and space are literally interlocked. For maritime peoples like the British, the tides become a primary figure for time.

Time and tide are discussed in detail in *Have His Carcase,* until Harriet points out that "You men [...] have let yourselves be carried away by all these figures and time-tables [...] But it's all machine-made. It creaks at every joint. It's like—like a bad plot, built up around an idea that won't work" (HHC 331; ch. 25). Pressing further, she declares accusingly that "whatever the explanation is, it must be simpler than that" (HHC 331; ch. 25). She is right. It *is* simpler than that. The plot turns entirely upon a mistake about the time of death, a mistake caused by one missing fact about the victim's blood, surely a figure for his life. Finally, Peter states: "The only thing we've found [...] is *Chamber's Dictionary* [...] We've found a lot of words marked with pencil" (HHC 334; ch. 25). These "words" are intended for use as "key-words to a cipher." The actual key-word turns out to be a central clue in the story, as the moment of solution draws closer.

Chapter XXVI, "The Evidence of the Bay Mare," begins with the cipher letter found on Alexis's body, printed in full for the reader, as an "inextricable jumble of letters" (HHC 339; ch. 26). To decode it, "a key-word of six letters" (HHC 341; ch. 26) must be found, and fitted into a square of five divisions in both the horizontal and vertical dimensions, a form of cipher called "Playfair."

The rest of the chapter is devoted to the bay mare, already identified by her replaced shoe. "She came up to be caught with remarkable readiness" (HHC 346; ch. 26) by the omnicompetent Peter, already fully established as an able horseman, who rides her along the beach. Suddenly, "she started as if she had been shot, flung up her head and slewed around so violently that Wimsey [...] was within an ace of being spun off altogether." Away she runs, "tearing back in her tracks as if the devil was after her" (HHC 347; ch. 26). The mention of the devil is not perhaps placed here only for emphasis. This animal has been forced to witness, and indeed to participate in, a bloody murder.

When Wimsey manages to slow and turn her, he finds that she still "would not go near the Flat-Iron" (HHC 348; ch. 26). Scowcroft points out the resemblance of this "curious behaviour"[55] to that of the mare Polly Flinders in Sayers's short story, "The Undignified Melodrama of the Bone of Contention," published in *Lord Peter Views the Body* (1928), who gives "a violent start [...] so sudden that it nearly unseated" Lord Peter (PVB 131). Oddly, there are characters in this short story named both Haviland and Martin.

Symbolically, "the horse pertains to the natural, unconscious, instinctive zone," when it appears in fairy tales; horses in such settings are seen as "clairvoyant [and] are often assigned the task of giving a timely warning to their masters." We have already seen above Sayers's use of "the belief that the horse-shoe brings luck"—an idea which "is derived from the magical nature of the horse."[56]

Wrongly convinced that a frightened horse would have been seen at two-o'clock by the offshore fishermen, in Chapter XXVII, "The Evidence of the Fisherman's Grandson," Inspector Umpelty urges Lord Peter to interview young Jem. Finding him at the Three Feathers—"it will be a black day for detectives when beer is abolished," the narrator comments—Wimsey gently interrogates the young man about "the Flat-Iron and the death of Paul Alexis" (HHC 355; ch. 27). What he discovers is that "Grand-dad" not only went fishing at two-o'clock (when Harriet saw him) but also "visited [another man's] lobster-pots, abstracted the greater part of their live contents, and replaced the pots" (HHC 356; ch. 27). "All this mystification," Lord Peter muses, "and nothing behind it but a trivial local feud." In this situation Jem has in fact seen "this chap on the Flat-Iron" looking as if "he's asleep or summat." Other than "this chap" ironically sleeping the sleep of death, "there wasn't a single soul come along that there shore" (HHC 357; ch. 27). Peter is profoundly puzzled. He spends the rest of the chapter helplessly reviewing the evidence without finding the truth.

Chapter XXVIII, "The Evidence of the Cipher," devotes ten pages of its content to the detailed deconstruction of the cipher. The description of this process may be one of the most unreadable passages in literature, but it culminates in the keyword, not only for the cipher but for the mystery; "MONARCH." Harriet exults, "Oh, Peter! How marvellous! Let's dance or do something," but instead they begin to read the passage, which begins; "'To His Serene Highness—'" (HHC 376; ch. 28). Not only does the solving of the cipher parallel the solving of a mystery; it also provides a figure for—indeed, an occasion of—Peter and Harriet's developing relationship. Their conceptions of one another have been scrambled. In the process of unscrambling the cipher, they also begin to unscramble their confused understanding of each other, a process of mutual cooperation and working in tandem, toward a shared goal. The key-word "Monarch" thus provides a clue to their future, suggesting the "King of Love" who is not only the ruler of lovers who face one another, but the Lord of friends who can work side by side.

Chapter XXIX, "The Evidence of the Letter," reveals that Paul Alexis has been duped into believing that he is "Paolo Alexandevitch, heir to the throne of the Romanovs" (HHC 379; ch. 29). Lacking the ironic corollary to this, that Alexis has inherited Hæmophilia, Peter and Harriet spend most of the rest of the chapter incorrectly rehearsing the murder at its imagined time. Peter concludes that "every theory [he] had so far formed about the case was utterly and madly wide of the mark" (HHC 389; ch. 29). According to *Websters Collegiate Dictionary* (1947) a cipher is a "method of secret writing," but it can also mean "zero," a numerical symbol for what "has no weight, worth, or influence," and is a "nonentity." Paul Alexis, who wanted to be a "Monarch," was in fact a nobody, a "cipher," most especially for his killers.

We join Mr. Mervyn Bunter in Chapter XXX, "The Evidence of the Gentleman's Gentleman." He has "bought himself a suit of horrible cheap serge, which it gave him acute agony to wear, and he had also purchased a disgusting bowler of curly shape and heavy quality" (HHC 390-91; ch. 30)—in other words, clothing that he would never otherwise wear, and, taking his own turn at disguise, he is tracking Bright (Morecambe in disguise) through Bloomsbury, a place of significant resonance for Sayers. He and an obliging taximan follow Bright until their quarry is glimpsed "vanishing down the subway to the Underground" (HHC 394; ch. 30). Bunter continues the hunt through a complex tour including Picadilly and elsewhere, finally trailing him to his lair in Kensington, where a local chemist states that

Bright is, in fact, a "gentleman in the City" (HHC 397; ch. 30), that is, in London's financial district. Learning that Morecambe is married to a woman who "used to be on the stage." Bunter telegrams Lord Peter with the news, "The chase has ended" (HHC 398; ch. 30). Along with Bunter's intolerable disguise, the motif of "the stage," with its feigned behavior and disguising makeup, emphasizes Morecambe's many false identities, even as they are being stripped away.

Superintendent Glaisher correctly sums up the discovery in Chapter XXXI, "The Evidence of the Haberdasher's Assistant"; thus: "If this here Bright is Morecambe, and Mrs. Morecambe is in cahoots with Weldon, then, likewise, Weldon and Bright—so to call him—are in cahoots together" (HHC 399; ch. 31). Consequently, Bright/Morecambe is no hairdresser and had "no legitimate call to buy that razor" (HHC 399; ch. 31). The very buying of the razor has offered an insult to the instrument, as well as to the "legitimate" order of things. A man who would buy a razor under false pretenses will do anything; at this point we touch the heart of this novel's symbolism of truth versus falsity.

Lord Peter cites the man's additional guises: "the bearded friend who came to stay with Weldon at Fourways Farm at the end of February," and "the bearded gentleman who approached Mr. Sullivan […] and asked him for the photograph" (HHC 400; ch. 31), using the name of Vavasour. Morecambe, says Lord Peter, "is the brains of the conspiracy" (HHC 401; ch. 31). He is the writer of the fateful letter to Alexis, signing his name as "Boris," yet another disguise. Alexis, acting under "the Imperial outlook" (HHC 402-403; ch. 31) as Wimsey puts it, has set aside his girlfriend Leila Garland, whom he has "pushed off on to our conceited young friend da Soto" (HHC 402; ch. 31) and has refused to take "large sums of money from Mrs. Weldon" (HHC 403; ch. 31). Peter concludes from all this that Alexis "has the instincts of a gentleman, if not necessarily of a prince" (HHC 403; ch. 31). Coming from Lord Peter, this may be a sober compliment, with no ironic overtone, but again, it may not.

Peter also analyzes Morecambe's various impersonations, noting that he had shaved off his beard to become Bright, and resorted to a false beard when pursued by Bunter. These disguises have been assisted by Mrs. Morecambe, the ex-actress who "knows something about makeup" (HHC 408; ch. 31). The chapter continues in this vein, but still the detectives think that the murder was committed in the afternoon.

Just as Harriet has taken a turn at feigned seduction, so Lord Peter pursues "the conquest of Leila Garland" in Chapter XXXII, "The Evidence of the Family Tree." The author notes parodically that Miss Garland "drove Wimsey almost to madness by the refinement of her table-manners" (HHC 413; ch. 32). From her, as he has hoped, he learns of Alexis's supposed noble birth, a subject on which Miss Garland deems him to have been "a little bit silly" (HHC 415; ch. 32), a term which not only means "foolish," but can carry the sense of "lower rank," a realistic judgment in the case of this easily fooled man who would be king.

Wimsey asks whether she has found any of his letters; "the beautiful eyes of Leila directed their beams like a pair of swivelling head-lamps rounding a corner on a murky night" (HHC 416; ch. 32). Leila is compared to a beautiful, desirable, and expensive object (an automobile) in this satirical simile. Off they go together to "Leila's crowded and untidy apartment" (HHC 417; ch. 32), where in the end Luis da Soto actually finds the document—the genealogy or "Family Tree" of the chapter's title-tracing Alexis back, on very shaky evidence, to Tsar Nicholas of Russia, through a morganatic marriage, that is, a marriage which could not make his consort queen. Every detail of this brief document is diagnosed by Lord Peter, whose speculations paint a romantic picture, while "Leila Garland yawned dreadfully" (HHC 422; ch. 32). Peter now knows "how the trap was baited" (HHC 423; ch. 32).

For their part, Inspector Umpelty and Chief Inspector Parker of Scotland Yard (Lord Peter's brother-in-law) interview Mrs. Morecambe about "Mr. Henry Weldon, to whom you gave a lift on Thursday morning" (HHC 423; ch. 32). She proves to be a very agile adversary, but is eventually forced to lead them upstairs to find "a small, red-bearded man" (HHC 426; ch. 32)—the so-called Bright—who responds with "Congratulations on your sleuthing" (HHC 427; ch. 32) in a cheerful voice. He has, he says, been writing a play for his wife; this explains his penchant for disguise, and supplies one more name, a *nom de plume,* for the Mr. Morecambe he actually is: "I've written a play or two before, under the name of Cedric St. Denis," he says (HHC 412; ch. 32). The theatrical motif so often reiterated here is both presented and parodied. One does not doubt that Morecambe is no more a playwright than he is a barber.

Just before the chapter ends, one final impersonation is revealed: a door opens, admitting "a respectable-looking working-woman and a large, stout man smoking a cigar" (HHC 429; ch. 32). The woman is asked if she can identify Morecambe, and responds: "Why yes, sir; this is Mr. Field, as was staying with Mr. Weldon down at Fourways in February. I'd know him anywhere" (HHC 429; ch. 32). The conspiracy of Morecambe and Weldon thus fully established, Inspector Umpelty solemnly announces:

> "Alfred Morecambe [...] alias William Bright, alias William Simpson, alias Field, alias Cedric St. Denis, alias Maurice Vavasour, I arrest you for being concerned in the murder of Paul Alexis Goldschmidt, otherwise Paul Alexis [...]" (HHC 429; ch. 32)

With this paroxysm of aliases, identities within identities, falsities within falsities, the chapter ends.

Lord Peter sums up the case in Chapter XXXIII, "Evidence of What Should Have Happened," stating that "Everything in the garden is lovely except the melancholy fact that none of the people engaged in the conspiracy could possibly have done the murder" (HHC 431; ch. 33). Harriet suggests that "you give the story one final shake, twist it around a fresh corner, and find [...] the real murderer" (HHC 431; ch. 33), which is what Sayers proceeds to do in the following and final chapter of *Have His Carcase*. Harriet then comments, "even if he had fifty kinds of Imperial blood in his veins instead of only one or two, it wouldn't help us to explain how he managed to get killed with nobody near him" (HHC 432; ch. 33). This, of course, is profoundly ironic, because it does and will explain this central problem.

Without yet realizing their import, all the intricate and interlocking disguises are rehearsed and explained. The theme of blood, the blood of the victim spilling on the terrified horse, is addressed by Lord Peter out of his own terrible war experiences—"Ever see a horse that has suddenly had fresh blood splashed all over it? Not pretty. Definitely not" (HHC 437; ch. 33). Finally, in the last line of this penultimate chapter, Lord Peter announces his conclusions, based precisely on the matter of blood, the blood of Paul Alexis: "We have no evidence at all [...] as to the time Alexis died" (HHC 441; ch. 33). This, too, is ironic, because the busy endeavours of the conspirators to provide themselves with alibis have made the actual time perfectly clear.

In Chapter XXXIV; "The Evidence of What Did Happen," Peter lays out the evidence for Alexis's Hæmophilia, concluding that "one may inherit other things besides Imperial crowns through the female line" (HHC 443; ch. 34). Harriet understands him first; Umpelty must have it explained. Hæmophilia, like colour-blindness, is "inherited through the female, and shows itself only, or practically only, in the male, and then only in alternate generations" (HHC 444; ch. 34). Because Hæmophiliacs risk with every cut the possibility of bleeding to death because their blood lacks the capacity to clot, Alexis "might have died at any time" (HHC 445; ch. 34). The carefully crafted alibis are meaningless because the liquid state of the blood suggested death at around two-o'clock in the afternoon. The Inspector groans, "It's so complicated [...] that I don't believe we'll ever get any jury to believe it" (HHC 447; ch. 34). There is one final factor: "Last night, Mrs. Weldon consented to dance with M. Antoine," Harriet reports, "and Henry Weldon didn't like it at all." Gigolo and heiress will now be in renewed danger, "If you let Henry Weldon and Morecambe loose again" (HHC 448; ch. 34).

At this point, the last page of the book, Peter declares the whole affair "a damned, awful, bloody farce," and takes Harriet "home" to Picadilly.

Conclusion

Beneath the bitter-flavored farce and razor-edged irony of *Have His Carcase,* there lies the mystery of transformation of life into death. This long novel teems with images of vanity, mortality, sterility, and loss. The old widow in love with the young dancer offers him no chance to become a father and every chance to become a faceless corpse. Their relationship is indeed a *danse macabre.* The widow's son kills her lover as well as the hoped for happiness of that lover, and in so doing, he causes her to lose her child (himself) to death by hanging. Alexis is duped into believing that he is to be Tsar, but all that his gold can do is weigh him down after his death.

Everything becomes other than it is perceived to be, and everything becomes worse than it was intended (or at least expected) to be. In a series of terrible metamorphoses, a respectable gentleman's razor becomes a murder weapon; a would-be king becomes a corpse; and the time of death is misidentified so that the calculated alibis become noticeable liabilities. Multiple disguises change the characters into one person after another, and all to no avail.

Cirlot states that "all transformations are invested with something at once of profound mystery and of the shameful, since anything that is so modified as to become 'something else' while remaining the thing it was, must inevitably be productive of ambiguity and equivocation. Therefore, metamorphoses must be hidden from view—and hence the need for the mask."[57] In the masque, disguises and revelations are inevitably interlocked, each requiring the others, each necessarily invoking the others. Death, which changes everything, not least the human body, is fundamentally ironic. One must live if one is to die, and one must die if one is to live. It is even possible that the author herself, striving to balance and maintain her roles as writer, mother, wife, and breadwinner, explored and expressed her own bitter feelings in this deeply ambivalent work. Certainly, as so many commentators say, she has used the novel to explore and develop the relationship of Lord Peter Wimsey and Harriet Vane.

In the end, it is the novel itself that must be judged. Taken on its own terms as a singular work of art, it stands alone of all Sayers's novels in its explicit contemplation of the ugliness of murder, the sharp consequences of falsity and betrayal, and the bitterness of death. No wonder its readers long to look away.

Notes

[1] Margaret Hannay, "Harriet's influence on the Characterization of Lord Peter Wimsey," *As Her Whimsey Took Her: Critical Essays on the Work of Dorothy L Sayers,* ed. Margaret Hannay (Kent, OH: Kent State UP, 1979) 41.
[2] Ralph E. Hone, *Dorothy L Sayers, A Literary Biography* (Kent, OH: Kent State UP, 1979) 81.
[3] James Brabazon, *Dorothy L Sayers A Biography* (London: Victor Gollancz, 1981) 149.

Notes

[4] Catherine Kenney, *The Remarkable Case of Dorothy L Sayers* (Kent, OH: The Kent State UP, 1990) 51.

[5] Kenney 159.

[6] Philip Scowcroft, "Sayers in Devon," *The Proceedings of the* 1992 *Seminar* (Hurstpierpoint, West Sussex; The Dorothy L Sayers Society, 1993) 27.

[7] Sharyn McCrumb, "Where the Bodies are Buried: the Real Murder Case in the Crime Novels of Dorothy L Sayers," *Dorothy L Sayers: The Centenary Celebration,* ed. Alzina Stone Dale (New York: Walker and Company, 1993) 88-89.

[8] Kenney 55.

[9] *The Letters of Dorothy L Sayers, 1899-1936: The Making of a Detective Novelist,* ed. Barbara Reynolds (1995; New York: St. Martin's Press, 1996) 330. Editor's note: Nephelocorcygia is properly spelled nephelococcygia.

[10] Northrop Frye, *Anatomy of Criticism* (1957; New York: Atheneum, 1967) 290.

[11] Frye 290.

[12] *The Letters of Dorothy L Sayers, 1899-1936* 330.

[13] Frye 107.

[14] Scowcroft, "Sayers in Devon" 27.

[15] Frye 292.

[16] Martial Rose, ed., "The Deliverance of Souls," *The Wakefield Mystery Plays* (New York: WW. Norton & Co., 1961) 372-84.

[17] Frye 233.

[18] Frye 233.

[19] Frye 366.

[20] Frye 317.

[21] Dorothy L. Sayers, *The Mind of the Maker* (1941; San Francisco: Harper and Row, 1979) 152.

[22] *The Letters of Dorothy L Sayers, 1899-1936* 311.

[23] *The Letters of Dorothy L Sayers, 1899-1936* 312.

[24] *The Letters of Dorothy L Sayers, 1899-1936* 316.

[25] *The Letters of Dorothy L Sayers, 1899-1936* 317.

[26] Dorothy L. Sayers, "Gaudy Night," *Titles to Fame,* ed. Denys Kilham Roberts (London: Thomas Nelson and Sons, 1937) 80.

Notes

[27] Sayers, "Gaudy Night" 81.

[28] For information about Beddoes, see Stephen P. Clarke, *The Lord Peter Wimsey Companion* (New York: The Mysterious Press, 1985).

[29] J.E. Cirlot, *A Dictionary of Symbols* (New York: Philosophical Library, 1962) 114.

[30] Cirlot 114-115.

[31] Julian of Norwich, *A Book of Showings to the Anchoress of Norwich Part Two,* eds. Edmund Colledge and James Walsh (Toronto, ON: Pontifical Institute of Mediaeval Studies, 1978) 294.

[32] Frye 220.

[33] Frye 221.

[34] Frye 367.

[35] Cirlot 28.

[36] C.G. Jung, *Symbols of Transformation*, Bollingen Series XX, CW vol. 5 (1956; Princeton, NJ: Princeton UP, 1967) 432, note 76.

[37] Cirlot 262.

[38] John Pinsent, *Greek Mythology* (London: Paul Hamlyn, 1967) 47.

[39] Robert Graves, *Greek Myths* (1955; combined edition London: Penguin, 1992) 143 no. 39.

[40] C.G. Jung, *Symbols of Transformation* 412, para. 638.

[41] C.G. Jung, *Symbols of Transformation* 413, para. 640.

[42] Kenney 51.

[43] Sayers, *The Mind of the Maker* 77.

[44] Joan M. Vastokas, "Are Artifacts Texts? Lithuanian Woven Sashes as Social and Cosmic Transactions," *The Socialness of Things: Essays on the Socio-Semiotics of Things,* ed. Stephen Harold Riggins (Berlin: Mouton de Gruyrer, 1994) 337.

[45] Vastokas 337.

[46] Vastokas 342.

[47] Cirlot 201.

[48] Sven Tito Achen, *Symbols Around Us* (New York: Van Nostrand Reinhold, 1978) 215-16.

[49] Barbara Reynolds, *Dorothy L Sayers: Her Life and Soul* (London: Hodder and Stoughton, 1993) 233-34.

[50] Robert Macoy, *A Dictionary of Freemasonry* (1869; Brattleboro, VY: Echo Point Books & Media, 1989) 536.

Notes

[51] Philip Scowcroft, "Some Pickings from *Have His Carcase,*" *Sidelights on Sayers,* Volume XXX (October 1989) (Hurstpierpoint, West Sussex: The Dorothy L Sayers Society, 1989): 18.

[52] William S. Baring-Gould and Cecil Baring-Gould, *The Annotated Mother Goose* (New York: Bramhall House, 1962) 224. Editor's note: The rhyme cited in Baring-Gould and Baring-Gould (no. 638, p. 253) is "Here we go round the bramble bush [...]"

[53] Baring-Gould and Baring-Gould 224.

[54] Cirlot 325.

[55] Scowcroft, "Some Pickings from *Have His Carcase"* 18.

[56] Cirlot 145.

[57] Cirlot 195.

Nancy-Lou Patterson, "Harlequin's Dive" and "Harlequin in the Tree."
First published in *Mythlore* 15.3 (Spring 1989): 24 and 24.
Further reproduction prohibited.

4. "A Comedy of Masks": Lord Peter as Harlequin in Dorothy L. Sayers's *Murder Must Advertise*

The masque of oddity he wore
Endeared the hidden beauties more.
When thrown aside, the shade was clear'd,
The real countenance appear'd
Where human kindness, candour fair,
And truth, the native features were.
How few like him could change with ease
From shape to shape and all should please!

——"On the Death of John Rich, Esq." (1761)

Peter Wimsey's harlequin disguise is a significant aspect of his inter-actions with Dian, the former lover of the murder victim in Murder Must Advertise. *Patterson analyzes Wimsey's use of this disguise in the novel and compares it with the historical Harlequin, the treatment of the character in G.K. Chesterton's Father Brown mystery "The Fly-ing Stars" (1911), C.G. Jung's writings, and Agatha Christie's Her-cule Poirot mystery "The Affair at the Victory Ball" (written 1923–1926), as well as Sayers's own "The Adventurous Exploit of the Cave of Ali Baba" (1928) and "The Incredible Elopement of Lord Peter Wimsey" (1933). Patterson concludes by noting the importance of Pe-ter's aliases to the discovery of the truth.*

Patterson also addresses the theme of falseness transforming into truth in "'Changing, Fearfully Changing': Polarization and Transformation in Dorothy L. Sayers's Strong Poison" *and "'Bloody Farce': Irony, Farce, and Mortality in Dorothy L. Sayers's* Have His Carcase," *and in the conclusion to "'A Ring of Good Bells': Provi-dence and Judgment in Dorothy L. Sayers's* The Nine Tailors."

"A Comedy of Masks" was first published in Mythlore *15.3 (Spring 1989): 22-28.*

In three chapters of *Murder Must Advertise*, Lord Peter, already in disguise as Death Bredon and an employee of Pym's advertising firm, dons the mask and costume of Harlequin in order to interview Dian de Momerie, whom he suspects of being involved with drug-trafficking, and perhaps of murder. In "Remarkable Acrobatics of a Harlequin," he has been invited to a ball by Pamela Dean, whose brother, Victor Dean, has been murdered. Wimsey/Bredon appears "in the harlequin black and white which had been conspicuous as he stepped into his car" (MMA 74; ch. 4).

The gathering is far from innocent; we read of the naked *danseuse*, "the amorous drunken couples" (MMA 75; ch. 4), and the "sinister little cubicles" each "furnished with a couch and a mirror" (MMA 75; ch. 4). The harlequin distinguishes himself in this frantic company by climbing a statue set in a pool. "Up and up went the slim chequered figure, dripping and glittering" (MMA 75; ch. 4). Dian, "in a moonlight frock of oyster satin," with "fair hair standing out like a pale aureole round her vivid face" (MMA 76; ch. 4), calls to him, "Come on Harlequin, dive!" and "The slim body shot down through the spray, struck the surface with scarcely a splash and slid through the water like a fish." Dian is delighted:

> "Oh, you're marvellous, you're marvellous!" She clung to him, the water soaking into her draggled satin.
> "Take me home, Harlequin—I adore you!" The Harlequin bent his masked face and kissed her. (MMA 76; ch. 4)

They make their departure together, as he cries, "'Let's run away, and let them catch us if they can'" (MMA 77; ch. 4). The reader is left to wonder what happened next until well into the following chapter, when Lord Peter remarks to his brother-in-law Charles Parker, Chief-Inspector of Scotland Yard, "She's a bad lot, that girl," and explains:

> I went incog. A comedy of masks. And you needn't worry about my morals. The young woman became incapably drunk on the way home, so I […] tucked her up on a divan in the sitting-room to astonish her maid in the morning. (MMA 85; ch. 5)

"Unsentimental Masquerade of a Harlequin" describes Lord Peter's second appearance as Harlequin. It begins with Dian behind the wheel of a friend's saloon, which is overtaken by "the glare of the enormous twin lights" (MMA 152; ch. 9) of another automobile. In a moment "She saw the black mask and skull-cap and the flash of black and silver" (MMA 152; ch. 9). The pursuit leads them into "a stretch of woodland" and shuts off all its lights. To Dian, "the darkness was Egyptian."[1] Far away she hears "a very high, thin fluting." The piping is explained by Lord Peter after its disembodied sound has led Dian into the dark woods:

> "The terror induced by forest and darkness," said a mocking voice from somewhere over her head, "was called by the Ancients, Panic fear, or the fear of the great god Pan. It is interesting to observe that modern progress has not altogether succeeded in banishing it from ill-disciplined minds."
>
> Dian gazed upwards. Her eyes were growing accustomed to the night, and in the branches of the tree above her head she caught the pale gleam of silver. (MMA 154; ch. 9)

In this position, Lord Peter questions the mesmerized Dian at length. She describes her affair with Victor Dean, and the boredom that led her to drop him. Harlequin refuses to descend from his tree; he calls Dian "Circe" and chides her, "You made him drink and it upset his little tummy. You made him play high, and he said he couldn't afford it. And you made him take drugs and he didn't like it" (MMA 157; ch. 9). Dian, in affirmation of the title Circe, replies, "He was a little beast, Harlequin, really he was" (MMA 157; ch. 9). The conversation continues until Lord Peter has learned that Tod Milligan is the drug-peddler who controls Dian.

Sister Mary Durkin (1980) remarks of this passage, "the mental picture of Lord Peter in the treetops and Dian huddled on the grass makes the scene grotesquely unreal."[2] There is indeed a certain sadistic element in this scene, and its darkness is not dispersed by dawn; Harlequin descends in the early daylight, which shows Dian "only a long implacable chin and the thin curl of a smiling mouth" and bestows upon her "kisses like deliberate insults" (MMA 160; ch. 9). Suddenly, her mood changes. "The hanged man," she cries: 'There's a hanged man in your thoughts. Why are you thinking of hanging?'" (MMA 161; ch. 9).[3] With this prescient outcry, she falls asleep. When he returns her to her door, "He kissed her gently this time and pushed her into the house" (MMA 162; ch. 9). Janet Hitchman (1975) too is offended by these scenes; she writes, "Wimsey who must by now be all of 43 [...] lures a fast woman with a penny whistle and she, poor soul, suffers a terrifying moment of E.S.P., or, as might be said today 'a bad trip.'"[4]

Lord Peter meets Dian de Momerie again in his Harlequin disguise.

[A]t the note of the penny whistle she would come out and drive with him, hour after hour, in the great black Daimler, till night turned into daybreak. He sometimes wondered whether she believed in him at all; she treated him as though he were some hateful but fascinating figure in a hashish-vision. (MMA 188; ch. 11)

He tells her frankly, "I am here because Victor Dean died," and muses, in a passage that probably reveals Sayers's intention in these symbol-laden passages:

She was the guardian of the shadow-frontier; through her, Victor Dean, surely the most prosaic denizen of the garish city of daylight, had stepped into the place of bright flares and black abysses, whose ministers are drink and drugs and its monarch death. (MMA 189; ch. 11)

In her search for entertainment, Dian persuades Milligan to gate-crash a party. Coincidentally, they choose the house of Lady Helen, Duchess of Denver and sister-in-law of Lord Peter, who is there as himself. "The shadow of a tall pillar-rose fell across his face and chequered his white shirt-front with dancing black; and as he went he whistled softly" (MMA 196; ch. 11). Dian recognizes the whistled air and knows him immediately as her Harlequin, but he pretends to be surprised; she has, he says, mistaken him for his "unfortunate cousin Bredon," a drug-smuggler, whom Dian and Milligan are to meet again (MMA 197; ch. 11).

In "Hopeful Conspiracy of Two Black Sheep," the couple watch as "The gentleman in the harlequin costume removed his mask with quiet deliberation and laid it on the table" (MMA 237; ch. 14), and takes him to be Lord Peter's imaginary cousin. When asked if he has a "Christian name" by Dian, he replies, "I have. It's spelt Death. Pronounce it any way you like." And he produces from his cloak a "dainty bag of oiled silk," calling it "Such stuff as dreams are made on" (MMA 241; ch. 14).[5] The bag contains a packet of dope obtained by the police when it was mis-delivered. The Harlequin and Milligan agree to set up a business partnership, and "Major Milligan dreamed that night that Death Bredon, in his harlequin dress, was hanging him for the murder of Lord Peter Wimsey" (MMA 246; ch. 14).

Lord Peter's costume makes a final appearance: Parker reports to him that

> Dian de Momerie was found this morning with her throat cut in a wood near Maidenhead. Beside the body was a penny whistle and a few yards away there was a black mask caught on a bramble bush [...] (MMA 322; ch. 19)

It is an obvious attempt to implicate the imaginary Bredon: "'I've done it,' said Wimsey [...] And so, in a sense, I have, Charles. If that girl had never seen me, she'd be alive today" (MMA 322; ch. 19). In a continuation of this mood, when the entire dope ring is gathered in by the police, Lord Peter declines to celebrate.

History of the Harlequin

In their detailed commentary on *Murder Must Advertise*, "The Agents of Evil and Justice in the Novels of Dorothy L. Sayers," R.D. Stock and Barbara Stock (1979) state that "Sayers represents their spiritual degeneration by their physical decay: she dilates on the blemished complexions of both Major Milligan and Dian de Momerie, setting them against Lord Peter's nearly super-human prowess— his acrobatics as harlequin."[6] By the principle of opposition implied in the Stocks's title, Lord Peter is the agent of Justice. "Disguise is employed to a point up the theme of deception,"[7] the Stocks continue, and therefore, "The levity and high-jinks are acceptable, for we know throughout the novel [...] that Peter's humanity is fully engaged in the personal tragedy which he has exposed and to which he has perforce contributed."[8]

The aptness of the Harlequin's "mask" for Lord Peter's complex role in *Murder Must Advertise* becomes cleared with an understanding of the *Commedia dell' Arte* and the history of the Harlequin figure. This traditional form of improvisatory comedy using stock characters, for which the English synonym, used by Lord Peter was "the comedy of Masks,"[9] began in the mid-sixteenth century.[10] The improvisation surrounded and filled out a loosely organized plot with a series of *lazzi* or sequences of comic business of ancient pedigree: "the devil in the Mysteries chased sinners off to Hell-mouth with blows as resounding as those inflicted by Arlecchino on his master's rivals."[11]

The major characters of the *Commedia dell' Arte* are Pantaloon, Harlequin, Scaramouche, and Columbine, the maid-servant of the Inamorata, who like her mistress and other female characters, was not masked. Also called Arlecchina, she was the object of amorous intentions, sometimes indecently expressed, by Harlequin.[12] Harlequin was one of the two *zanni*, Harlequin and Brighella,[13] both men-servants. These two roles contributed to the development of the modern clown. Each of the characters is called a "mask," a term which refers to the complete costume.

The character of Harlequin probably derives from "spectre-devils" and "clown-devils of the early Middle Ages."[14] A French play of 1275 mentions a "King of the devils named Harlequin," and there is a comic devil in Dante's *Inferno* named Alechino, which Sayers translates "Hellkin,"[15] probably from Harlequin's French name, "Hellequin."[16] Harlequin "has the [...] arduous task of maintaining the even rhythm of the comedy as a whole,"[17] and like Peter, he engages in activities that "sometimes involve [...] the most daring and perilous acrobatics."[18] In the sixteenth century his costume was "overlaid with irregular coloured patches" which came to be made up of "regular diamond-shaped lozenges of many colours"[19] and his mask showed a fierce dark face with a carbuncle on the forehead, a wrinkled brow, an aquiline nose, and heavy eyebrows.[20] In his belt, he bore a leather purse and wooden sword,[21] which developed into the "bat" and finally into the "slapstick," a device of wood with two thin slats which produced a resounding whack when a blow was delivered with it.

Even after the *Commedia dell' Arte* migrated to England in the eighteenth century, becoming part of the English Pantomime tradition, Harlequin retained his colorful costume and black half-mask. The "custom began of interspersing short mimed scenes and dances played by characters of the *Commedia dell' Arte*, led by Harlequin, between the plays, or the acts of plays, in London theatres."[22] This "Harlequinade" became a major feature until Harlequin's centrality was superceded in the early nineteenth century, as the "Clown" began to dominate. By then, Harlequin's character had become firmly fixed in the British imagination.

Precursors: G.K. Chesterton, C.G. Jung, and Agatha Christie

There are interesting prefigurations or parallels for Sayers's use of the Harlequin figure in two short stories, one of them by G.K. Chesterton. Barbara Reynolds (1984) points out that "If we read these incidents"—Lord Peter's escapades as Harlequin—without having Chesterton's 'The Flying Stars' in mind, we miss an important point. It is all part of a literary game and of the same kind of artistry."[23] In "The Flying Stars," published in 1911, a young woman is to be given a gift of diamonds at a Christmas party, and an impromptu Harlequin-ade is planned. "I can be harlequin, that only wants long legs and jumping about,"[24] says a Mr. Blount. As part of the action, he beats one of the actors—who is dressed as a policeman—in a traditional *lazzi*, and at the end of the performance,

> danced slowly backwards out of the door into the garden, which was full of moonlight and stillness. The vamped dress of silver paper and paste, which had seemed too glaring in the footlights, looked more and more magical and silvery as it danced away under a brilliant moon.[25]

In the excitement, the diamonds have been stolen, but Father Brown has guessed where they have gone. He goes into the garden, where among the trees, "a strange figure is climbing, who looks not so much romantic as impossible. He sparkled from head to heel, as if clad in ten million moons." It is the arch-criminal, Flambeau. The clubbed policeman, Father Brown tells him, who in pursuit of his duty "could be kicked, clubbed, stunned and drugged by the dancing harle-quin"[26] because such violent actions are expected in a harlequinade. This action was demeaning, a downward step for Flambeau. The "sil-ver bird" in the tree relents, and drops "three flashing diamonds" onto the turf beside the priest. [27]

Among the parallels between this story and that of Sayers are the images of Harlequin in a tree, and his glittering garb. In his essay on "The Philosophical Tree" (1954), C.G. Jung discusses a woman patient's painting of a figure "swathed in multicoloured wrappings" perched in a tree, which suggested to her "the harlequin motif." Jung interpreted this figure as representing "a panic fear that [the patient

...] is slipping helplessly into some kind of madness."[28] The painting[29] shows an image remarkably similar to that of Flambeau perched in a tree in "The Flying Stars," and to that of Lord Peter similarly placed in *Murder Must Advertise*, with the exception that the Harlequin motif is expressed by multicolored patches of diamond shape rather by glitter.

As we have seen, the multicolored garb is a long-associated element of Harlequin's "mask": his glittering aspect originated with the costume of James Byrne, who performed at Covent Garden in 1805 "entirely covered with over three hundred pieces of cloth sewn with nearly 50,000 spangles. [...] The black vizard was replaced by an eye-mask. The Bergamask yokel was now a very fine gentleman indeed, as he flashed about the stage, a glittering quicksilver figure that caught every eye."[30] One writer called him "the knight of the spangles."[31]

In *Murder Must Advertise*, Sayers associates the motif of glitter with a fish-like appearance. There is a distinctly sexual element in her description of Lord Peter as Harlequin, "dripping and glittering like a fantastic water-creature" (MMA 75; ch. 4) who, when he dives, "slid through the water like a fish" (MMA 76; ch. 4). The fish in traditional European symbolism suggested "every conceivable form of devouring *concupiscentia*,"[32] according to Jung. These fish and pool images are reinforced by Lord Peter in his guise as cousin Bredon, when he falsely explains to Milligan his presence at Pym's:

> "I received information [...] that Dean was on to something fishy about Pym's. So, since most fish have gold in their mouths like St. Peter's, I thought it wouldn't do any harm to try a cast or two over that particular pool." (MMA 240; ch. 14)[33]

The reference is to Matthew 17.27, in which Jesus directs Peter to cast a hook into the sea, "and when thou hast opened [the fish's] mouth, thou shalt find a piece of money," which is to be used to pay the tribute required by the state. This oddly negative image is appropriate to the feigned intentions of cousin Bredon.

Jung points out that the sign of Pisces shows two fish, that, among other things, suggests its "splitting into the figures of Christ and Antichrist."[34] Perhaps this dichotomy is implied in Lord Peter's "harlequin black and white." There is a binary structure in *Murder*

Must Advertise with its paired and linked dichotomies of advertising world versus drug world and "city of daylight" / city of night. Sayers wrote that "The idea of symbolically opposing two cardboard worlds—that of the advertiser and the drug-taker—was all right, and it was suitable that Peter, who stands for reality, should never appear in either except disguised."[35] In Sayers's Piscine structure, Lord Peter's Harlequin is a judgmental fish who will gobble Miss de Momerie up.

A second short story with a Harlequin motif is Agatha Christie's "The Affair at the Victory Ball," written between 1923 and 1926.[36] In her autobiography, Mrs. Christie remarks of the Harlequin that "he was a friend of lovers, and connected with death."[37] This is the way Lord Peter portrays Harlequin, and this is what Dian de Momerie senses. The elements of a ball, a Harlequin, a Lord (Lord Cronshaw), a woman of questionable morals (Coco Courtenay), and cocaine, are united in this story, which well pre-dates Christie's stories of Mr. Harley Quin, as well as the publication of *Murder Must Advertise*. Hercule Poirot solves the mystery by examining the costumes of a set of porcelain figures, from which the actual ball costumes have been copied. The solution turns on the possibilities of disguise provided by the various "masks" of the Harlequinade, and the truth is revealed when "There in the limelight stood glittering Harlequin!"[38]

The spangles that glitter on Harlequin's costume are a token, in all of these works, of falsity. This theme is echoed in Major Milligan's contemptuous phrase used on Lord Peter as Harlequin to Dian: "this theatrical gentleman in tights" (MMA 245; ch. 14) and Poirot says to the people watching his reconstructed parade of the masks, "Your eyes have lied to you,"[39] because the Harlequin "must have been an impersonation."[40] The double meaning of this phrase—since all living Harlequins are ordinary human actors impersonating the Harlequin mask—is related to the plot but also to the symbolism. Even when Harlequin seems to reveal his identity to Major Milligan and Dian, he is impersonating cousin Bredon, whom he has accused of frequently impersonating him.

Precursors: Sayers's Short Stories

There are also precursors for Lord Peter's Harlequinade in two of Sayers's own short stories, one of which pre-dates *Murder Must*

Advertise. In both, Lord Peter assumes a disguise. In "The Adventurous Exploit of the Cave of Ali Baba" (1928), he is disguised first as the servant Rogers and second as one of a criminal gang whose members only appear to one another covered in black velvet masks. The events of the story take place at a false ball that is really a meeting of criminals. The *Commedia dell' Arte* is alluded to in this story in a remark of Lord Peter's as he is threatened with torture: "I shall not guess any the better for being stimulated with hot irons, like Pantaloon" (PVB 308). One of the last motifs to survive in the harlequinade was "the red-hot poker to be applied to Pantaloon's backside."[41]

Comic business that turns out to be genuinely violent has already been described from "The Flying Stars"; it also appears in *Murder Must Advertise*. When an arrest of Lord Peter in his persona of cousin Bredon is staged for the benefit of the press, "Wimsey tapped the sergeant lightly but efficiently under the chin and sent him staggering, tripped Parker as neatly as he jumped from the running-board, and made for the gate like a hare" (MMA 324; ch. 19). This is truly Harlequinesque *lazzi*. The sequence concludes with a comic exchange on the theme of truth versus falsity:

> "Rather prettily done, I flatter myself," said Wimsey.
> "Ar!" said Lumley, caressing his jaw. "You didn't need to have hit quite so hard, my lord."
> "Verisimilitude," said Wimsey, "verisimilitude. You looked lovely as you went over." (MMA 325; ch. 19)

This is slapstick, which David Madden calls "the comedy of force." A blow in the jaw is only funny in a comedy.[42]

In the second story, "The Incredible Elopement of Lord Peter Wimsey" (1933),[43] Lord Peter travels to rescue an ill-used woman in the Pyrennes, posing as a magician. His performance in this role resembles that of charlatans thought to have contributed to the development of the Doctor mask in the *Commedia dell' Arte*. Wimsey quotes Homer and Euripides, metamorphoses pigeons and a crystal tree from a metal pot, and prescribes "enchanted wafers" (HH 77), which in fact cause the wife to be healed. The feigned performance conceals genuine medicine. Winifred Smith (1912; 1964) states that

> The central figure in every group of charlatans, the quack doctor, half astrologer, half magician [...] traded on the supersti-

tions of his audience in his long-winded nonsensical speeches about the more than natural powers of his drugs.[44]

The motif of magical transformation in Lord Peter's performance is associated with Harlequin, whose bat possessed "magic powers,"[45] in its nineteenth century form, "working such marvels as converting a beehive into a statue, a coach into a wheelbarrow."[46]

These tricks and devices from the most antique to those contemporary with today, share in the symbolism of sham, feigning, artifice, and mummery. Playing Arlecchina to Lord Peter's Arlecchino is Dian de Momerie. Her surname "de Momerie" means "mummery," while her Christian name Dian, which refers to the moon goddess, Diana, is used here in her negative form suggestive of fickleness and mutability, of night and the eclipse of consciousness. The virginity of the goddess Diana, who corresponds to the profoundly archaic Artemis of the Greeks, symbolizes her state of being independent of external control, rather than of being sexually intact. Certainly, Dian de Momerie is not a virgin, but neither is she independent. She is a slave to dope and to the men who can provide it to her; Major Milligan is able to order her out of the room when he and cousin Bredon wish to speak privately.

Sayers was inclined to use the moon as a symbol of illusion or falsity; she made Lord Peter's Uncle Delgardie write:

> And then in his last year at Oxford, Peter fell in love with a child of seventeen [...] He treated that girl as if she was made of gossamer [...] [T]hey made an exquisite pair—all white and gold—a prince and princess of moonlight, people said. Moonshine would have been nearer the mark. (UBC 8; Biographical Note)

After Peter has gone to war, gallantly releasing Barbara from their engagement in case he should return mutilated, he comes back "to find the girl married—to a hardbitten rake of a Major Somebody" (UBC 9; Biographical Note). Dian too is the companion of a rakish Major. Are Lord Peter's bitter kisses intended in memory of his lost moonlight princess? May we interpret his relative inhumanity to Dian as a sort of psychic blind spot, a patch of emotional scar tissue?

Sayers, who actually had observed and to a degree participated in the bohemian life of her period, wanted to say that it was a mum-

mery, a world of falsity, artifice, and inhumanity. She is compassion-
ate in her judgment of the creative artists living on the edge of this
world, but savage in judging those who control or feed upon it. Dian
seems a pitiful figure, her fragile beauty already fading, her commanding stature and leadership abilities wasted, her wits, of which
she has perhaps once had more than an ordinary supply, dulled, distorted, and diffused. That she responds so intuitively to Lord Peter in
his Harlequin's guise suggests not only his skills, but her natural sensitivity. Her boredom is not only weakness, but an appropriate response to her empty and meaningless life.

Her "hair standing out like a pale aureole" and her "moonlight
frock of oyster satin" reinforce the image of her name. As the moon is
the symbol of night, so all Lord Peter's meetings with Dian are noc-
turnal. The moon also symbolizes mutability, because its appearance
is continually changing. In her second appearance Dian's decline has
already begun, as she stumbles among the briars of the woodland, and
the brambles tear at her clothing. Dian does not see herself in negative
terms, however. When Lord Peter chides her for being out for all she
can get in her relationship with the murder victim, she retorts: "I'm
terribly generous. I gave him everything he wanted. I'm like that when
I'm fond of anybody" (MMA 157; ch. 9). In the same conversation,
she tries to warn Harlequin against Milligan: "You'd better keep clear
of him" (MMA 159; ch. 9). One of Lord Peter's three kisses at the end
of this interview is given for her "disinterested effort to save [him]"
(MMA 160; ch. 9). When he takes her home, she tells him, weeping,
"I'm afraid of you. You aren't thinking about me at all" (MMA 161;
ch. 9). This entirely accurate accusation reminds us that Dian herself
is a victim.

Could Wimsey have saved her, had his attentions been meant
rather than feigned? Would she have found him a worthy partner, one
who could have given her a chance for renewal, the promise of the
full moon? The writer cannot tell us. She has evoked this vivid image
of squandered wealth, increasing helplessness, and waxing decadence,
only to let her be crushed underfoot like a beautiful doomed moth.
Dian has used her men and they her; Lord Peter is but the last man to
approach her for his own needs rather than hers.

Precedents: The Trickster

The exact meaning of Harlequin cannot be expressed entirely in words, but the visual elements of his mask can reveal something of that meaning. Harlequin originally embodied an old stereotype of a low city dweller, "gluttonous, stupid, and lazy."[47] But the developed figure is neither stupid nor lazy. The earliest picture of Harlequin, circa 1600, shows him in a cap with a rabbit's scut attached. The scut, a short upraised tail, is shown by a fleeing rabbit or hare to its pursuer. Mentions of rabbits and hares occur in *Murder Must Advertise* when cousin Bredon is said to be less rabbity-looking than Lord Peter, and when Wimsey fakes his arrest by running "like a hare." The "racy, native humour" of Harlequin's character diminished in the nineteenth century, as he became the "artificial creature, recognisable by his costume alone," as seen in the illustration of the period.[48]

Despite the attenuation of the Harlequin figure in her own time, Sayers incorporates his antique elements by referring to Pan. Thelma Niklaus (1956) expatiates upon Harlequin's mask, with its vivid impression of "sensuality and cunning, of diabolism and bestiality,"[49] and remarks upon "the assumption of masks at religious festivals, as when men covered their faces with vine leaves to honour the great god Pan."[50] In her impassioned book, *Harlequin Phoenix*, she describes her first encounter with an early Arlecchino mask: "this feral ancestor of the shining Harlequin forever associated in my mind with the little black mask, the spangles, and the white frill."[51] This is Lord Peter's Harlequin to the last detail.

A being who is at once "feral" and "shining" may be identified as Trickster, whom Jung describes as "God, man, and animal at once. He is both subhuman and superhuman, a bestial and divine being:[52] Karl Kerenyi (1972) says he is "inimical to all boundaries,"[53] and Alan Garner (1975) calls him "the shadow that shapes the light."[54] Trickster's character is the fullest embodiment of human ambivalence. Lord Peter continually crosses boundaries in *Murder Must Advertise*, managing at least three separate identities beyond his own. When he disguises himself, he dives downward into deep waters; he becomes a man-servant, a novice advertising copy-writer, a false copy-writer in a world based on falsehood. Harlequin represents an inferior and unconscious element in the human personality, which perverts and betrays the consciousness he appears to serve. Lord Peter's own character thus reveals odd, even sinister depths as Sayers portrays him in his Harlequin role.

The plunging descent of Harlequin, glittering as he falls, suggests the saying of Jesus, "I beheld Satan as lightning fall from heaven" (Luke 10.18). Satan is the name, which in Hebrew means "adversary," given to the agent of God who acts as tempter. In some terrible way, Lord Peter's Harlequin is the Tempter, even the Satan, who with brutal kisses and contemptuous banter lures Dian to reveal herself and die. Indeed, at one point she calls him "You devil!" (MMA 160; ch. 9). The Harlequin figure here meets fully Jung's dictum that a true symbol will be ambivalent. Lord Peter by his falsity reveals the truth, and by his tricks triggers the punishment demanded by justice. There may be an implacable justice active here; there is very little mercy.

Notes

[1] This simile may derive in part from Rudyard Kipling's "The White Man's Burden" (1899) with its echo of the lament of the Israelites against Moses in Exodus 16.31 "Why brought ye us from bondage,/ Our loved Egyptian night?"

[2] Mary Brian Durkin, OP, *Dorothy L. Sayers* (Boston: Twayne Publishers, 1980) 66.

[3] Sayers's use of the term "the hanged man" may merely refer to a man executed by the hangman, but it may refer to the Tarot card of that title, made famous by T.S. Eliot in "The Waste Land" (1922); that sinister card is a symbol of upheaval and change in occult meaning and of betrayal in its Renaissance origins.

[4] Janet Hitchman, *Such a Strange Lady* (London: New English Library, 1975) 105-106.

[5] Lord Peter is quoting the line spoken by Prospero in *The Tempest* (Act IV, Scene I) "We are such stuff / As dreams are made on, and our little life / is rounded with sleep." The passage is an example of the Petrine penchant for literary allusion and a witty simile for drugs, but may also be a reference to Prospero's meditation on the unsubstantial pageant of life. In the same scene of *The Tempest*, Ariel lays out Prospero's "glittering apparel."

Notes

[6] R.D. Stock and Barbara Stock, "The Agents of Evil and Justice in the Novels of Dorothy L. Sayers," *As Her Whimsey Took Her*, ed. Margaret P. Hannay (Kent, OH: Kent State UP, 1979) 19.

[7] Stock and Stock 20.

[8] Stock and Stock 21.

[9] Winifred Smith, *The Commedia dell' Arte* (1912; New York: Benjamin Blom, 1964) 3.

[10] Giacomo Oreglia, *The Commedia dell' Arte* (1961; London: Methuen, 1968) 1.

[11] Smith 4.

[12] David Madden, *Harlequin's Stick—Charlie's Cane: A Comparative Study of Commedia Dell'arte and Silent Slapstick Comedy* (Bowling Green, OH: Popular Press, 1975) 16.

[13] Madden 10.

[14] Oreglia 56.

[15] *The Comedy of Dante Alighieri, Cantica I Hell*, trans. Dorothy L. Sayers (Harmondsworth, UK: Penguin Books, 1949) Canto XXI, line 118, "Stand forward, Hacklespur and Hellkin there!" and Canto XXII, line 112, "Here Hellkin got completely out of hand."

[16] Oreglia 56.

[17] Oreglia 58.

[18] Oreglia 3-4.

[19] Oreglia 57.

[20] Madden 111.

[21] Oreglia 58.

[22] George Speight, "The Pantomime Tradition," *The Illustrated London News* (Christmas Number, 1975): 9.

[23] Barbara Reynolds, "G.K. Chesterton and Dorothy L. Sayers," *The Chesterton Review* X.2 (May 1984): 151.

[24] G.K. Chesterton, "The Flying Stars," *The Innocence of Father Brown* (1911; Harmondsworth, UK: Penguin Books, 1950) 83.

[25] Chesterton, "The Flying Stars" 83.

[26] Chesterton, "The Flying Stars" 90.

[27] Chesterton, "The Flying Stars" 91.

[28] C.G. Jung, "The Philosophical Tree," *Alchemical Studies* (Princeton, NJ: Princeton UP, 1967) 261.

Notes

[29] Jung "The Philosophical Tree" figure 20.

[30] Thelma Niklaus, *Harlequin Phoenix* (London: The Bodley Head, 1956) 157.

[31] Niklaus 157.

[32] C.G. Jung, *Aion: Researches into the Phenomenology of the Self* (1959), second edition (Princeton, NJ: Princeton UP, 1969) 112.

[33] St. Peter is Lord Peter's patron saint, and a fellow fisherman.

[34] Jung, *Aion* 114.

[35] Dorothy L. Sayers, "Gaudy Night," *Titles to Fame*, ed. Denys Kilham Roberts (London: Thomas Nelson and Sons, 1937) 77.

[36] Nancy Blue Wynne, *An Agatha Christie Chronology* (New York: Ace Books, 1976) 187. The story was first published in *The Under Dog* (1952) and most recently in *Poirot's Early Cases* (1974).

[37] Agatha Christie, *An Autobiography* (1977; London: Fontana/Collins, 1978) 447.

[38] Agatha Christie, "The Affair at the Victory Ball," *Poirot's Early Cases* (London: Collins, 1974) 21.

[39] Christie, "The Affair at the Victory Ball" 21.

[40] Christie, "The Affair at the Victory Ball" 22.

[41] Niklaus 172.

[42] Madden, see chapter heading VII: "Lazzi (Slapstick) and the Comedy of Force."

[43] Editor's note: "The Incredible Elopement of Lord Peter Wimsey" is one of four Whimsey stories included in *Hangman's Holiday* (1933; London; Victor Gollancz, 1971) 47-86, along with "The Image in the Mirror" (7-46), "The Queen's Square" (87-114), and "The Necklace of Pearls" (115-32). This book also includes eight Montague Egg stories.

[44] Smith 35-36.

[45] David Mayer III, *Harlequin in His Element: The English Pantomime 1806–1836* (Cambridge, MA: Harvard UP, 1969) 5.

[46] Mayer 5.

[47] Cyril W. Beaumont, *The History of Harlequin* (1926; New York: Benjamin Blom, 1967) 46.

[48] Beaumont 62.

[49] Niklaus 33.

[50] Niklaus 36.

Notes

[51] Niklaus 14.

[52] C.G. Jung, "On the Psychology of the Trickster Figure," in Paul Radin's *The Trickster* (New York: Schocken Books, 1972) 203.

[53] Karl Kerenyi, "The Trickster in Relation to Greek Mythology," in Paul Radin's *The Trickster* (New York: Schocken Books, 1972) 188.

[54] Alan Garner, *The Guizer: A Book of Fools* (London: Hamish Hamilton, 1975) 1.

5.   "A Ring of Good Bells": Providence and Judgment in Dorothy L. Sayers's *The Nine Tailors*

"Well," said Wimsey, "I used at one time to pull quite a pretty rope. But whether, at this time of day—"

"Treble Bob?" inquired the Rector, eagerly.

"Treble Bob, certainly. But it's some time since—"

"It will come back to you," cried the Rector, feverishly. "It will come back. Half an hour with the handbells—"

"My dear!" said Mrs. Venables.

"Isn't it wonderful?" cried the Rector. "Is it not really providential? That just at this moment we should be sent a guest who is actually a ringer and accustomed to ringing Kent Treble Bob?"

———Dorothy L. Sayers, *The Nine Tailors*

In "A Ring of Good Bells" Patterson examines The Nine Tailors *as a novel in which the cause of death of the supposed murder victim is God. She notes that the long opening is not merely local color, as many readers assume: it establishes the unusual circumstances and extraordinary timing that involve Wimsey in the mystery such that his participation seems to be divinely prescribed. The death of the victim is, as Patterson shows, directly related to the ritualistic actions of Wimsey and the bell-ringers.*

Patterson also emphasizes the unusual "character" and role of man-made objects and structures in a murder and in disguising a murder in "'Beneath That Ancient Roof': The House as Symbol in Dorothy L. Sayers's Busman's Honeymoon." *She addresses the theme of falseness transforming into truth in "'Changing, Fearfully Changing': Polarization and Transformation in Dorothy L. Sayers's* Strong Poison" *and "'Bloody Farce': Irony, Farce, and Mortality in Dorothy L. Sayers's* Have His Carcase," *and in the conclusion to "'A Comedy of Masks': Lord Peter as Harlequin in* Murder Must Advertise."

"A Ring of Good Bells" was first published in Mythlore *16.1 (Autumn 1989): 50-52.*

Agatha Christie wrote one detective novel in which the murderer was the narrator, and one play in which he was the detective. In a sense, *The Nine Tailors* falls into the latter category, but in another sense, Dorothy L. Sayers takes the blame one step higher. The ultimate cause of death in this novel, which some would claim as her finest, is God.

Appropriately to such an august and dismaying subject, the book begins with an accident; by the third sentence the word "accident" has been uttered: "Peering through a flurry of driving flakes, Wimsey saw how the accident had come about." An "accident," we note, must have a cause. His car has gone "nose deep in the ditch" on a New Year's Eve, and equally deep in the fen country. The hour is "past four o'clock" (NT 9; ch. 1; part 1) and night is not far off. Bunter declares that he and Lord Peter are "near Fenchurch St. Paul," and as if summoned, "the sound of a church clock, muffled by the snow, came borne upon the wind; it chimed the first quarter." The engine of execution, the bell tower, has spoken, though it is recognized only as a time-piece by Lord Peter, whose response is entirely prophetic: "'Thank God!' said Wimsey. 'Where there is a church, there is civilisation'" (NT 10; ch. ch. 1, part 1). God is thus perceived to be active on the first page of the novel, and named in thanks for having placed a church so conveniently close to the accident scene on the second. Sayers, like all proper mystery writers, has placed her clues in plain sight, or in this case, sound.

After a bitter walk of a mile and a half against the wind, the two men reach a signpost announcing "Fenchurch St. Paul" (NT 10; ch. 1, part 1), and as they turn toward the church, "they heard the clock again—nearer—chiming the third quarter." Throughout the first chapter, the twin themes of accident and bells are reiterated: "The gentlemen have had an accident with their car" (NT 11; ch. 1, part 1), the village pubkeeper's wife tells "an elderly parson," who is, by coincidence, visiting in her parlor. This benign character invites Lord Peter and Bunter to spend the night at the vicarage, and, remarking "Bless my heart, there's five o'clock striking," he ushers them into his car and drives them homeward. Wimsey exclaims, "'Great Heavens!' […] 'is that your church?'" as "there loomed out of the whirling snow a grey, gigantic bulk" (NT 13; ch. 1, part 1), and the major player in the story makes its first visual appearance.

Welcomed to tea and muffins, after still other references to accident, Lord Peter and his host begin a cheerful conversation. "Perhaps you do not mind the sound of bells?" the parson enquires, and immediately announces his plan, central to the plot, "to ring the New Year in" (NT 16-17; ch. 1, part 1) with Fenchurch bells, a matter of nine hours and 15,840 Kent Treble Bob Majors. Lord Peter and Mr. Venables affably talk bells until interrupted by a knock. The Influenza—a name based upon the same concept of "influence" as that attributed to the stars and planets by astrology has struck, and one of the ringers, Will Thoday, cannot attend. "An irreparable disaster," the rector says, using another astrological term; disaster means "ill-starred."

"Well," says Wimsey, not unexpectedly, perhaps, "I used at one time to pull quite a pretty rope" (NT 20; ch. 1, part 1). And the matter is settled. "Nothing would please me more than to ring bells all day and all night." The relationship between coincidence, accident, and providence is openly expressed by the parson in his response: "Positively, I cannot get over the amazing coincidence or your arrival. It shows the wonderful way in which Heaven provides even for our pleasures, if they be innocent" (NT 21; ch. 1, part 1).

The practice for the ring is ready to begin; Sayers emphasizes the ceremonial nature of the event. The ringers are arranged in a circle, and "in the centre, the Rector stood twittering like an amiable magician" (NT 23; ch. 1, part 1). Each of the ringers, and each of the bells they are to ring, are introduced by name: there are no inanimate actors in this event. Warming to her campanological subject, the author calls change-ringing an "intricate ritual faultlessly performed" (NT 26; ch. 1, part 1), as the ringers wield their handbells in preparation for the greater effort to follow.

The reader, perhaps, accepts all these passages as the necessary paraphernalia of local color: the frequent reiteration of "accident" as an excuse for the usual coincidence by which a detective happens to be present at the scene of a murder; the bell-ringing as a picturesque background to the proceedings. But such is not the case. Lord Peter has been brought by "Heaven," as the Rector plainly states, to participate in an execution, although all the participants are (as an executioner supposedly is), again in the parson's words, "innocent." These ritual preparations, this ritual activity, is to lead to the death of a villain, and it will be Lord Peter's Heaven-sent task to find out how and why the man has died.

Chapter One moves toward its conclusion with an emphasis upon the inherent goodness of the bells and their ringers who are to be the instruments of death. As the rehearsal ends, the man in "charge of the bells and ropes" remarks that Lord Peter is not as tall as the man he is to replace, and his lordship retorts "In the words of the old bell-motto, I'd have it to be understood that though I'm little, yet I'm good" (NT 27; ch. 1, part 1). Good here is a pun upon good in the sense of skilled and good in the sense of innocent. The same double sense, used first of a bellringer (Lord Peter), is immediately repeated in regard to the bells themselves; Mr. Venables escorts his guest to view the church and its bell-chamber with the remark, "To my mind, Lord Peter, the sight of a ring of good bells—" (NT 28; ch. 1, part 1) when he is interrupted by his wife. But the word "good" has been applied to the human and brazen agents of the coming night's work: the divine intervene is therefore also, by implication, good.

In the bell-chamber Lord Peter is introduced to the bells by their sounds, as he raises his own—the second bell, Sabaoth, whose voice is rendered as "tan-tan" (NT 30; ch. 1, part 1), second to the highest. The purpose of the intended peal is to ring out the old year, and the book's title is explained by Hezekiah Lavender, "I rings the nine tailors [...] for Old Year, see" (NT 31; ch. 1, part 1). Nine tolls of a bell signify the death of a man, and it is the dying year who is mourned on New Year's Eve, even as the New Year is welcomed. As this peal will in fact cause the death of a man, the title is doubly appropriate.

Peter and his escort the Rector are prevented, by a final coincidence, from actually examining the bells themselves. If they had mounted the tower to do so, they would have discovered the bound prisoner unknowingly awaiting his execution there. Mr. Godfrey who has declared he has brought all the necessary keys is suddenly discovered by the Rector to have departed with them, along with the other bell-ringers, and to signal this final intervention of Providence, "the clock in the tower chimed the three quarters" (NT 31; ch. 1, part 1). Even at this point the Rector makes a last attempt to call back Jack Godfrey—repeating his name several times—"But Jack, unaccountably deaf, was jingling the church keys in the porch, and the Rector, sighing a little, accepted defeat" (NT 32; ch. 1, part 1).

Unaccountably, indeed! But there is a long wait before Lord Peter (and the reader) learn how fateful, or rather, how providential, this unaccountable deafness is to be for the man who is bound above the bells. In the meantime the Rector begins to trot toward the rectory and supper, apologizing for losing count of the time, as Wimsey politely and with remarkable prescience replies, "Perhaps [...] the being continually in and about this church brings eternity too close" (NT 32; ch. 1, part 1). Eternity thus poised as near as possible on the moment of transition from one year to the next and from this life to the other, the pregnant chapter ends.

This complex symbolic structure has not, of course, gone unnoticed. Geoffrey Lee (1987) finds that God is particularly "involved in the action" of *The Nine Tailors* in Parts I and IV. In part I, God brings Lord Peter "to Fenchurch St. Paul to execute vengeance upon the impenitent thief and double murderer," Deacon, and in Part IV God causes the flood which brings about the "redemptive death of Will Thoday," and shows Lord Peter "the solution to the mystery."[1] For Lee, the specific symbol of God's presence and direct activity in these two Parts is the tenor Bell, Tailor Paul, which "stands for God" and is pulled by Hezekiah Lavender.

The bells themselves are the cause of Deacon's death, but they are operated by the bell-ringers, of whom Lord Peter is, providentially, one. Sayers says that in *The Nine Tailors* "Peter himself remained [...] extraneous to the story and untouched by its spiritual conflicts."[2] If this is true, it may be so because while Lord Peter is an instrument in the hands of God to execute justice, he is also "an eighteenth-century Whig gentleman, born a little out of his time, and doubtful whether any claim to possess a soul is not a rather vulgar piece of presumption."[3]

Lionel Basney (1979) says that the mystery in *The Nine Tailors* is "virtually unguessable"[4] because it is "committed by no one, or rather by several people, as innocently and indifferently as if it were a natural catastrophe."[5] But for Basney, in contrast with Sayers, "Wimsey is as much involved in the death as the other bell ringers," and is thus "robbed involuntarily of his detective's distance and objectivity."[6] Basney concurs with Lee that "there are definite similarities between the murder and the flood,"[7] and concludes that "the bells' indifference to Wimsey's presence and suffering" as he climbs the tower during the flood and experiences first-hand their awful clamor, "clinches the ambiguity of Deacon's death at the same moment that it explains its mechanism."[8] Wimsey is thus "one of the murderers and, through their shared experience of the bell chamber, the murdered as well."[9]

So far from being, as his own creator Sayers would have it, "extraneous" and "untouched," Lord Peter bears in his own body the agony, brief enough not to be lethal, which in the nine long hours of Deacon's ordeal, have already killed their man. It seems to me that this scene, which sounds horribly real in the novel, whether or not a peal of bells could actually kill, is the central key to the greater mystery of God's innocence or guilt which haunts this novel from beginning to end, and causes it to provide the most profound frisson of any novel I have ever read.

Agatha Christie has defined the detective story as "the old Everyman morality tale, the hunting down of evil and the triumph of Good."[10] In this particular morality tale, the murder victim is himself a double murderer, and his death is a just reward for these crimes. As Basney puts it, "the bells are associated explicitly with moral retribution."[11] It is, I think, Lord Peter's innocence that is indicated by his suffering in the presence of the bells:

> He felt himself screaming, but could not hear his own cry. His ear-drums were cracking; his senses swam away. It was infinitely worse than any roar of heavy artillery. That had beaten and deafened, but this unendurable shrill clangour was a raving madness, an assault of devils. (NT 344; ch. 4, part 2)

It is after this frightful revelation, signaled in part by a reference to Lord Peter's personal ordeal of shell-shock which has been resolved through his detective's vocation, that he is able to explain to the police who the murderers were: "Gaude, Sabaoth, John, Jericho, Jubilee, Dimity, Batty Thomas and Tailor Paul" (NT 349; ch. 4, part 3).

The Superintendent is horrified as the revelation sinks in, and he calls upon precisely the names he should, beginning with the first of the quotation:

"My God!" said the Superintendent. "Why then, you were right, my lord, when you said that Rector, or you, or Hezekiah might have murdered him."

"I was right," said Wimsey. "We did." (NT 350; ch. 4, part 3)

The Rector's comment upon the revelation is this: "Perhaps God speaks through those mouths of inarticulate metal, He is a righteous judge, strong and patient, and is provoked every day" (NT 350; ch. 4, part 3).

If Lord Peter is innocent (as God is innocent) despite their direct role in causing the death, then why does Lord Peter suffer in the process of uncovering the mystery? Sayers's admitted mentor, Charles Williams, has something to say about this. In his extremely significant essay, "The Cross," he explains that "popular doctrine in the Church has rather taken the view that we did not consciously choose [...] original sin, but [...] There remains for us the eternal dying that is its result."[12] The God who made the world in this regrettable manner then proceeded to submit (as the incarnate deity, Jesus) to "the will which is He." That is, "He deigned to endure the justice he decreed." Lord Peter is not only the instrument of that justice, and the discoverer of the fact that justice has taken place, but also a victim, albeit not to the death, of that justice as well. He has thus been the chief actor, whether he admits to a soul or no, in what may be Sayers's most profound morality play.

But when somebody kills anybody in a novel, it is always the creator who is the cause—the creator, that is, of the novel itself. *The Nine Tailors* can be read as a meditation not only upon divine justice and the mysterious operations of providence, but upon the creative process itself, a subject which Sayers has addressed elsewhere. She said more than once that the only Christian work is good work well done, and she compared creative humankind with its creative Maker in the great speech with which she concluded her play, *The Zeal of Thy House* (1937):

> Praise Him that He hath made man
> in His own image, a maker and
> craftsman like Himself. [13]

The same play begins with a line announcing the nature of the Creator: "Disposer supreme, and judge of the earth." This introductory speech includes the same image which concludes the action in *The Nine Tailors*, a massive flood, in a description of the power of God over clouds and winds, "They thunder, They lighten, the waters o'erflow."[14] These passages and indeed the whole theme of *The Zeal of Thy House* are related to Sayers's profound theological study of human creativity as a model of the Trinity, *The Mind of the Maker*.

In that book she suggests, as she does in her essay "Gaudy Night," that the human creator, in her case, the novelist, finds, just as God does, that her creations, the characters in her novels, exhibit free will.[15] They develop, after her initial creative act in inventing them, into persons with an inner logic of their own. They cease to be puppets, so that, even if the author later wishes to, they cannot be so used without the result being not only forced but false. For this situation, too, the bell is a metaphor. It must ring true, and utter its own particular note (with all its complex inner structure of overtones and undertones) and no other.

The creator must work by means of the very rules she has created, and it is precisely by possession of free will that humankind can be said to have been created in the image of God. This mystery, for which the bells are a profound figure, is still more profoundly embodied in the human characters of *The Nine Tailors*. The life patterns of these people are intermixed not by mechanical means, or even by the actions of a divine bell-ringer, but through their own human actions and relationships as free persons, however inexorable or providential the context in which they sound their intricate sequences of notes. As the novelist, Sayers has both signified and embodied the complexities of human experience in this novel. Her art can be judged by its ring of truth.

Notes
[1] Geoffrey Alan Lee, *Lord Peter Rings the Changes: A Study of Change Ringing in* The Nine Tailors (Hurstpierpoint, West Sussex: The Dorothy L. Sayers Historical and Literary Society, 1987) 14.
[2] Dorothy L. Sayers, "Gaudy Night," *Titles to Fame*, ed. Denys Kicham Roberts (London: Thomas Nelson and Sons, Ltd., 1937) 77.

Notes

[3] Dorothy L. Sayers, *The Mind of the Maker* (1941; Westport, CT: Greenwood Press, 1970) 131.

[4] Lionel Basney, "The Nine Tailors and the Complexity of Innocence," *As Her Whimsey Took Her*, ed. Margaret P. Hannay (Kent, OH: Kent State UP, 1979) 24.

[5] Basney 24.

[6] Basney 25.

[7] Basney 33.

[8] Basney 34.

[9] Basney 34.

[10] Agatha Christie, *An Autobiography* (1977; New York: HarperCollins, 2011) 437.

[11] Basney 27.

[12] Charles Williams, "The Cross," *The Image of the City*, ed. Anne Ridler (London: Oxford UP, 1958) 132.

[13] Dorothy L. Sayers, "The Zeal of Thy House" (1937), *Four Sacred Plays* (London: Victor Gollancz, 1948) 103.

[14] Sayers, *Four Sacred Plays* 15.

[15] Sayers, "Gaudy Night," *Titles to Fame* 78-79.

Nancy-Lou Patterson: top: "Talboys"; middle "Bedroom Casement" & "Chimney"; bottom: "Kitchen" & "Door and Drain." First published in *Mythlore* 10.3 (Winter 1984): 39-46 and 48. Further reproduction prohibited.

6. "Beneath That Ancient Roof": The House as Symbol in Dorothy L. Sayers's *Busman's Honeymoon*

The New House is almost a major character in my story.

——C.S. Lewis, *Surprised by Joy*[1]

In "Beneath That Ancient Roof" Patterson examines the house at Tal-boys in Busman's Honeymoon, *notably its garden, three storey structure, drains, chimney, chimney pots, indoor plants, and the goose-feather bed and other furnishings, in relation to the character of the previous owner Noakes and that of the new owners Harriet and Peter Wimsey, and in relation to the action of the story. She mentions other houses and their furnishings in connection with the characters associated with them, including Peter's mother, Agnes Twitterton, and Frank Crutchley.*

Patterson also emphasizes the unusual "character" and role of man-made objects and structures in a murder and in disguising a murder in "'A Ring of Good Bells': Providence and Judgment in Dorothy L. Sayers's The Nine Tailors."

"Beneath that Ancient Roof" was first published in Mythlore *10.3 (Winter 1984): 39-46, 48.*

Dorothy L. Sayers's last detective novel, *Busman's Honeymoon*, began as a play of the same name, and was set in the conventional stage interior, with the murder weapon in full view. It is not surprising, then, that the setting—an Elizabethan farmhouse in a country village—figures largely in the novel. But it plays a role more significant than that of mere setting. It is a symbol in its own right, structuring the action and giving a three-dimensional order to the relationships of the major characters.

The Wimseys Arrive at Talboys

The novel opens with an epistolatory Prothalamion which includes "Extracts from the Diary of Honoria Lucasta, Dowager Duchess of Denver" as she records the preparations for the marriage of her son Lord Peter Wimsey (an amateur detective) and his bride Harriet Deborah Vane (a detective novelist). The Dowager Duchess describes her efforts to prepare a fine eighteenth-century house for the couple to use in London. In between mentions of bed-draperies, servants, and chandeliers, we learn of another house:

> Harriet, who has been down to the country to look at a water-mill (something to do with her new book), said she had motored back through Herts, and paid a visit to her old home at Great Pagford. (BH 31-32; Prothalamion)

There follows the first mention of Talboys:

> H. said her own childish ambition had been to make enough money to buy quaint old farmhouse called Talboys in the next village. […] Elizabethan, very pretty. (BH 32; Prothalamion)

Herts is the abbreviation of Hertfordshire, the easternmost of the "Western Home Counties," and lies to the immediate northwest of Greater London. Needless to say, there is no Great Pagford there. The area has been inhabited for centuries: a horse cut in white chalk in that county dates from the tenth century, and before that the Romans built roads and settlements. Most of the medieval villages were built of "grey or golden-tinted stone."[2]

Harriet asks Peter to buy the house for her: the Dowager Duchess reports that "she thought Peter 'liked giving people things'" (BH 32; Prothalamion) and remarks that Peter will at last be repaid for his "five-and-a-half years' arrears of patience" in waiting for Harriet to forgive him the gift of her life. This passage makes clear the centrality of Talboys as a symbol of Peter and Harriet's relationship.

By August 24, Lord Peter's agent has been instructed to negotiate for Talboys with its present owner, a "man called Noakes" (BH 33; Prothalamion). By September 20 the price is settled. "Many alterations and repairs needed, but fabric sound" (BH 36; Prothalamion). Talboys is to be used for the honeymoon, "nobody to know anything about it," and the furniture will be lent for the use of the honeymooners: "own roof more suited to English gentleman" (BH 37; Prothalamion) than a hotel, as the Dowager Duchess quotes Lord Peter. Valet Bunter's plan to make Talboys ready is aborted when reporters begin to shadow him in hopes of discovering where the honeymoon is to be: "better take Talboys (including drains) on trust" (BH 38; Prothalamion). And, the payment made, the house is theirs. The concern with drains is a common-place in British life. C.S. Lewis wrote of his boyhood home: "the drains were wrong, the chimneys were wrong, and there was a draught in every room."[3]

As a result of the lack of an advance visit, Bunter prepares to depart still "anxious about the arrangements—or lack of them—at Talboys" (BH 44; ch. 1). On the trip to great Pagford Harriet recalls the beginning of her own and Lord Peter's delicate marital negotiations—their talk about "this question of children" (BH 47; ch. 1). Her recollections are interspersed with childhood memories:

> [T]his is Great Pagford, where we used to live. Look! that's our old house with the three steps up to the door—there's a doctor there still, you can see the surgery lamp ... After two miles you take the right hand turn for Pagford Parva, and then it's another three miles to Paggleham, and sharp left by a big barn and straight on up the lane. (BH 50; ch. 1)

The progress to Talboys is from larger to smaller—from London to the country. Great Pagford is, as its name suggests, located on an old ford or river crossing: "A town, with a wide stone bridge, and lights reflected in the river" (BH 49; ch. 1). The River (which Lord Peter calls the Rubicon, suggesting that he, like the conqueror of Rome, is passing within the near limits of his goal) is the River Pagg (246; ch. 12), perhaps suggesting the Latin word *pagus*, or country district. Great Pagford gives way to Pagford Parva (Pagford minor or lessor). Paggleham is a hamlet or very small village, there, at last is the house. Though the couple, escorted by Bunter, arrives in darkness, the house is described as Harriet remembers it:

> Yes—the house—a huddle of black gables, with two piled chimneystacks, blotting out the stars. One would open the door and step straight in through the sanded entry into the big kitchen with its wooden settles and its great oak rafters, hung with home-cured hams. Only, Darby and Joan were dead by now [...] (BH 50-51; ch. 1)

But in fact, "there was no light in any of the windows at Talboys" (BH 51; ch. 1). The arrival is awkward: Harriet is anxious, and Bunter silently reproachful. There is a gate, there are "flowerbeds, carefully tended and filled with chrysanthemums and dahlias." Nobody answers Lord Peter's "brisk fantasia upon the horn" of his car. Harriet blames herself. "Her idea in the first place. Her house. Her honeymoon.

Her—and this was the incalculable factor in the thing—her husband" (BH 52; ch. 1). Idea, house, honeymoon, husband: these are equated in Harriet's mind.

Peter, meanwhile, sensibly reflects his country upbringing by suggesting they try the rear door. In the end, the party is admitted, albeit reluctantly, by Mrs. Ruddle, a neighbor. Noakes, who "Got some kind of squeeze on the old people and put the brokers in" (BH 59; ch. 1), is away, she says. Peter and Harriet drive off to fetch the key from Noakes's niece, whose cottage is described as being "like the uglier kind of doll's house" (BH 61; ch. 2). The London house prepared by the Dowager Duchess has suggested Lord Peter's identity—"My dear lady, Peter is not the Ideal Man; he is an eighteenth-century Whig gentleman, born a little out of his time"[4]—and "a very handsome block of flats with sunshine balconies and vita-glass and things" (BH 60; ch. 1) has pictured the urban side of his life. In the same way, Agnes Twitterton's ugly little house announces her even before she appears in person.

With the key in hand, the newlyweds return to Talboys and, with Bunter lighting the way with an electric torch:

> the party stepped into a wide stone passage strongly permeated by an odour of dry-rot and beer. On the right, a door led into a vast, low-ceilinged, stone-paved kitchen, its rafters black with time […] (BH 65; ch. 2)

This unpleasant reality contrasts with Harriet's warm memory, quoted above. The stone entry and the kitchen rafters are seen, and in a moment "Two ancient oak-settles" (BH 66; ch. 2) appear in the sitting-room, moved there, we presume, from their earlier position in the kitchen by the usurping Noakes. A settle is a large high-backed bench which serves to reflect the heat of a fire-place or grate, while protecting the back of a seated person from draughts, which we have seen already to be a problem in British houses. Sayers lingers over the rest of the furniture, which was Noakes's own—"auction-sale bargains"—reflecting his taste and life-style. Among "this collection of bric-a-brac" is "an unnaturally distorted cactus" (BH 66; ch. 2) which is important to the "detective interruptions" of the novel, but not to the "love story" mentioned in the novel's subtitle.

The house itself, however, is important. Among its features, mentioned in Harriet's memory description, are its chimneys: these too are a subject of concern in British households. Mrs. Ruddle reports that "these here great chimbleys ate up too much of the 'eat" (BH 66-67; ch. 2). Noakes used oil-stoves instead. Two other features are also reported, and we achieve a sense of the lower and upper extent of the house: Mrs. Ruddle says "Bert—jest shet that cellar door as you goes by—sech a perishin' draught as it do send up," and "if your ladyship will come this way [...] I'll show you the bedrooms." She opens "a door in the panelling" and admonishes, "Mind the stair, m'lady, but there—I'm forgettin' you knows the house" (BH 67; ch. 2).

These chambers are to be made ready for the wedding night: Mrs. Ruddle promises to "jest pop the bed again the fire" (BH 67; ch. 2)—"the sheets is aired beautiful, though linen" (BH 68; ch. 2). Bunter takes a hand as well: he empties and relines drawers, sets out new candles, and, in a beautiful passage that pays homage to his as well as Lord Peter's taste,

> He took away Mr. Noakes's chunk of yellow soap, his towels and the ewer, and presently returned with fresh towels and water, a virgin tablet of soap wrapped in cellophane, a small kettle and a spirit lamp [...] (BH 70; ch. 2)

Despite these preparations with their echoes of cleanliness, warmth and light (as well as virginity and spirit), Harriet notes that "The room, though spacious and beautiful in its half-timbered style, was cold." She hopes "a good roaring fire" will cure the problem (BH 70; ch. 2). But the chimneys prove to be recalcitrant. When Lord Peter comes in from the woodshed he finds "smoke billowing out into the passage" (BH 71; ch. 2). The chimneys are blocked. Peter, however, is undaunted.

> Send for the sweep tomorrow, Bunter. Heat up some of the turtle soup on the oil-stove and give us the *foie gras*, the quails in aspic and a bottle of hock in the kitchen. (BH 72; ch. 2)

In the meantime, Harriet has discovered that they are to lie on a goosefeather bed. The reference is to a British folk ballad, but the goosefeather bed functions as a secondary symbol in this novel: the house represents the marriage relationship and the bed is the place of its consummation. Goosefeathers were a feature of medieval rural life.[5] Bunter adds the additional discovery that the chimney "in her ladyship's room was clear," because "nothing had been burned in it since the days of Queen Elizabeth" (BH 73; ch. 3). The bedroom, then, is directly related to the medieval past, along with lordship and ladyship. In fact, Bunter has "succeeded in kindling upon the hearthstone a small fire of wood" (BH 74; ch. 3)—a new fire for a new marriage. Supper ordered by Lord Peter and prepared by Bunter proceeds in a jolly manner, with Bunter included at the table.

When Harriet enters her room, she finds heated water, "two brass candlesticks [which] bore their flaming ministers bravely," and the four-poster bed with "its patchwork quilt of faded blues and scarlets" (BH 79; ch. 3). The candles increase the sense of a spiritual element in the events: they refer to Psalm 104.4: "who maketh his angels spirits; his ministers a flaming fire." Patchwork, a British custom, makes its earliest appearance in the Levens Hall bedcoverings of Cumberland, England, dated at the beginning of the eighteenth century.[6] "The sheets, worn thin by age, were of fine linen, and somewhere in the room there was a scent of lavender" (BH 80; ch. 3). In this room and in this bed, redolent of traditional comforts and securities, Peter joins his lady.

Bunter's bed is less comfortable: he is wrapped in great-coats and a rug and lies on "a couple of arm-chairs" (BH 80; ch. 3). He is to be more satisfactorily settled later on: "Mrs. Ruddle had made up a bed for him in one of the back rooms" (BH 227; ch. 10). But on this first night at Talboys, despairing of early sleep, he pens a letter to his mother. The chapter closes with a prophetic sentence: "of the sleepers beneath that ancient roof, he that had the hardest and coldest couch enjoyed the quietest of slumbers" (BH 81; ch. 3). The reader is to discover that Sayers is not referring to the contrast between Bunter, sleeping alone on arm-chairs, and Peter and Harriet on a goosefeather bed in their nuptial embraces, but between all these living occupants and the corpse of Noakes in the cellar, on the "hardest and coldest couch" of a stone floor, whose "quietest slumbers" are those of death.

In these introductory chapters, the house has served to focus the action. The plan to buy it is carried out, and the honeymoon of the novel's title is to take place there. The entranceway of Talboys becomes the entrance of the couple into their wedded state: Harriet,

Lord Peter, and Bunter each responding in their own way. The kitchen is presented both as Harriet remembers it from her childhood and as it is at the time of the novel's action. Lord Peter's childhood is represented by his sensible countryfied reactions to the physical problems. The Elizabethan setting presents a background of the stable past, while the oil-stoves and motley furniture provide a foreground of the temporary present. The reference to the cellar door and its perishing draught gives the first hint of the macabre discovery which awaits, and the repeated mentions of the recalcitrant chimneys prepare us for what will prove to be a significant clue. The murder weapon is in sight all the time.

The most obvious images of the honeymoon situation, the bedroom and the fourposter goosefeather bed with its chintz hangings and lavender-scented sheets, its candle-fire, warm water, virgin soap (Peter comes to bed freshly washed in cold water—like a schoolboy—from the scullery pump) and a fireplace fire of wood, pile sensory signal upon sensory signal of cozy comfort: fragrance, softness, warmth, and delicate light. Here in the height of the house, up a stair, the lovers unite at last, while Bunter reposes on the main floor, where the kitchen and sitting room are located, and the corpse lies in the cellar belowstairs. The three-level structure of the house relates to the old three-story universe: the day-to-day affairs of middle-earth occur on the main floor. Sayers knew this universe well: it furnished the stage setting of medieval religious drama. In the beginning of the York Pageant of the Creation, God's speech sets out the structure:

> Here underneath me now an isle I neven,
> Which isle shall be earth. Now all be at once:
> Earth, wholly, and hell; this highest be heaven.[7]

and in the action of the York Cycle, "God the Father, on the Heavenly level above, casts down Lucifer and his evil angels through a trap door into Hell, depicted on the lower level of the pageant."[8] At Talboys, Hell, or the cellar, occupied by a murdered sinner, yawns below, with a cold draught pouring from its door; hell is icy cold at its depth in *The Divine Comedy*:

> The Emperor of the Sorrowful realm was there,
> Out of the girding ice he stood breast-high,[9]

It is Satan's wings which create the cold wind:

105

[…] as they flapped and whipped
Three winds went rushing over the icy flat
And froze up all Cocytus […][10]

The upper level of the medieval universe, Heaven, suggested by the "flaming ministers" of the candles, by the spirit lamp, by water, by fragrant herbs and sweet-burning wood, offers a paradisal marriage bed out of the Song of Songs. Sayers is orthodox here too, of course, in making marriage a celestial and supernal symbol. To assure the precision of the imagery, Sayers makes Peter call Harriet "my Shulamite" at the beginning of the next chapter when they awaken in bed together in the morning. The epithet "Shulamite" appears in the Song of Solomon 6.13 in the same chapter which contains the sentence, "I am my beloved's, and my beloved is mine" (6.3).

The First Day at Talboys

Daylight thus introduced, the new day reveals more about the house. Peter's window is so located that he can sit in it and call out to the people below, looking down upon his domain like a whimsical image of God looking down upon His Creation in the medieval mystery play. Meanwhile, the chimney sweep has been summoned. Harriet discovers a backstairs—which becomes nicknamed the "Privy Stair" and reappears in the short story "Talboys"[11]—leading to the "modern convenience" as well as "at length into the scullery and so to the back door" (BH 91; ch. 4). Outside, there is a well-kept garden:

> There were cabbages at the back, and celery trenches, also an asparagus bed well strawed up and a number of scientifically pruned apple-trees. There was also a small cold-house sheltering a hearty vine with half a dozen bunches of black grapes on it and a number of half-hardy plants in pots. (BH 91; ch. 4)

The front of the house (seen by electric torch the night before) gives in daylight "a good show of dahlias and chrysanthemums and a bed of scarlet salvias" (BH 91; ch. 4). The combination of vegetable, fruit, and flower is part of a tradition of Western literature concerning the *locus amoenus* or "pleasant place" which probably begins in European literature with the garden of Alcinous in *The Odyssey*: "Beyond the last row of vines were neat beds of all kinds of garden-stuff, ever fresh and green."[12] Harriet and Peter (who looks down from the window above) engage in a witty conversation full of garden quotations to emphasize the paradisal scene.

When the sweep arrives to clear the chimneys, Peter cries, "All my life I have waited to hear those exquisite words, *Peter darling, the sweep's come*. We are married, by god! We are married" (BH 96; ch. 4). For him too, the house embodies the marriage. Noakes has sold the Tudor chimney pots and replaced them with small, unsuitable contemporary pots. Since the Tudor setting symbolizes the importance and role of time, we are not surprised that the pots have been sold to make sundials. The emphasis in the novel upon chimneys and hearths calls attention again and again to the house and its symbolism. Oliver Marc (1977), in his *The Psychology of the House*, states that "the hearth was placed in the house as a symbol of the vital core of the human being."[13] He continues, "In Europe until the Renaissance, the hearth, like the chimney on the roof, was elaborately decorated by architects and artists, thus emphasizing its importance in the collective psyche of the times."[14] Furthermore, and exactly apposite to the novel: "Today we consider the fireplace the symbol of country life, which is indicative of the severance from nature which city life has imposed."[15] This explains why the bedroom fire was laid by Bunter of wood "upon the hearthstone," rather than of coal in a grate.

In the midst of this scene of domestic turmoil, with the sweep hard at work, and Peter, Harriet, and Miss Twitterton watching him from indoors, a new character appears. He is Frank Crutchley, and he is, significantly, "peering in the window" (BH 101; ch. 5). That is, he is *outside* the house while more innocent characters are inside. Like Aggie Twitterton with her ugly "doll's house," Frank Crutchley is given a domicile in the novel, but it is not a house. He works at a garage and sleeps in a room above it, which he shares with the other garageman, Williams. The room has a small dormer but no other amenities (BH 234; ch. 11). When he courts Polly Mason he resorts to "a big old barn with a tiled roof" (BH 355; ch. 18) and his ill-fated affair with Aggie Twitterton has been pursued, significantly, in the churchyard; that is, in the village cemetery (BH 358; ch. 18). Otherwise Crutchley's environment, the garage, includes a canal and a gas-works, all reinforcing the industrial motif, the sense of something alien to countryside and Tudor period alike. All of this is expressed in advance by his glance through the window of Talboys.

Once inside the house, Crutchley searches "over the room as though seeking counsel from the dust-sheets" (BH 103; ch. 5). Like Adam (who also fell) he is the gardener, and he is looking nervously for the former master of the garden. He is introduced to the new owners, and proceeds to water the plants, whereupon Mr. Goodacre, the Vicar, arrives, and is also introduced: "You see, padre, we are old-fashioned country-bred people" (BH 112; ch. 5). Lord Peter is not joking and neither is Sayers. *She* was an old-fashioned country-bred person, and her villages in *Busman's Honeymoon* depict elements of her own childhood. In her sensitive biography of Sayers, Nancy M. Tischler (1980) has commented:

> An artist with Dorothy L. Sayers' kind of imagination takes the stuff of her life and transforms it into art. She was four years old when her family moved from their comfortable life in Oxford to Bluntisham Rectory in the fen country. Here she came to understand the town without the gown—the small English village. [16]

Sayers passed her later life in another village, "Witham, just outside London."[17] Many commentators have remarked on the similarity of Harriet D. Vane to Dorothy L. Sayers: they are both women, both detective novelists, both reared in the country. Tischler comments on the "established roles and set patterns" of village life: Sayers's father was a vicar, a role paralleled to that of Harriet's father. "He [the vicar] works with his mind like the doctor, but he heals the spirit rather than the body. Like the doctor, he may be one of the few educated men in the community."[18]

Eventually the entire group, including Bunter and Mrs. Ruddle, watches as the sweep fires a shotgun up the chimney, and in full view of them all, a second central piece of evidence—a fragment, indeed, of the murder weapon, drops upon the hearth. The house is giving up its secrets, or at least coughing them forth. In traditional house symbolism in primitive cultures, the chimney or smokehole was the route to the upper world,[19] so there is a certain *deus ex machina* element in this event. Into the sooty scene comes a creditor, Mr. MacBride, to seek repayment of a loan: Noakes's possessions are threatened with being carried away, leaving the house closer to its primaeval state.

The Body in the Cellar

Finally, in Chapter VI, after a long "financial" conversation between Lord Peter and the newcomer, the house gives up its deepest secret.

> "Excuse me, my lord." Bunter stood on the threshold empty-handed.
>
> "I'm afraid we have found Mr. Noakes." (BH 135; ch. 6)

Wimsey is aghast. "Where? Down the cellar?" (BH 135; ch. 6). And so he proves to be. Within moments yet another character arrives: Constable Joe Sellon. Most of the company are now onstage.

In the following chapter, Harriet notes with entertainment that her husband, back at his detectival task, has changed his clothes: "Someone has died in our house, so we put on a collar and tie" (BH 140; ch. 7). Death has found a place in the house, along with marriage. Peter meditates on this theme—"you know, that bed must be pretty nearly as old as the house—the original bits of it anyhow. It could tell a good many tales of births and deaths and bridal nights" (BH 140-41; ch. 7). So the house and its bed symbolize the full round of human life and of the generations in their endless repetition. Harriet asks him about the cellar—"there weren't *rats* [...]" (BH 141; ch. 7)—and he reassures her that it is "Just a perfectly good cellar." In the end they decide to stay in their honeymoon house. "Country people are very matter-of-fact about life and death. They live so close to reality" (BH 142; ch. 7). The house is the house of country people: the house, then *is* reality.

In support, as it were, of this conception, there follows a brief description of its rooms and passages, filled with activity necessitated by the finding of a corpse within its walls. The sitting-room is cleared, a fire kindled, a table set, the cellar door shut, the kitchen used to make sandwiches, the scullery cleared of its contents to ready a table on which to lay the body. Bunter stands at the back door and Mr. MacBride strolls the backyard: "he had the air of inventorying its contents" (BH 143; ch. 7). The house is presented as a fully developed representative of its type. The sixteenth century, the period of the Tudors "opened in the spirit of the Middle Ages."[20] Writing of "the small informal house or cottage of brick, stone, cob or half timber" associated with the sixteenth century, A.H. Gardner (1948) remarks: "There is no more charming sight than this 'vernacular' architecture, preserved in cottage and small house in many a country town and village."[21] Writing in the same vein, Stephen Gardiner (1976) describes "the familiar Tudor house period" in which the "timber frame structure was revived; it was a peacetime theme."[22] Sayers is appealing to a widely-received convention in choosing the architecture and style of the house.

When Superintendent Kirk arrives to take up the case, all is in order. Peter, Harriet, and MacBride enjoy an amicable supper— Harriet reflects that he is their first dinner guest. They are joined by Kirk for an after-dinner conversation of shared quotations. Then, Kirk begins his enquiries with a question about the house. "About them doors, now. You're sure they were both locked when you arrived?" The mystery is the classical locked-door puzzle, and the house provides the doors. Many of the details that supplied elements of atmosphere when the couple arrived, now provide clues to the events of the murder. This is the beginning of the "detective interruptions," and the house plays a part in them as well as in the "love story." Three chapters later, Bunter returns from his own investigations at the village pub, tidies the bedrooms, and the newlyweds retire, this time to Peter's room.

But the detectival interruption stretches on. At one point Harriet and Peter escape for a drive in the country, and there they discover a sun-dial made from one of their own Tudor pots. "I think the luck went out of the house with the chimneypots, and it's our job to bring it back" (BH 291; ch. 14), Peter opines, and his notion is echoed by a carter they meet: "The very man wot sold vicar the chimbley-pot, 'e wos found dead in his own 'ouse only yesterday" (BH 299-300; ch. 14). The dismantling of the house has brought about its own revenge.

Miss Twitterton suffers a little too at the hands of the house, for she is trapped upstairs after arguing with Crutchley when the couple return. The sounds of domestic comfort terrify her, as they once delighted Harriet: "Next door she heard the crackle of a kindled fire, the rattle of curtain rings upon the rods, a subdued click, the pouring of fresh water into the ewer" (BH 325-26; ch. 16). She flees down the stairs and creeps past the door, where she sees "framed in the glowing circle of the lamplight, the two figures […] bright and motionless as a picture" (BH 326-27; ch. 16). She is discovered, and pours out her heart-broken story of Frank Crutchley's betrayal of her love for him.

There follows an absolute confrontation between Lord Peter and his wife in which they consider—and reject—the idea of running away. Peter proposes it, thinking it is her wish, and she refuses: "Whatever marriage is, it isn't that" (HB 343; ch. 17). In that moment, she gives him the freedom he has given her, and they are fully equals.

> Harriet looked at the clock. It seemed to her that she had lived through interminable ages of emotion. But the hands stood at a quarter past eight. Only an hour and a half had gone by since they had entered the house. (HB 345; ch. 17)

So the house is the place where the couple obtain the "Crown Imperial" which entitles the chapter.

Adapting Talboys and Solving the Mystery

In the next chapter Peter is already planning "a workable hot-water system" and "a bathroom over the scullery" (BH 346; ch. 18). The problem of drains has been addressed: he is ready to take full possession. Harriet suggests a new kitchen range (for Bunter's sake) and there is a discussion of dogs. At this point a second creditor arrives—Mr. Solomons—and proposes to take away the furniture. He and MacBride are invited to supper and the matter approaches settlement. Kirk arrives, and during his conversation with the couple the murder moves close to its solution. Night brings Peter and Harriet to bed again. "The window was still open; for October, the air was strangely mild and still" (BH 362; ch. 18). A cat cries out but Peter stays his hand: he "drew the casement to and fastened it." Below, Bunter "flung a boot from the back bedroom" (BH 362; ch. 18). The stillness and strange warmth as well as the casement contain echoes of Keats's "casement" in "The Eve of St. Agnes" and of the closing image of C.S. Lewis's *That Hideous Strength*. The rich sexuality of Keats's poem climaxes as Porphyro gazes on his love, Madeline, where

> A casement high and triple-arch'd there was,
> All garlanded with carven imag'ries
> Of fruits, and flowers and bunches of knot-grass,
> And diamonded with panes of quaint device (xxiv, lines 1-4)

and

> Full on this casement shone the wintry moon
> And threw warm gules [red] on Madeline's fair breast.
> (xxv, lines 1-2)

The lovers see her first at her prayers and then, letting down her hair and slipping off her clothing, she takes to her bed. In C.S. Lewis's *That Hideous Strength*, Jane, escorted by mating elephants (instead of mating cats) goes through a night "impossibly hot for the time of year"[23] to the cottage where her husband awaits her:

> Then she noticed that the window, the bedroom window, was open. Clothes were piled on a chair inside the room so carelessly that they lay over the sill: the sleeve of a shirt—Mark's shirt—even hung over down the outside wall."[24]

In this passage, it is the male who has disrobed.

But the night is not peaceful. Lord Peter is afflicted with a terrible nightmare. Something the house has shown him is teasing at his unconscious. He awakes to find Bunter preparing for the "village funeral" of Noakes (BH 365; ch. 19). The matter of Solomons and MacBride approaches completion too: the furniture is to be taken away, while the wedding couple absent themselves for the weekend. Harriet watches the departure of the furnishings.

> Then, smitten by a sudden pang, she hastened into the pantry. It was already stripped. With the furies at her heels, she bounded down the cellar steps, not even pausing to remember what had once lain at the foot of them. (BH 373; ch. 19)

But all is well: his lordship's "two-and-a-half-dozen of port lay carefully ranged upon racks" (BH 374; ch. 19). Harriet's concern for her husband's port has exorcised any ghosts that might have lingered in the cellar.

As item after item is carried out of the house, little remains except the plants—the huge cactus among them—which are to go to the Vicar. He comments that this especially ugly plant is "on a longer chain." Dream and reality come together, and "Peter's gasp was like a sob." The house's final contents have made the secret known. After a few moments of investigation, Peter gives his orders. "Here are the housekeys. [...] Make sure that Ruddle and Puffett and Crutchley are

112

all inside" (BH 392; ch. 20). Harriet tiptoes about the house on these orders: "She locked the front door, and the house was fast, as it had been on the night of the murder" (BH 393; ch. 20).

In the locked house, Lord Peter shows how Noakes met his death by re-enacting the murder process, and the murderer, shouting in frenzy, is dragged "from the room" (BH 401; ch. 20). Peter watches from within as the killer is "hauled past the window, still struggling in the four men's hands" (BH 402; ch. 20). Again, being outside the house is a symbol of the separation from others, of the guilty from the innocent.

The discovery of the killer is not quite the end of the novel; there is an Epithalamion. Peter and Harriet plan to go "up to Town," after leaving orders for the recovery of the displaced chimney pot, and a conversation about "that bathroom extension." Peter proposes to hire Thipps, a character from the first of Sayers's novels, *Whose Body?* Harriet is glad to hear that her husband has not "taken [...] a misliking to Talboys." "While I live," Lord Peter declares, "no owner but ourselves shall ever set foot in it" (BH 409; Epithalamion, part 1). And indeed, though *Busman's Honeymoon* is the last of Sayers's novels, the last (and posthumously) published of her short stories describes Peter and Harriet living in Talboys with their three sons, Bredon, Roger, and Paul, having left behind "the stately publicity of town life" for "a really small place in the country,"[25] where Harriet took her husband into her own room (the furthest of the two bedrooms from the main part of the house) and put the two older boys in the dressing-room, making room for an elderly house-guest, Miss Quirk.

In the end, the couple does not go up to town in *Busman's Honeymoon*: instead they drive to Duke's Denver, Lord Peter's ancestral home. "At the far end of the avenue, the great house loomed grey against the sunlight—a long Palladian front, its windows still asleep, and behind it the chimney and turrets of rambling wings and odd, fantastic sprouts of architectural fancy" (BH 417; Epithalamion, part 2). In this house, which of course symbolizes Lord Peter's origins, the most fantastic moment of the fourteen novels occurs: Harriet sees the family ghost, cousin Gregory. Here the house of Lord Peter's childhood both reveals his past and embodies his identity, the last of the series of houses Sayers has used to personify a person in this novel.

At Home at Talboys

    Peter and Harriet complete their honeymoon in Spain while the Dowager Duchess arranges to send furniture from the Hall up to Talboys, and sees to the painting and plastering. The bathroom will be added when the frosts are over. Talboys has one last image to offer in the novel. While the murderer awaits execution, Peter and Harriet return to their Tudor farmhouse, "admiring the arrangement of the house and furniture" (BH 436; Epithalamion, part 3), and continuing to search for missing chimney pots. On the night before the hanging, Peter goes for a long desperate drive in his car, alone, while Bunter and Harriet await his return.

> The old house was Harriet's companion in her vigil. It waited with her, its evil spirit cast out, itself swept and garnished, ready for the visit of devil or angel. (BH 441; Epithalamion, part 3)

The reference is to Matthew 12.44 and 11.25:

> When an unclean spirit is gone out of a man, he walketh through dry places, seeking rest, and findeth none. Then he saith, I will return into my house from whence I came out; and when he is come, he findeth it empty, swept, and garnished. Then goeth he, and taketh with himself seven other spirits more wicked than himself, and they enter in and dwell there; and the last state of that man is worse than the first. (Matthew 12.43-45)[26]

But the last state of Talboys is better than the first: Lord Peter returns. Harriet waits for him to come to her: "She held her breath till she heard his footsteps mount slowly and reluctantly and enter the next room" (BH 442; Epithalamion, part 3). At last he enters, coming into the bedroom, the heart of the house and its meaning. "[Y]ou're my corner and I've come to hide" (BH 443; Epithalamion, part 3), he confesses. The corner is the house: Gaston Bachelard writes in his meditation on *The Poetics of Space* (1958):

> [...] every corner in a house, every angle in a room, every inch of secluded space in which we like to hide, or withdraw ourselves, is a symbol of solitude for the imagination; that is to say, it is the germ of a room, or of a house.[27]

Peter and Harriet spend the long night together, waiting in torment for the morning. Their bedroom window appears for the last time: "Through the eastern side of the casement, the sky grew pale with the forerunners of the dawn" (HB 445; Epithalamion, part 3). We last see Lord Peter in the novels, weeping upon the breast of his wife. Idea, house, husband, wife: the images are complete.

Notes

[1] C.S. Lewis, *Surprised by Joy: The Shape of My Early Life* (1955; New York: Harcourt, Brace, Jovanovich, 1966) 10.

[2] *Book of the British Villages* (Basingstoke, Hampshire: Drive Publications, 1980) 427.

[3] C.S. Lewis, *Surprised by Joy* 10.

[4] Dorothy L. Sayers, *The Mind of the Maker* (1941; New York: HarperCollins, 1987) 131.

[5] Dorothy Hartley, *Lost Country Life* (New York: Pantheon Books, 1979). See 234-37 for a description of goosefeather beds.

[6] Patsy and Myron Orlofsky, *Quilts in America* (New York: McGraw Hill, 1974) 6-7.

[7] A.C. Cawley, ed., *Everyman and Medieval Miracle Plays* (London: J.M. Dent and Sons Ltd., 1956) 4.

[8] E. Martin Browne, Introduction, *Religious Drama 2, Mystery and Morality Plays* (New York: Meridian Books, 1958) 11. C.S. Lewis wrote wryly of Bishop J.A.T. Robinson's attempts to topple this ancient symbolic structure: "We have long abandoned belief in a God who sits on a throne in a localized heaven." C.S. Lewis, "Must Our Image of God Go?" *God in the Dock* (Grand Rapids, MI: William B. Eerdmans, 1970) 184.

[9] *The Comedy of Dante Alighieri*, Cantica I, Hell, trans. Dorothy L. Sayers (Harmondsworth, UK: Penguin, 1949) Canto XXXIV, 11, 28-29.

[10] *The Comedy of Dante Alighieri*, Cantica I, Hell, Canto XXXIV, 11, 50-52.

[11] "Talboys" is one of the three final Wimsey stories published in *Striding Folly* (London: New English Library, 1972) 92-123. The other two are "Striding Folly" and "The Haunted Policeman."

[12] *The Odyssey*, trans. W.H.D. Rowse (New York: Mentor, 1960) 78.

Notes

[13] Olivier Marc, *Psychology of the House*, trans. Jessie Wood (London: Thames and Hudson, 1977) 98.

[14] Marc 99.

[15] Marc 99.

[16] Nancy M. Tischler, *Dorothy L. Sayers, A Pilgrim Soul* (Atlanta, GA: John Knox Press, 1980) 8.

[17] Tischler 8.

[18] Tischler 8.

[19] Marc 100.

[20] A. H. Gardner, *Outline of English Architecture*, third edition (London: B.T. Basford, 1948) 62.

[21] Gardner 67.

[22] Stephen Gardiner, *Evolution of the House* (Frogmore, St. Albans: Paladin, 1976) 153.

[23] C.S. Lewis, *That Hideous Strength* (1945; Hammersmith, London: HarperCollinsPublishers, 2003) 301; ch. 14.

[24] C.S. Lewis, *That Hideous Strength* 380; ch. 17.

[25] Dorothy L. Sayers, "Talboys," *Striding Folly* (1972; London: New English Library, 1973) 108.

[26] The story is told in Luke in almost the same words.

[27] Gaston Bachelard, *The Poetics of Space*, trans. Maria Jolas (1958; Boston: Beacon Press, 1969) 136.

7. "Eve's Sharp Apple": Five Transgressing Women in the Novels of Dorothy L. Sayers

None may touch my lips
while on his own hangs still the fatal taste
of Eve's sharp apple.

———Dorothy Sayers, *The Devil to Pay*

In "Eve's Sharp Apple" Patterson examines five of Sayers's most unsympathetic female characters in the order of their appearance in her novels: Mary Whittaker (Unnatural Death 1927), *Margaret Harrison* (The Documents in the Case 1930), *Gilda Farren* (Five Red Herrings 1931), *Annie Robinson* (Gaudy Night 1935), *and Martha Ruddle* (Busman's Honeymoon 1937). *All of these novels, except* The Documents in the Case, *involve Lord Peter Wimsey. Patterson emphasizes that these female characters are unsympathetic because they commit acts of betrayal and thus fail in their relationships to others. She then associates each betrayal with a violation of one or more of the biblical commandments discussed by Sayers herself in "The Other Six Deadly Sins" (1941), an essay in which she observed that women were more likely to be judged for these sins than men.*

In her other papers on Sayers's detective fiction, Patterson frequently draws attention to Sayers's use of betrayal and failures of relationship as motives for murder. The well-known exception is The Nine Tailors, *which Patterson addresses in her "'A Ring of Good Bells': Providence and Judgment in Dorothy L. Sayers's* The Nine Tailors." *Patterson takes up the relevance of sin in Sayers's own life as another influence on her novels in "'A Bloomsbury Blue-Stocking': Dorothy L. Sayers's Bloomsbury Years in Their Spatial and Temporal Context" and in "'Cat o' Mary': The Spirituality of Dorothy L. Sayers."*

"Eve's Sharp Apple" was first published in The Sayers Review *3.3 (April 1980): 1-24.*

———————

The female characters in Dorothy L. Sayers's detective fiction are, like her clergy, generally sympathetic. Few of them are mere stereotypes and some of them are deeply sensitive and powerful portraits of a woman's reality. This being so, one may examine her unsympathetic female characters to see why she has led us to dislike or disapprove of them. The most famous of these women is probably Annie Robinson, the scout of *Gaudy Night*. Sayers herself wrote about her at some length in *The Mind of the Maker* and another writer has even defended her, so I shall put her to one side for the moment and address myself to her predecessors in the order of their appearance.

1. Mary Whittaker, from *Unnatural Death* (1927)
2. Margaret Harrison, from *The Documents in the Case* (1930)
3. Gilda Farren, from *Five Red Herrings* (1931)
4. Annie Robinson, from *Gaudy Night* (1935)
5. Martha Ruddle, from *Busman's Honeymoon* (1937)

The first of these characters, Mary Whittaker, is by far the most evil, followed closely by the second, Margaret Harrison. Gilda Farren is perhaps unintentionally but very definitely a cause of suffering, while Annie Robinson, though a cause of considerable disruption, is a disturbed personality and not altogether to blame for her acts. Martha Ruddle is hardly a sinner at all, a mere jest on Sayers's part, but a revealing one. They all have one trait in common, however, and that is a failure of understanding. They are ladies who are not "intelligent in love" (to use Dante's phrase from *La Vita Nuovo*).

In each of the novels somebody dies by somebody's hand—and in describing the parts of the plots relating to the five women, I have tried not to reveal exactly who has killed whom, in order to abide by the rule that the reviewer of detective novels is not allowed to reveal the killer. Readers will have to consult the novels to find out for themselves. I have been concerned here with the women and their particular sins or moral failures as *women*, or persons, in their relationships with other people. Death in the novels of Dorothy L. Sayers is always a by-product of failures in human relationships.

1. Mary Whittaker

In *Unnatural Death* (1927), an elderly woman, Miss Agatha Dawson, a victim of cancer, has suddenly died. Her nurse, who is also her niece, Mary Whittaker, is first described to Lord Peter Wimsey by the old lady's doctor:

Oh, a very nice, well-educated, capable girl, with a great deal more brain than her aunt. Self-reliant, cool, all that sort of thing. Quite the modern type. The sort of woman one can trust to keep her head and not forget things. (UD 21; ch. 1)

That seems to augur well, though the words "cool" and "modern" may suggest certain ominous or at least ambivalent traits to some readers.

A second description of Mary Whittaker is provided by Nurse Philliter, who has been dismissed from her former position as Miss Dawson's nurse—Mary Whittaker dismissed her because of her romantic involvement with the doctor. She is asked by Lord Peter, "What is Miss Whittaker like?"

"Tall, handsome, very decided in nature," she said, with an air of doing strict justice against her will, "An extremely competent nurse— [...] we both knew good hospital work when we saw it, and respected one another." (UD 51; ch. 4)

Both "decided" and "extremely competent" add to the images of "cool" and "modern" to create a sense of force, rigid self-control, and capacity to act under the guidance of the will. As Lord Peter says later. "I'm perfectly sure she was a very capable woman indeed" (UD 66; ch. 6). What is lacking in these traits as attributed to a nurse (by a doctor and a nurse) is any mention of compassion.

We now meet Mary Whittaker. She is first encountered by Miss Climpson, the extremely clear-eyed spinster who is perhaps Sayers's most delightful female character.

The first impression which Miss Climpson got of Mary Whittaker was that she was totally out of place among the tea-tables of S. Onesimus. With her handsome, strongly marked features and quiet air of authority, she was one of the type that "does well" in City offices. She had a pleasant and self-possessed manner, and was beautifully tailored—not mannishly, and yet with a severe fineness of outline that negatived the appeal of a beautiful figure. (UD 59; ch. 5)

Miss Climpson is puzzled. "This was no passionate nature, cramped by association with an old woman and eager to be free [...] " (UD 59; ch. 5). Rather, "meeting Mary Whittaker's clear, light eyes under their well-shaped brows, she was struck by a sudden sense of familiarity" (UD 59; ch. 5).

At this point we are introduced to another character who is very important in Mary Whittaker's life: her companion, Vera Findlater. She is "gushing," she comes "romping over," and sits "plumped down on the end of the sofa." She is "fair and bobbed and rather coltish" (UD 60; ch. 5). A remark of hers surprises Mary Whittaker into an ejaculation which shows something to us: "Miss Climpson was startled to recognize in eye and voice the curious quick defensiveness of the neglected spinster who cries out that she has no use for men" (UD 62; ch. 5). She writes to Lord Peter in her report on the interview that "The lady doth protest *too much*" (UD 62; ch. 5).

Later on in this story, the relationship between Vera Findlater and Mary Whittaker is discussed in another of Miss Climpson's letters.

> I *really think* she means to set up farming *with Miss Findlater*, though what Miss Whittaker can see in that very gushing and really *silly* young woman I cannot think. However, Miss Findlater has evidently quite a "pash" (as we used to call it at school) for Miss Whittaker, and I am afraid none of us are above being *flattered* by such outspoken admiration. I must say I think it rather *unhealthy* […] It has such a bad effect, as a rule, upon the *weaker character* of the two—[...] (UD 91; ch. 8)

This may be Sayers's way of saying that the relationship was, at least latently, a homosexual one, but she is objecting particularly to the destructive or manipulative elements, not to the sexual implications in themselves.

In her relationship with her aunt, too, Mary Whittaker has been a manipulator. Parker (the policeman) says, "There's no doubt about what happened there. Miss Whittaker was trying to get the old lady to sign a will without knowing it" (UD 128; ch. 11).

Lord Peter's own interview with Mary Whittaker comes in a quite unexpected form and it reinforces the lesbian elements mentioned above. He is disguised as Mr. Templeton and she is disguised as Mrs. Forrest. On admitting him to her apartment,

Mrs. Forrest nodded her fantastically turbanned head. Swathed to the eyebrows in gold tissue, with only two flat crescents of yellow hair plastered over her cheek-bones, she looked, in an exotic smoking-suit of embroidered tissue, like a young prince out of the Arabian Nights. (UD 177; ch. 15)

They talk, and he "became uncomfortably aware that she was watching him." Like Miss Climpson he is drawn to her eyes, which "were the eyes of a person who expects something. Something alarming, he decided, yet something she was determined to have." Then, "suddenly he became aware that she was trying—clumsily, stupidly and as though in spite of herself—to get him to make love to her" (UD 180; ch. 15).

He ponders this prospect, and finds that "she had not a particle of attraction for him." Indeed, "she struck him as spinsterish—even epicene [...] Wimsey [...] felt her as something essentially sexless" (UD 180; ch. 15). Nevertheless,

> He coaxed his voice into the throaty, fatuous tone of the man who is preparing to make an amorous fool of himself.
>
> He felt her body stiffen as he slipped his arm round her, but she gave a little sigh of relief.
>
> He pulled her suddenly and violently to him, and kissed her mouth with a practiced exaggeration of passion.
>
> He knew then. No one who has ever encountered it can ever again mistake that awful shrinking, that uncontrollable revulsion of the flesh against a caress that is nauseous. He thought for a moment that she was going to be actually sick. (UD 181-82; ch. 15)

The interview has been a failure from both participants' point of view: each leaves the other still in disguise. As he looks back, Wimsey sees her again: "She stood in the middle of the room, watching him, and on her face was such a fury of fear and rage as turned his blood to water" (UD 182; ch. 15).

This striking and revelatory passage—in which Mary Whittaker, masked, is unmasked—is followed by another of Miss Climpson's analyses. She

> felt sure that Vera Findlater was being "preyed upon" [...] by the handsome Mary Whittaker. "It would be a mercy for the

girl" [...] "if she could form a genuine attachment to a young man. It is natural for a schoolgirl to be *schwärmerish*—in a young woman of twenty-two it is thoroughly undesirable. That Whittaker woman encourages it—she would, of course. She likes to have someone to admire her and run her errands. And she prefers it to be a stupid person, who will not compete with her. If Mary Whittaker were to marry, she would marry a rabbit." (UD 183; ch. 16)

A conversation about friendship follows between Vera Findlater and Miss Climpson, which gives a clear picture of the moral problem involved here:

> "But a great friendship does make demands," cried Miss Findlater eagerly [...] "Instead of being centred in one-self, one's centred in the other person. That's what Christian love means—one's ready to die for the other person."
>
> "Well I don't know," said Miss Climpson. "I once heard a sermon about that from a most *splendid* priest—and he said that that kind of love might become *idolatry* if one wasn't very careful. He said that Milton's remark about Eve—you know, 'he for God only, she for God in him'—was not congru-ous with Catholic doctrine. [...]"
>
> "One must put God first, of course," said Miss Findlater, a little formally. (UD 188; ch. 16)

There is a bitter irony in this passage, for Miss Findlater does indeed "die for the other person": she is found dead by Parker, while her companion, Parker thinks, must have been kidnapped. Again, a significant clue to the true course of events comes through the agency of Miss Climpson. She finds a note, which she has scooped up in church along with her prayer book (one probably has to be an Anglo-Catholic to know how accurately Sayers has described the contents of Miss Climpson's prayerbook): and it proves to be a list of sins which Vera Findlater has prepared for confession. The words "Jealousy" and "Idol" appear, and Miss Climpson reconstructs the sad quarrels they reflect: "Humiliating degrading, exhausting, beastly scenes. Girls' school, boarding-house, Bloomsbury-flat scenes. Damnable selfish-ness wearying of its victim. Silly *schwärmerei* swamping all decent self-respect. Barren quarrels ending in shame and hatred." Miss

Climpson is outraged: "It's too bad," she tells herself; "She's only making use of the girl" (UD 259; ch. 22).

This passage makes explicit the precise nature of the sins, which in Vera Findlater's case, have been shriven before her death, and in Mary Whittaker's case, lead to damnation. The operative word is "barren" not simply because the relationship between the two women could not be what Miss Climpson earlier calls "a *fruitful* affection" (UD 188; ch. 16), but because idolatry, selfishness, and the use of one person by another are occasions of death rather than life. They are the death of true worship, true selfhood, and true relationship, in every case, and in this particular case they are the death of three—no, four—women.

Following up this clue, Miss Climpson attempts to search out Mary Whittaker. She has the wit to disguise herself, but she is recognized; the searcher and the sought, in fact, encounter one another when they are both in disguise, Miss Whittaker having reassumed the role of Mrs. Forrest. There is a confrontation:

> Suddenly, something which had been troubling Miss Climpson for weeks crystallised and became plain to her. The expression in Mary Whittaker's eyes. (UD 268; ch. 22)

She recalls a young man who had forged a bad check: "She remembered the odd, defiant look with which the young man had taken up his pen for his first plunge into crime. And to-day she was seeing it again—an unattractive mingling of recklessness and calculation. It was the look which had once warned Wimsey and should have warned her" (UD 269; ch. 22).

These eyes are a central image of the novel, and when we last see Mary Whittaker, her "blue eyes were bleared with terror and fury" (UD 281; ch. 23). The commandments which have been broken in the novel (beyond the Sixth, "Thou shalt not kill") are the First: "Thou shalt have no other gods but me," to which Vera Findlater has been tempted, and the Tenth: "Thou shalt not covet," broken along with a number of others by Mary Whittaker. She has coveted her aunt's money and her companion's adulation. From these seemingly moderate and understandable (if unattractive), desires, she descends from being a "self reliant," "cool," "tall, handsome, very decided" woman with a "quiet air of authority," to the desperate-eyed spectacle she finally becomes. The capacity of covetousness to erode the mind and corrupt the will have been given vivid expression in *Unnatural Death*.

2. Margaret Harrison

Dorothy L. Sayers's novel *The Documents in the Case* (1930) is the only one in which Lord Peter does not appear, though it takes place in his world, for several characters from the other novels appear in it. It is also the only one of her novels to have a collaborator in its final form, Robert Eustace (although her novel *Busman's Honeymoon* emerged from a collaborative play, and she contributed to several detectival *jeux d'esprit* in which a number of writers took part). The novel is pure Sayers through and through, however; a deep analysis of morality presented in witty and complex terms.

The story concerns a married couple. The husband dies of muscarine poisoning after eating a dish of mushrooms that he has apparently prepared for himself. In the course of the novel, the character of his wife, Margaret Harrison, and the part she plays in his death, is gradually revealed through a variety of witnesses. The book is in epistolatory form. We first hear of Margaret Harrison from her housekeeper, Agatha Milsom:

> "[…] fond though I am, and always will be, of dear Mrs. Harrison, I do sometimes wish she was just a little more practical […] she always says she should have been born to ten thousand a year […]" (DC 13; ch. 1)

Miss Milsom is fonder of Mrs. Harrison than of Mr. Harrison, whom she regards as "a dry sort of man and so lacking in sympathy" (DC 12; ch. 1). Mrs. Harrison is Mr. Harrison's second wife, we learn from Miss Milsom, and "she never loses hope, but goes on, day after day, trying to be brave and devoted and to keep up her interest in life. And she has such a vivid, alert mind—she is keen on everything, even on things like Einstein" (DC 17; ch. 2).

There are roomers in the house, including John Munting: "with a lot of thick hair and one of those rather sulky, handsome faces" (DC 19; ch. 3), whom Miss Milsom, whose words these are, obviously dislikes, and Mr. Lathom, of whom Hiss Milsom thinks rather better. The descriptions of the Harrisons and their boarders appear in inverted form, like Uncle Screwtape's view of reality in *The Screwtape Letters*, and the characters with whom we later learn to

124

sympathize—John Munting, for instance—appear unattractive under Miss Milsom's pen. We ought to be warned by this against entirely trusting her, then, when she says that Mr. Harrison is "such a stick" (DC 17; ch. 2). Our knowledge of Lathom is increased as we get to know Munting personally through his letters to his fiancée, Elizabeth Drake. We also see Margaret Harrison in another, if sardonic, light:

> "[…] she's a sort of suburban vamp, an ex-typist or something, and entirely wrapped up, I should say, in her own attractions, but she's evidently got her husband by the short hairs. Not good-looking, but full of S.A. and all that." (DC 24; ch. 5)

Sayers not wishing to press us too closely at the outset with revelations of the plot to come, has made Munting's remarks about her almost as repellant to us as Mrs. Harrison is to him. But a letter or two later he expresses a certain sympathy for her, and an objection to the way her husband treats her, fussing over his dinner made "uneatable" (DC 30; ch. 7) by her lateness, when she has been out shopping for his anniversary gift. Nonetheless, Munting presciently remarks "there's something wrong in this house—something more than a little misunderstanding about dinner time. I shouldn't wonder if she gives this man a devil of a time—probably without meaning it, that's the rub" (DC 31; ch. 7).

Harrison is certainly not the ideal husband, and the various epistilators show us his annoying traits in considerable detail: he is stuffy, boring, and inhibiting to his wife's wish to return to office work. She, on the other hand, is shown to us by Munting as "a perfect example of [...] dramatisation" (DC 42; ch. 11).

> "If she reads [...] about the modern woman who finds spiritual satisfaction in a career, she *is* that woman [...] if on the other hand, she reads about [...] a "complete physical life" [...] then she is the thwarted, maternal woman, who would be all right if only she had a child [...] And so on. What she really is, if reality means anything, I do not know." (DC 42; ch. 11)

He plays a mischievous trick on her, saying that he can "see her in a cloister, walking serenely among the lilies" (DC 43; ch. 11), and

"Next day I met her in the hall, dressed in a demure grey frock, with a long veil swathed nun-like about her cloche hat. She saluted me with a grave and far-away smile." (DC 44; ch. 11)

We learn of Mr. Harrison's own view of his wife when he calls her "a thorough little town-bird" (DC 53; ch. 15) who doesn't care to go on country sketching trips with him. His study of wild foods and his making of little water-color paintings of natural subject-matter, is the greatest pleasure of his life, but she refuses to share it with him. In his absence, Lathom, who is a professional artist, makes ready to paint Mrs. Harrison's portrait. Miss Milsom explains:

"It is to be a blue, green and bronze colour-scheme—blue dress, green background and a big bowl of those bronze chrysanthemums. It gave Mr. Latham a great deal of trouble deciding it. Of course Mrs. Harrison is very attractive-looking, but you couldn't exactly call her pretty with those greeny eyes and her rather pale complexion." (DC 56; ch. 16)

The result is a success; Harrison himself deems it "a handsome piece of *coloratura*," though he refuses to expose it to public exhibition because he fears that it will "attract a great deal of comment" (DC 63; ch. 20). As he explains naively to the painter, "My wife would hardly like to be put on show, you know" (DC 66; ch. 21).

He is defeated in the end, however, in a manner explained by John Munting:

"She was not, he [Harrison] said, like the ordinary woman. She had a remarkable gift for artistic appreciation. He felt sure that if he put it to her in the right light she would see that it was not a personal question at all. [...] His attitude about the thing was preposterous of course, but I have a queer feeling about Mrs. Harrison. [...] It is that she is clever enough to see it and adopt it when it is pointed out, and to make it into a weapon of some kind for something or other. Not knowing that it was a weapon, either; practising a sort of ju-jitsu, that overcomes by giving way." (DC 82; ch. 27)

As the work is exhibited, along with another which Lathom has painted of Miss Milsom, Munting describes the portrait of Margaret Harrison for us: "Almost the first thing I saw, as we surged through the crowd, was the painted face of Mrs. Harrison, blazing out from a wall full of civil worthies and fagged society beauties, with the loud insistence of a begonia in a bed of cherry-pie" (DC 115-16; ch. 37). And he gives us, too, the appearance of the portrait's subject at the exhibition's opening: "Mrs. Harrison glowed. For the first time I saw her in full prismatic loveliness, soaked and vibrating with colour and light" (DC 119; ch. 37).

Mrs. Harrison is late for dinner a second time, with a consequently disagreeable scene at table with her husband, Munting comments,

> "Love makes no difference. Harrison would cheerfully die for his wife—but I can't imagine anything more offensive than dying for a person after you've been rude to them. It's taking a mean advantage. And what's the good of it all to him, if he loves her so much that everything she says gets on his nerves? I like Harrison—I think he's worth a hundred of her—and yet, every time there's a row she ingeniously manages somehow to make him appear to be in the wrong. She is completely selfish, but she takes the centre of the stage so convincingly that the whole scene is engineered to give her the limelight for her attitudes.
>
> This house is becoming a nightmare [...]" (DC 85-86; ch. 28)

Precisely: and poor Harrison does, in fact, die for his wife.

She and Lathom have become lovers, and we read of the love affair between Margaret Harrison—"Lolo"—and her "Petra"—Harwood Lathom—which has taken place "even under the Gorgon's eye—such a cold stony eye, darling, and with all those people around" (DC 121; ch. 38), as she writes. Their pet names are derived from "the real Laura and Petrarch—did you know, she was really only a little girl and that he hardly saw her at all?" (DC 128; ch. 39). Lathom has left the household in order to conceal the relationship, and Mrs. Harrison writes him a series of pleading letters. Harrison would never, she says, allow her to divorce him, and she could not bear to allow him to divorce *her*—"You used to say you wanted to stand between me and trouble, and couldn't bear to think of anything touching our pure and lovely passion" (DC 129; ch. 40). If there were a divorce proceedings, "It would all sound so different to their worldly, coarse, horrible minds—and our love would seem Just a vulgar, nasty—I don't like to write the word they would call it, even to you—instead of the pure, clean, divine thing it really is" (DC 129; ch. 40).

The couple is reunited briefly—"our evening of marvelous love"—"and even then, if it hadn't been the girl's night out, we shouldn't have been safe" (DC 134; ch. 42). Mr. Harrison, his wife writes, "never touches me—you know what I mean—and I wouldn't let him" (DC 134; ch. 42). The result of this brief reunion after a long separation is biologically predictable: "Oh, Petra, I am so frightened. Darling, something dreadful has happened. I'm sure—I'm almost quite sure. Do you remember when I said Nature couldn't revenge herself? Oh, but she can and *has*, Petra." Mrs. Harrison has "tried things, but it's no good." She has even "tried to be nice to [Harrison] and make him love me, but it wasn't any good" (DC 138; ch. 44).

She is desperate—"Darling, darling, do *something*—anything" and writes "How cruel God is! He must be on the conventional people's side after all" (DC 138-39; ch. 44). It is the fault of Nature or God, not of the lovers, she is saying. The broken commandment, the Seventh, against adultery, leads to the shattering of the Sixth as well. But when Harrison is found dead, Margaret Harrison writes: "Oh, Petra—didn't I tell you that God was on our side? Our love is so beautiful—so *right*—He had to make a miracle happen to save it. Isn't it wonderful—without our doing anything at all" (DC 165-66; ch. 46). As far as she knows, Harrison has died of his own cooking.

Margaret Harrison is described after her husband's death by Paul Harrison, the dead man's son by his first wife: "She was dressed in deep mourning, very fashionably cut, and came up to me with the gushing manner which I had always so greatly disliked" (DC 185; ch. 49). She defends herself to him: "In the beginning I was ready to give him all the love and affection that was in me. But he didn't like it. He dried me up. He broke my spirit, Paul." Paul replies that "If you had heard him speak of you as I have heard him—" (DC 187; ch. 49).

> "Ah!" she said quickly, "but I never did. That was the trouble. What is the good of being praised behind one's back if one is always being scolded and snubbed to one's face." (DC 187-88; ch. 49)

In the end of the book there are final comments about Margaret Harrison, one by Munting, pondering Lathorn's view of her—"the only real part of her was vulgar and bad, and the rest merely the brilliant refraction of himself" (DC 283; ch. 52), and one by Paul Harrison, who is given the last word:

> "The unsatisfactory part of the case is [...] that which concerns the woman, Margaret Harrison. [...] she has taken pains to protect herself against any suspicion of complicity. Although, morally, she is quite equally guilty [...] it will probably be difficult to bring home to her a guilty knowledge of the actual commission of the crime." (DC 284; ch. 53)

Although adultery is obviously committed in this novel. Sayers is telling us that this is not the most serious sin in the story. As she says elsewhere, "Perhaps the bitterest commentary on the way Christian doctrine has been taught in the last few centuries is the fact that to the majority of people the word 'immorality' has come to mean one thing and one thing only."[1] This best-known sin—Lust—is called in Latin, *Luxuria*. Sayers says "it may be through sheer exuberance of animal spirits";[2] but more "commonly" today, "men and women may turn to lust in sheer boredom and discontent."[3] This seems to be the case with Margaret Harrison and her lover.

She also suffers from the "close companion" of Covetousness—"*Invidia* or *Envy*—which hates to see other men happy." Sayers says

> In love, Envy is cruel, jealous, and possessive. My friend and my married partner must be wholly wrapped up in me, and must find no interests outside me. That is my right. No person, no work, no hobby must rob me of any part of that right. If we cannot be happy together, we will be unhappy together—but there must be no escape into pleasures that I cannot share. If my husband's work means more to him than I do. I will see him ruined rather than preoccupied; if my wife is so abandoned as to enjoy Beethoven or dancing; or anything else that I do not appreciate, I will so nag and insult her that she will no longer be able to indulge these tastes with a mind at ease.[4]

This is the nightmare of suffocation which is the Harrison's marriage.

But one cannot understand sin or vice as if it were a positive force, or a specific set of actions to take or not take as one chooses. Sin and vice are negative, not positive. Traditional Christianity expresses this through the seven Virtues, and these include the three Theological Virtues—Faith, Hope, and Charity, which last is, C.S. Lewis says. "Love, in the Christian sense,"[5] and the four Cardinal Virtues, which are Prudence, Temperance, Justice, and Fortitude. Margaret Harrison's failures include a neglect of Prudence: as Lewis says, "because Christ said we could only get into His world by being like children, many Christians have the idea that, provided you are 'good', it does not matter being a fool."[6] But "Christ never meant that we were to remain children in intelligence."[7] The reference by Margaret Harrison to Petrarch's child-love Laura is related to this: Mrs. Harrison, who hated being treated like a child by her husband, behaves like a child in her relationship with her lover.

The sexual relationships of the two novels we have been discussing are both of them barren. The operative image of coldness in *Unnatural Death* is one sort of barrenness: the love of the two women cannot bear fruit of any sort for it is a winter love in which fertility is impossible. And in *The Documents in the Case* there is in fact no baby. Margaret Harrison's supposed pregnancy proves to be a false alarm. In the latter novel the symbol of dryness is used to represent barrenness. In ancient culture (and in medieval thought based upon ancient sources) dryness was one of the primary causes of infertility and one of the primary attributes of death. That is why Near Eastern religions (which must include Christianity) make rain, springwater, dew, and other forms of moisture—divine sputum, divine tears, divine semen, and the waters of the divine womb—operative images of salvation and spiritual renewal. And that is why Dame Julian of Norwich expatiates upon the terrible dryness of the crucified Christ: she saw him hung upon the cross "as people hang up a cloth to dry,"[8] turned by the loss of his "vital fluids" into a "shriveled image of death."[9] It is in this sense that Mr. Harrison is a "dry sort of man" (DC 12; ch. 1), and what Agatha Milsom calls a "*stick*" (DC 17; ch. 2). His dryness provides no moisture to sustain the woman "blazing [...] with the loud insistence of a begonia" (DC 116; ch. 37)—his flowering wife. "He dried me up" (DC 187; ch. 49), she says. She looks elsewhere (and in vain) for the waters of life.

A final image in *The Documents in the Case* is that of refraction: Margaret Harrison's "full prismatic loveliness, soaked and vibrating with colour and light" (DC 119; ch. 37) seems fair enough, but her truth is that she is "merely the brilliant refraction" of Lathom. This is not a passing image used for coloration: it is the centrally operative motif of the book, for the specific form of muscarine which has caused the death of George Harrison can only be determined by the refraction of light through a piece of tourmaline:

> If, when we put the muscarine solution in the polariscope, we get light, it proves nothing. Either the stuff is natural, or else the synthetic preparation has already been split up into two active forms, and we can make no pronouncement about it. But if we get darkness—then it's a pretty dark business [...]" (DC 277-78; ch. 52)

Sayers says elsewhere, "In the orthodox Christian position [...] the light is primary, the darkness secondary and derivative."[10] "In thy light shall we see light," the Psalmist says. Munting looks into the instrument and sees "Dead blackness." The love which had seemed to show "all the colours of the rainbow" (DC 281; ch. 52) leads to an absense of any light at all.

3. Gilda Farren

In *Five Red Herrings*, Lord Peter, investigating the finding of a dead painter's body at the bottom of a ravine, visits the dead man's acquaintances. At the home of Hugh Farren, he finds Gilda Farren: "Mrs. Farren, looking like a ghost painted by Burne-Jones in one of his most Pre-Raphaelite moments, extended a chill hand." Her husband is out, and she invites Wimsey in.

Mrs. Farren led the way into the little sitting-room with the sea-green and blue draperies and the banks of orange marigolds.

> "Or is it scarves this morning?" Mrs. Farren wove hand-spun wool in rather attractive patterns. "I envy you that job, you know. Sort of Lady of Shalott touch about it. The curse is come upon me and all that sort of thing." (FRH 65; ch. 6)

Mrs. Farren has been friendly to the dead man, Sandy Campbell, and her husband, Wimsey thinks, objected to the friendship. In any event, Farren is absent. Wimsey notices that

> [...] the cushions were crushed, a flower or two here and there was wilted; there was a slight film of dust on the window-sill and the polished table. In the houses of some of his friends this might have meant mere carelessness and a mind above trifles like dust and disordering, but with Mrs. Farren it was a phenomenon full of meaning. To her, the beauty of an ordered life was more than a mere phrase; it was a dogma to be preached, a cult to be practised with passion and concentration." (FRH 65-66; ch. 6)

Wimsey observes that

> Mrs. Farren was a very beautiful woman, if you liked that style of thing, with her oval face and large grey eyes and those thick masses of copper-coloured hair, parted in the middle and rolled in a great knot on the nape of the neck. (FRH 66; ch. 6)

The narrator continues: "Mrs. Farren came back and sat down in a high, narrow-backed chair, looking out and past him like a distressed beggar-maid beginning to wonder whether Cophetua was not something of a trial in family life." Mrs. Farren denies that her husband was troubled by her friendship with Campbell, and Wimsey muses,

> she was the kind of woman who, if once she set out to radiate sweetness and light, would be obstinate in her mission. He studied the rather full, sulky mouth and narrow, determined forehead. It was the face of a woman who would see only what she wished to see—who would think that one could abolish evils from the world by pretending that they were not there. Such things, for instance as jealousy or criticism of herself. A dangerous woman, because a stupid woman. Stupid and dangerous, like Desdemona. (FRH 69; ch. 6)

We have already been shown Campbell's own feeling about Gilda Farren and Hugh Farren as well, in his drunken soliloquy near the beginning of the novel: he had "only wanted [...] to go and sit among the cool greens and blues of Gilda Farren's sitting-room and be soothed by her slim beauty and comforting voice. And Farren, with no more sense or imagination than a bull, must come blundering in, breaking the spell, putting his own foul interpretation on the thing, trampling the lilies in Campbell's garden of refuge" (FRH 17; ch. 1).

In fact Farren has quarreled with his wife, threatened Campbell in a public-house, and after the death, has gone into hiding.

In a second interview, Lord Peter sees the lady again:

> Gilda Farren sat, upright as a lily stalk, in the high-backed chair, spinning wool. Her dress was medieval, with its close bodice and full, long skirt, just lifted from the ground by the foot that swayed placidly upon the treadle. It had a square neck and long, close-fitting sleeves, and it was made of a fine cream-coloured serge which gave her an air of stately purity. Besides, it had the advantage of not showing the fluff of white wool which settles all over the spinning-woman and tends to give her the appearance of a person who has slept in her clothes. Lord Peter Wimsey […] noted this detail with sardonic appreciation. (FRH 201; ch. 20)

Wimsey and Mrs. Farren talk about her marriage:

> "I have always done my duty as his wife."
> "Too true," said Wimsey. "He put you up on a pedestal, and you have sat on it ever since. What more could you do?"
> "I have been faithful to him," said Mrs. Farren, with rising temper. "I have worked to keep the house beautiful and—and to make it a place of refreshment and inspiration." (FRH 205; ch. 20)

But Sandy Campbell too had sought consolation in her house, and Lord Peter gently reproaches her for offending her husband's feelings. He wouldn't have been suspicious of her himself, he says:

> "If I were married to you, for example, I should know that under no circumstances would you ever be unfaithful to me. For one thing, you haven't got the temperment. For another, you would never like to think less of yourself than you do. For a third, it would offend your aesthetic taste. And for a fourth, it would give other people a handle against you."

"Upon my word," said Mrs. Farren, "your reasons are more insulting than my husband's suspicions."

"You're quite right," said Wimsey, "They are." (FRH 206; ch. 20)

His gentle brutality reaps its reward: Mrs. Farren reveals her husband's hiding place to him—"the postmark was Brough in Westmoreland" (FRH 206; ch. 20). Farren has been working there as an itinerant painter.

The symbolic references used to create the image of Gilda Farren can be listed as follows: ghost, Burne-Jones, Pre-Raphaelite, chill hand, sea-green and blue draperies, hand-spun wool, Lady of Shalott, thick masses of copper-colored hair, high, narrow-backed chair, beggar-maid, Cophetua, Desdemona, trampling the lilies, garden of refuge, upright as a lily stalk, medieval dress, cream-colored serge. The image Sayers depicts is a kind of malignant Goldberry, as Tolkien describes her in *The Fellowship of the Ring*:

> In a chair, at the far side of the room facing the outer door, sat a woman [...] her gown was green, green as young reeds, shot with silver [...] and her belt was of gold, shaped like a chain of flag-lilies [...] About her feet in wide vessels of green and brown earthenware, white water-lilies were floating [...][11]

These are the quintessential lilies of Art Nouveau sensibility and the cream is not lacking: Tom Bombadil exclaims, "Here's my Goldberry clothed all in silver-green [...] Is the table laden? I see yellow cream and honeycomb, and white bread, and butter [...]"[12]

Burne-Jones was a member of a group of artists who called themselves the Pre-Raphaelite Brotherhood. King Cophetua and his beggar-maid, and the Lady of Shalott were the subjects of paintings by artists associated with this group. The beggar-maid sits serenely gazing at the viewer while the king, his crown on his bended knees, looks up at her, and the Lady of Shalott works frenziedly at her enchanted loom, gazing into a mirror for a glimpse of Camelot.

Desdemona, strangled by Othello because of his insane jealousy, is relatively familiar because English majors still read Shakespeare, but modern students are less likely than was Sayers to have read Tennyson's "The Beggar Maid."

> Her arms across her breast she laid;
>> She was more fair than words can say:
> Bare-footed came the beggar maid
>> Before the king Cophetua.
> In robe and crown the king stept down,
>> To meet and greet her on her way;
> "It is no wonder," said the lords,
>> "She is more beautiful than day."
> As shines the moon in clouded skies,
>> She in her poor attire was seen;
> One praised her ankles, one her eyes,
>> One her dark hair and lonesome mien.
> So sweet a face, such angel grace,
>> In all that land had never been.
> Cophetua swore a royal oath:
>> "This beggar maid shall be my queen!"

Sayers was later to use the theme of the king stooping to marry a beggar maid in expressing Harriet Vane's fears of marriage to Lord Peter Wimsey.

The theme of the man driven to murder by his wife's suspected infidelity appears elsewhere in Sayers, in *Clouds of Witness*, where the farmer Grimethorpe's beautiful wife is the object of Lord Peter's brother, the Duke of Denver's attentions, with dangerous results; she has

> a broad white forehead under massed, dusky hair, black eyes glowing under straight brows, a wide, passionate mouth—a shape so wonderful that even in that strenuous moment sixteen generations of feudal privilege stirred in Lord Peter's blood. (CW 113; ch. 4)

The description could be that of William Morris's adulterous wife, as she was portrayed by her lover, Dante Gabriel Rossetti, another Pre-Raphaelite. There is also a genuinely terrifying story by H.G. Wells, anthologized by Sayers in one of her omnibi, in which a jealous husband drops his wife's lover onto the top of a blast furnace. The motif is in a sense a stock item in detective and thriller formats.

Tennyson also wrote "The Lady of Shalott," in which he says of the Lady:

> There she weaves by night and day,
> A magic web with colours gay.
> She has heard a whisper say
> A curse is on her if she stay
> > To look down to Camelot.

She hears Sir Lancelot singing by the riverside, and

> She left the web, she left the loom,
> She made three paces through the room,
> She saw the water lily bloom,
> She saw the helmet and the plume,
> > She looked down to Camelot.

And, as Lord Peter says,

> The curse is come upon me, cried
> > The Lady of Shalott.

As the curse is fulfilled, the poem moves toward its conclusion while the Lady lies dying in the river:

> Lying robed in snowy white
> That loosely flew to left and right—
> Through the noises of the night
> > She floated down to Camelot.

Many of the visual motifs in this poem are used by Sayers to describe Gilda Farren, including the loom, the lilies, and the long white dress. The lady at her loom includes echoes of the wife of Ulysses, Penelope, weaving her web by day and unraveling it by night in order to discourage her suitors in her husband's absence. As well, the spinning Gilda Farren suggests the even more ancient motif of the woman as spinner of fate: the Norns spun and then cut the thread of human life. The whole image of woman as the spinner and weaver is extremely ancient, bound up in Neolithic culture and all that is derived from it and this symbolism is closely associated with the Mother Goddess. The woman with her lilies, her loom, her water, and her heavy hair, is profoundly complex, and deeply sexual image, and Sayers has invoked it in a negative way. Like all archetypes, that of the woman is ambivalent.

Sayers has created, by mentioning a series of motifs relating to late nineteenth-century art and poetry, a portrait of a self-regarding manipulative woman. Her sin is that, while playing the role of the domestic, artistic, blameless wife she has

1) allowed her husband and Campbell too, to worship her and
2) has driven her husband to rash acts which might lead him to be charged with murder.

The particular commandments involved are the First and Second, against idolatry (she has tempted two men to commit idolatry in regards to herself) and the Ninth, against false witness. The particular vices, or selections from the seven deadly sins, are of course, Pride, but also *Acedia*: Sloth, that little understood Sin of not bothering, not quite managing to stay out of trouble. Sayers says in her trenchant essay, "The Other Six Deadly Sins," that "in the world it calls itself Tolerance, but in hell it is called Despair."[13] She continues: "Let us take particular notice of the empty brain. [...] Sloth persuades us that stupidity is not our sin, but our misfortune."[14] The kind of stupidity meant here is not a lack of intellectual capacity, but the kind of which Lord Peter accuses Gilda Farren: insensitivity to other people's feelings and needs, a self-satisfied self-love which dismisses other people's fears and insecurities as inconsequential or undeserving of consideration.

It is a kind of guilty innocence, which refuses to admit responsibility for inflaming another person's weaknesses. Christians are enjoined to avoid the appearance of evil, to refrain from acts which offend the scruples of others: St. Paul is particularly clear on this point: Christians need not fear to eat any sort of food, he says, in dismissal of millennia of dietary law. But they should refrain from eating sacrificial meats because that might mislead non-Christian Gentiles. It is a difficult thing to practice Charity: one must free oneself from scruples while regarding those of other people!

4. Annie Robinson

There is no murder in *Gaudy Night*, but there is a death, and not from natural causes. The dead man is Arthur Robinson. His wife, who works as a scout (a maid) in Shrewsbury College at Oxford, to which Harriet Vane has returned for a reunion—the Gaudy Night of the title—makes her first appearance extremely unobtrusively as Harriet takes coffee with the scholar Miss Lydgate.

> "Annie!—I think I hear my scout in the pantry—Annie! Would you please bring in a second cup for Miss Vane." (GN 47; ch. 3)

This refreshment is "brought in by the smartly uniformed maid" (GN 47; ch. 3). Miss Lydgate remarks, after Annie has gone out,

> We may have to lose Annie from this staircase. Miss Hillyard finds her too independent; and perhaps she *is* a little absent-minded. But then, poor thing, she is a widow with two children, and really ought not to have to be in service at all. Her husband was in quite a good position, I believe, but he went out of his mind, or something, poor man, and died or shot himself […] leaving her very badly off, so she was glad to take what she could. The little girls are boarded out […] Annie is able to go and see them at weekends. (GN 47; ch. 3)

This lengthy description is only one of several describing functionaries of the college as Miss Lydgate brings Harriet up to date about old acquaintances, including other scouts.

On Annie's next noted appearance, Harriet remembers what she has been told:

> A cold lunch was brought up to the self-appointed in-vigilator [Harriet, looking for the "College Poltergeist," a poison-pen writer who has turned to vandalism as well]. A napkin covered […] a plate of ham sandwiches […] Harriet recognised the scout.
>
> "It's Annie, isn't it? Are you on the kitchen staff now?"
>
> "No, madam. I wait upon the Hall and Senior Common room."
>
> "How are your little girls getting on? I think Miss Lydgate said you had two little girls?" (GN 126; ch. 6)

They chat about children and motherhood, and Annie remarks, "it seems to me a dreadful thing to see all these unmarried ladies [the academic women] living together. It isn't natural, is it?" (GN 127; ch. 6). Harriet seems to see her clearly for the first time: "she had large light blue eyes, and Harriet thought she must have been a good-looking woman before she got so thin and worried-looking" (GN 127; ch. 6).

The conversation continues to purse the matter of "these clever ladies" (GN 128; ch. 6), whom Annie finds "a bit queer" (GN 128; ch. 6). (Harriet recalls that Annie has had "misunderstandings with Miss Hillyard" and attributes her animosity to that.) But when Annie quotes the Bible—"much learning has made thee mad," Harriet's attention is caught again: she "looked up sharply and caught an odd look in the scout's eyes" (GN 128; ch. 6). Annie, in fact, is implying that "one of these learned ladies" is responsible for the recent disruption in the College. Harriet, offended, dismisses the scout: "I feel quite sure you must be mistaken, Annie; I should be very careful how you spread about a tale of that kind. You'd better run along back to the Hall, now; I expect they'll be needing you" (GN 128-29; ch 6). Harriet is condescending to Annie, of course. She remarks to herself, "So that was what the servants were saying," and dismisses Annie from her thoughts.

On their next meeting, Harriet is looking for someone—Jukes, a general factotum with the College. "The S.C.R. scout came in, carrying a pile of clean ash-trays, and Harriet suddenly remembered that her children lodged with the Jukeses" (GN 175; ch. 8). In questioning her about Jukes, she draws out another of Annie's opinions:

> "I'm the last person to wish to put difficulties in the way of respectable married women," went on Annie, slapping an ash-tray smartly down, "and naturally she's right to stick by her husband. But one's own children must come first, mustn't they?"
>
> "Of course," said Harriet, rather inattentively. (GN 175; ch. 8)

Meanwhile the Poison Pen continues to wreak havoc in the closely-knit little academic community, and Harriet's search for the culprit continues. In fact, she calls in Miss Climpson to help her, and even, finally, Lord Peter. The oppressions of the Poison Pen grow increasingly more sinister and take a more dangerously physical form.

Harriet's next encounter with Annie takes place by phone, and again Harriet's attention is not directed specifically toward the woman herself, but toward the business at hand.

A voice answered her; not the same person's that had rung her up before.

"Is that Dr. Baring's maid?"

"Yes, madam. Who is speaking, please?"

("Madam"—the other voice had said "miss." Harriet knew now why she had felt vaguely uneasy about the call. She had subconsciously remembered that the Warden's maid said "Madam." (GN 385; ch. 18)

Annie assures Harriet that she has not called before and Harriet continues in her investigation, finally hanging up the phone.

Very late in the novel we learn more detail about Annie's dead husband, Arthur Robinson. Lord Peter has been looking for him, and he tells Harriet the man's story. Arthur Robinson "in a weak moment married his landlady's daughter." He "was an M.A. of York University" but he "came up against the formidable memory and detective ability of your Miss de Vine [...] on the examining body" (GN 396; ch. 19). Lord Peter points out that this is "the only thing [Miss de Vine] ever mentioned that might suggest a personal enmity" (GN 397; ch. 19). Miss de Vine has been a major object of the Poison Pen's attacks.

In the next act of vandalism, a beautiful chess set which Lord Peter has bought for Harriet is destroyed: "It's horrible, Peter. It's like a massacre. It's—it's rather frightening, somehow—they've been hit so hard" (GN 423; ch. 20). Lord Peter agrees: he looks "grave," and exclaims, "Blind, bestial malignity. Not only broken but ground to powder. There's been a heel at work here, as well as the poker; you can see the marks on the carpet. She hates you, Harriet" (GN 423; ch. 20). Harriet answers a knock at the door. It is Annie, summoning Lord Peter. He shows her the wanton damage, warning her of the danger to herself as well as others, and she remarks of the destruction, "Yes, I see, sir. What a pity, isn't it?" (GN 425; ch. 20). Lord Peter dismisses her and she leaves, saying, "Good night, sir. Thank you." Lord Peter says to Harriet, "You never know whether to warn people or not. Some of them get hysterics, but she looks fairly level-headed" (GN 425-26; ch. 20).

Finally, Harriet is attacked personally: the Poison Pen tries to strangle her, but Lord Peter has provided her with a protective collar and she is knocked unconscious instead, awakening to find herself in

140

the College infirmary. Annie too has come to grief, for "We found her in the coal-hole, my dear," the Dean says, "in such a state, what with coal-dust and hammering her fists on the door; and I wonder she wasn't clean off her head, locked up there all that time" (GN 445; ch. 21).

Soon after Lord Peter outlines the process of offense and detection as it has developed in the novel: we are close to the revelation of the culprit. In the process he tells the full story of Arthur Robinson. He had been deprived of his M.A. when caught falsifying the facts in his research, and had followed a descending path (while married to Charlotte Anne Clarke—Annie—and fathering two children) from drink to suicide. The events at the College have been a revenge against the whole of female academia (or a significant segment of it) for the act of Miss de Vine in bringing Arthur Robinson's unscholarly falsification out into the open. While the revelation continues, we hear of Annie's own response to her husband's tragic story.

> "I have been down to see Jukes," began Peter; when the entrance of Annie interrupted him. Neat and subdued as usual, she approached the Warden:
> "Padgett said you wished to see me, madam." Then her eye fell on the newspaper spread out upon the table, and she drew in her breath with a long, sharp hiss, while her eyes went round the room like the eyes of a hunted animal. (GN 467; ch. 22)

She accuses Miss de Vine of killing her husband.

> "I say you murdered him. What had he done to you? What harm had he done to anybody? He only wanted to live and be happy. You took the bread out of his mouth and hung his children and me out to starve. [...] He told a lie about somebody else who was dead and dust hundreds of years ago. Nobody was the worse for that. Was a dirty bit of paper more important than all our lives and happiness? You broke him and killed him—all for nothing. Do you think that's a woman's job?"
> "Most unhappily," said Miss de Vine, "it was my job." (GN 468; ch. 22)

Annie continues to round upon the assembled women: "It would do you good to learn to scrub floors for a living as I've done, and use your hands for something, and say 'madam' to a lot of scum" (GN 469; ch. 22). Turning upon Harriet, with "fierce eyes," she cries: "You don't know what love means. It means sticking to your man through thick and thin and putting up with everything." And as for Peter—"Wives and mothers may rot and die for all you care, while you chatter about duty and honour" (GN 470; ch. 22).

> She suddenly burst out crying—half dreadful and half gro-tesque, with her cap crooked and her hands twisting her apron into a knot. (GN 471; ch. 22)

Miss de Vine confesses her repentance, "Not for my original action, which was unavoidable, but for the sequel." She should have "made it her business to see what became of that unhappy man and his wife" (GN 472; ch. 22).

The last we see of Annie, she is in the care of Miss Barton and the Bursar, who are recommending aspirin and a rest and, remonstrating, "What would the children think if they saw you now?" And we hear no more of her sad life, which presumably continues on beyond the end of the novel, employed, perhaps, by some non-academic institution or household, and probably the recipient of tardy but heartfelt charity. Throughout the novel, Annie Robinson appears, except for her final scene, as a subservient and unmemorable element in the background of the main action. That is, she is not made one of a number of possible suspects, of whom we hear much, until one is revealed as the actual culprit, in the usual manner of a detective novel. Rather, Annie is a minor and scarcely noticed figure, whom Harriet treats off-handedly, absent-mindedly. Had she been noticed, truly seen as a real person, by Harriet or anybody else in the novel at some earlier point, much suffering might have been prevented.

The operative images used to describe her follow a veering sequence: from "smartly uniformed" and "too independent," to "thin and worried-looking," with an "odd look in her eyes"; from "slapping and ash-tray smartly" and looking "fairly level-headed" to being in "such a state, what with coal-dust"; from "Neat and subdued as usual," to having "the eyes of a hunted animal." The last image of her, "with her cap crooked and her hands twisting her apron into a knot," is the most pitiful of all, for it carries the full and crushing load of class discrimination. Some readers may recognize its remarkable similarity to a description of the boarding-school slavey Becky in Frances Hodgson Burnett's *A Little Princess* (1905): Becky is presented "with a coal smudge on her nose and several on her apron, with her poor little cap hanging half off her head," as "an ugly, stunted, worn-out little scullery drudge."[15]

This is the fate of Annie Robinson, "a woman in whom the emotions had gained control over the reason,"[16] as Sayers has described her in another place. The image is drawn from the most extreme version of the fate of women, to stand with her head in a servant's cap and her body in a servant's apron, humiliated and helpless, before the privileged and the powerful. She has chosen to play the woman's role of servant to husband and children and her punishment is, precisely, to play that role. I realize that this image opens Sayers to charges of snobbery and class-consciousness, and in fact she has been accused of making her various novels' villains guilty most of all of striving to better themselves. Nevertheless the image is an apt, even terrifying one.

Annie's primary sin (she is clearly a disturbed personality, but she has made *some* conscious choices, especially of the precise manner in which she sticks by her husband and makes her children come first) is against herself. It is the sin of "*Ira* or *Wrath*," and in a particular form which Sayers describes: the Englishman, she says, "is peculiarly liable to attacks of righteous indignation. While he is in one of those fits he will fling himself into a debauch of fury and commit extravagances which are not only evil but ridiculous."[17] Sayers further describes "the harsh, grating tone and the squinting, vicious countenance"[18]—and this is Annie, castigating the academic women for their chosen life-style, which is different from hers. She makes her husband's falsehood the fault of its discoverer, and places the responsibility for his weaknesses upon the community he betrayed. She is possessed by her own rage: she has surrendered her selfhood and her sanity to it. The use of the term "Poltergeist" for the explosive destructions of the Poison Pen is an exact thematic parallel for Annie's situation: they have been the side-effects of a psychological storm. The precise border between insanity and crime is a matter of law in our society but both states can lead to a loss of liberty, spiritual as well as physical. Annie is a slave as well as a slavey.

5. Martha Ruddle

Having created the tragic character (I am using the word "tragic" not only in the classical sense of a person of high degree fallen through *hubris* or by fate, but as we use it today for something to which, in the words of the wife of Willy Loman in *The Death of a Salesman*, "attention must be paid") of Annie Robinson, Sayers produced no more villainesses or heedless female causers of much evil. But she did create the character of Martha Ruddle, a somewhat disagreeable lady who is perhaps the closest to a caricature of any of her female figures.

We first meet Martha Ruddle as Lord Peter and his bride Harriet arrive at their honeymoon cottage, Talboys, in *Busman's Honeymoon*.

> The speaker, now emerging into the blaze of the headlights, was a hard-faced angular lady of uncertain age, dressed in a mackintosh, a knitted shawl, and a man's cap secured rakishly to her head with knobbed and shiny hatpins. [...] [A]dvancing with a snort to Harriet's side, she said, belligerently:
> "Now then, 'oo are you and wot d'you want, kicking up all this noise?" (BH 54-55; ch. 1)

She takes Lord Peter and his new Lady for "film actors" and says of Harriet, "no better than you should be, I'll be bound." Herself she describes as "a respectable married woman with a grown son of her own." Of her husband, dead fifteen years, she says, "a good 'usband 'e was, when he was himself, that is" (BH 55; ch. 1). When she hears of the marriage and recognizes Harriet as daughter of the local doctor, her manner changes:

> She wiped a bony hand on the mackintosh and extended it to bride and groom in turn. "'Oneymoon—well, there!—it won't take me a minnit to put on the clean sheets, which is laying aired and ready at the cottage." (BH 56; ch. 1)

Mrs. Ruddle is not really a villainess. In some ways she is like the coarsely-spoken but good-hearted Nurse in *Romeo and Juliet*. But she is not entirely honest either. There is an interrogation scene revealing this. The scene begins:

And the lady who now entered rubbing her hands on her apron and crying in self-important tones, "Did you want me, mister?"—there was nothing in *her* to music the silent string of chivalry. Kirk [the policeman], however, knew where he was with the Mrs. Ruddles of this life and attacked the position confidently (BH 194; ch. 9)

It emerges that she has been known to "borer a drop of paraffin" from Noakes from time to time. (Noakes, who owned the cottage Lord Peter has bought as a honeymoon gift for his wife, is the victim in *Busman's Honeymoon*; paraffin is an inflammable fluid used for cooking-stoves and lamps.) Mrs. Ruddle is an important witness because her theft has placed her in a position to see an essential clue. Lord Peter concludes the interview by

> driving her gently before him like a straying hen. "We know we can rely on you, Mrs. Ruddle, thou foster-child of Silence and slow Time. Whatever you do," he added earnestly, as he propelled her over the threshold, "don't say anything to Bunter—he's the world's worst chatter box." (BH 201; ch. 9)

Lord Peter's irony in comparing Mrs. Ruddle to the Grecian urn of Keats's *Ode* is obvious. He is also speaking ironically of her talkative ways. The scene then moves on to an even more shocking revelation: the local policeman has been blackmailed by Noakes for the theft of a purse: he exclaims of Mrs. Ruddle, "I didn't know that old cat had seen me" (BH 201; ch. 9). Words like "hen" and "cat" are common epithets for women, comparing them to domestic animals that are usually considered to be feminine in our culture—"hen" is the feminine term for chicken, but "cat" has a female implication so that we say "tom-cat" when we mean a male.

Mrs. Ruddle has played a part in the plot beyond the matter of the paraffin and the constabulary, however; she has (innocently) delayed the process of detection. In this role she appears at the very moment when the murderer has been revealed. Looking at the vital clue,

> "Why, there!' she cried, triumphantly. "That's a funny thing, that is. That's the way it was when I came in 'ere Wednesday morning to clear for the sweep. I took it off meself and throwed it down on the floor."

She looked about her for approbation, but Harriet was past all power of comment and Peter still stood unmoving. Gradually, Mrs. Ruddle realised that the moment for applause had gone by, and shuffled out. (BH 402; ch. 20)

We last hear of Mrs. Ruddle with her son Bert, "having a sumptuous six o'clock tea with Mrs. Hodges and a few neighbors, eager to have their news served up piping hot" (BH 408; Epithalamion 1).

Hers is not a malignant figure, and of all the female characters discussed here, she best represents that snobbery of which Sayers is often accused. There is no reason why she should be a little dishonest, a little talkative, a little stupid. And certainly Lord Peter condescends to her, as Harriet had condescended to Annie Robinson. One such figure in a great catalog of women is not, perhaps, a bad record: there *are* ridiculous and dishonest women in the world. If there has been a commandment broken it is the Eighth, "Thou shalt not steal," and Mrs. Ruddle endures no judgment within the confines of the story. Sayers is merely having sport with her.

The title of the present essay, "Eve's Sharp Apple," was suggested to me by a line in Sayers's verse play, *The Devil to Pay*. A long-standing misinterpretation of the meaning of the Eve myth is that women are naturally sinful. What Sayers is saying in her novels may be that women are as free as men to sin or not to sin, but that when they *do* sin, they do it in a characteristically female way. That is, women's sins are especially inclined to be sins against relationships, and perhaps especially sins in cases of sexual relationships, where men are, indeed, especially vulnerable.

> None may touch my lips
> while on his own hangs still the fatal taste
> of Eve's sharp apple.[19]

So says Helen, the heart's desire of this world, and to gain her in Sayers's version of the Faust legend, "Faustus denies the reality of evil and of personal responsibility for evil."[20] But the fatal taste is the inheritance of every descendant of the first to soil his lips on that apple (despite his disclaimer, "The woman gave it to me and I did eat"). The universality of guilt, or the capacity of guilt, in men and women, is what is meant by the doctrine of Original Sin, Christians say "Forgive us our trespasses," in the Lord's Prayer because they are all, in various ways, guilty of trespassing. And they make their own forgiveness dependant upon their own ability to forgive others. In the above essay I have concentrated not directly upon the central plots of the novels with their crimes, criminals, and inevitable detections. Rather, I have been talking about the depiction by Dorothy L. Sayers of human weakness and sin in particular women's lives.

I said at the beginning that these women had not been intelligent in love: their failures are in the sphere of human relationships. They are all of them married women except for Mary Whittaker, who has a female companion in a relationship which some people would consider a form of marriage, and they betray these relationships in some fatal way. Mary Whittaker uses Vera Findlater and then throws her away like a spent toy. Margaret Harrison brings about the death of two men while never even imagining her own guilt. Gilda Farren encourages an intemperate man to acts that cost him his life, and endangers the life of her husband as well. Annie Robinson, one suspects, helped to drive her husband toward suicide. Perhaps if she had helped him to face, accept, and surpass his own guilt, he might have lived a fulfilled life. Instead she reinforced his resentments and became an accomplice in his self-destruction. Finally, Martha Ruddle, a very small offender in such company, blunderingly removes a vital piece of evidence and delays the process of detection, causing a series of more or less innocent people to be suspected of murder. The truth is almost still-born.

Notes
[1] Dorothy L. Sayers. "The other Six Deadly Sins" (1941), *Christian Letters to a Post-Christian World* (Grand Rapids, MI: William B. Eerdmans. 1969) 138.
[2] Sayers, "The other Six Deadly Sins" 138.
[3] Sayers, "The other Six Deadly Sins" 139.
[4] Sayers, "The other Six Deadly Sins" 149.
[5] C. S. Lewis, "The Great Sin," *Mere Christianity: A revised and amplified edition.* 1952; New York: Harper Collins, 2000) 127.
[6] C. S. Lewis, "The Three Parts of Morality," *Mere Christianity* 75.

Notes

[7] C. S. Lewis, "The Three Parts of Morality," *Mere Christianity* 75.

[8] Julian of Norwich, *Showings*, Edmund Colledge O.S.A. and James Walsh, S.J., trans., (New York: Paulist Press, 1978) 208.

[9] Julian of Norwich, *Showings*, 84,

[10] Dorothy L. Sayers, "The Faust Legend and the idea of the Devil," *Christian Letters* 225.

[11] J.R.R. Tolkien, *The Fellowship of the Ring* in *The Lord of the Rings* with illus. by Alan Lee (Hammersmith, London: HarperCollins Publishers, 1991) 138; ch. 7.

[12] Tolkien, *The Fellowship of the Ring* 139; ch. 7.

[13] Sayers, "The Other Six Deadly Sins," *Christian Letters* 152.

[14] Sayers, "The Other Six Deadly Sins," *Christian Letters* 153.

[15] Frances Hodgson Burnett, *A Little Princess* (1905), Gutenberg Ebook #146, ch. 5.

[16] Dorothy L. Sayers, *The Mind of the Maker* (1941; New York: HarperCollins, 1987) 76

[17] Dorothy L. Sayers, "The Other Six Deadly Sins," *Christian Letters* 140.

[18] Sayers, "The Other Six Deadly Sins" *Christian Letters* 140.

[19] Dorothy L. Sayers, "The Devil to Pay," *Four Sacred Plays* (London: Victor Gollancz, 1948) scene II, 162.

[20] William Reynolds, "Dorothy Sayers and the Drama of Orthodoxy," 3.1 *The Sayers Review* (October 1978): 37.

8. "The Perilous Synthesis": Sacred and Profane Love in Dorothy L. Sayers's *Thrones, Dominations*

> For by him were all things created, that are in heaven, and that are in earth, visible and invisible, whether they be thrones, or dominions.
>
> ——Colossians 1:16

Patterson argues that the marriage theme in Sayers's manuscript fragment Thrones, Dominations *was meant to be intertwined with a detective plot. She chooses the probable victim and murderer of this plot by comparing the fragment's characters with the victims and murderers in Sayers's other works. She analyses the marriage theme by comparing Peter and Harriet's relationship with that of Laurence and Rosamund Harwell, and considering Sayers's personal experiences as lover and wife as sources for her fictional characters. Patterson's speculations on this fragment long predate Jill Paton Walsh's version of the finished novel (Hodder & Stoughton, 1998).*

Patterson raises the subject of influences from the author's own life on her fiction in several papers, including this one and "'A Bloomsbury Blue-Stocking': Dorothy L. Sayers's Bloomsbury Years in Their Spatial and Temporal Context."

"The Perilous Synthesis" was delivered at the 17th Annual Mythopoeic Conference, August 8-11th, 1986, California State University, Long Beach, California. This copy was retrieved from the Archives at the University of Waterloo.

In London On October 8, 1985, *The Times* carried the following report under the caption "Golden Wedding":

> Wimsey-Vane—On the 8th October at St. Cross Church Oxford, Peter Death Bredon Wimsey, second son of the late Gerald Mortimer Bredon Wimsey 15th Duke of Denver to Harriet Deborah Vane, only daughter of the late Henry Vane MD of Great Pagord, Herts.[1]

Readers of the detective novels of Dorothy L. Sayers will have smiled at this formal recognition of the marriage of these beloved but fictional characters. The earliest days of this celebrated marriage were explored in her novel *Busman's Honeymoon* (1937) which has been called her "most erotic published work."[2] The commentator—Nancy M. Tischler—adds intriguingly that "(the unpublished *Thrones, Dominations* takes it a step further)." It is the purpose of my paper to explore this additional step.

Historical Context

The last to be published of Sayers's twelve novels of detection, *Busman's Honeymoon* appeared in 1937, but it had been preceded by a play of the same title, which went into rehearsal October 19, 1936, and opened November 9, 1936, in Birmingham. Alzina Stone Dale (1985) has suggested that when Sayers wrote the novel *Gaudy Night* (published in 1935), in which her amateur detective Lord Peter Wimsey and his future wife, detective novelist Harriet Vane, become engaged, she had already planned the sequel in which the couple enjoy their honeymoon. Sayers began work on the play, *Busman's Honeymoon* (published like the novel in 1937), in February 1935,[3] and in February 1936 she sent some of the opening chapters of the novel to her producer.[4] If we assume that the whole of the novel *Busman's Honeymoon* was in manuscript form in 1936, there may just have been time in the same year for Sayers to begin work upon another novel with a nuptial theme, which resulted in the manuscript fragment, *Thrones, Dominations*.

This unfinished work is built around a pivotal historical event, the death of King George V on January 20, 1936, a watershed which occurred when Sayers was engaged in writing her novel *Busman's Honeymoon* and which may have suggested itself as the symbolic key to a further exploration of the marital relationship of Lord and Lady Peter, to wit: what was their new-made marriage like after the honeymoon? Dale (1978) thinks it likely that this combination of themes—the death of George V and the marriage relationship of the Wimseys—became unusable when, on December 11, 1936, the king's son and heir, Edward VIII, abdicated in order to marry the divorced American commoner, Wallis Simpson, because it would have been seen as a commentary by Sayers on this second watershed event, rather than a meditation on marriage in general, as she had intended it to be.[5]

The Characters and Detectival Plot

As the manuscript stands, it is filled with sexual tension and a sense of delicate balance, as the Wimseys explore the further ramifications of their new-made bond, while a second couple, whose marriage is a bitter contrast to that of the Wimseys, provides a foil for this exploration. The major characters in the novel may be represented by the following diagram:

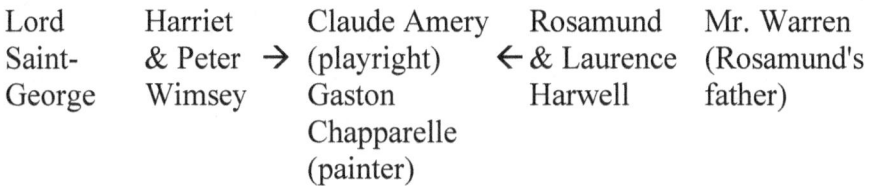

| Lord Saint-George | Harriet & Peter Wimsey | → | Claude Amery (playright) Gaston Chapparelle (painter) | ← | Rosamund & Laurence Harwell | Mr. Warren (Rosamund's father) |

There are other characters, chief among them Lord Peter's maternal uncle Paul Delagardie, who is very important to the subject of sexuality. These include the Duke of Denver (Peter's elder brother) and his wife Helen, who are the parents of Lord Saint-George, and whose dinner party for the Wimseys is evidently meant to be a set piece in the novel. Others are servants, a pair of dressmakers, and Lady Severn, Lord Peter's ninety-year-old godmother whose letter to Peter's mother opens the novel *Busman's Honeymoon*.

In my diagram I oppose the Wimseys to the Harwells and place between them the names of two men: the one the playwright Claude Amery and the other the painter Gaston Chapparelle, both of whom are sources of contact and conflict between the two couples in general as well as forming sources of conflict between Rosamund and Laurence Harwell in particular. The placing of Lord Saint-George beside the Wimseys and Mr. Warren beside the Harwells indicates my conclusion that their difficulties also had some bearing upon the projected plot. The problem is that although the marriage relationship is an obvious subject of this novel, the detective story it must have been intended to tell is not.

I am convinced that there *was* a detective plot in the author's mind and that it was intended to be related to the marriage theme, just as, in *Busman's Honeymoon*, the doomed relationship of Frank Crutchley and Aggie Twitterton forms a pathetic counterpoint to the glorious nuptials of the Wimseys, and *Gaudy Night* the disordered loyalties of Annie Robinson to her tragic husband are contrasted with the slowly developing relationship of Harriet to Lord Peter. Before exploring the nuptial theme, therefore, I shall examine the detectival possibilities of the cast of characters as Sayers has presented them in *Thrones, Dominations*.

The majority of the sequences in the manuscript are written from Harriet's point of view. In my proposed detective plot, she would have continued to dominate. In one possible scenario, Claude Amery, the weak but importunate playwright, is the victim. Since Harriet has aided in his efforts to get his play performed, she feels an obligation to uncover his murder. Lord Peter helps her but he is "in a rather irresponsible mood as a detective."[6] It is presumably from the "new" characters in the novel (aside from the Wimsey household servants and selected guests at the Denver dinner) that the murder suspects must be chosen: these are Gaston Chapparelle, Rosamund and Laurence Harwell, and "old Mr. Warren." The dressmakers are not likely to be implicated unless Sayers planned an extreme example of the "least likely person" syndrome.

I chose Claude Amery as the victim because he is an unattractive character and a bone of contention. Chapparelle is a very attractive personality (too attractive to be killed), but he may be a suspect because he could be thought (briefly and, I think, incorrectly) to have been involved with Rosamund. The latter's father, Mr. Warren, would make a pathetic victim, and an unlikely-seeming murderer, although he is an ex-convict. It is just possible that he could be suspected of holding a grudge or having an obligation to the playwright since he had been a director before his imprisonment for mismanagement of funds. Rosamund and Laurence Harwell seem headed toward conflict over Amery, and either of them is sufficiently disagreeable to be the murderer: Laurence is the obvious choice, through jealousy, and Rosamund is called a "siren," one who lures people to their doom. Frankly, I would prefer a denouement in which she is directly the murderer, perhaps in a fit of sudden rage.

Sayers's murder victims are for the most part either unpleasant or dispensable people; that is, we either feel unsympathetic towards them or they are minor figures in the story. (I am not concerned with exceptions such as the lack of a victim in *Gaudy Night* and the quite blameless victim in *Whose Body?*) While her murderers are often not only unsympathetic but downright malignant, the exceptions to this rule are perhaps more important. There is a sense in which God (or at least his bell-ringers) killed the victim—himself very much a villain—in *The Nine Tailors*, and the murderer in *Murder Must Advertise* is a pathetic figure, as is the "poison pen" in *Gaudy Night*. There is no murderer in *Clouds of Witness*, and the death in *Five Red Herrings* is accidental. What Sayers does not do is to give us a murderer whose identity offends, shocks, annoys, or dismays us, as P.D. James does so frequently and with such evident glee. A Sayers villain or villainess, where there is one, is usually driven by overmastering concerns of fear, or more commonly, of jealousy or greed. Therefore if Claude Amery is the victim in *Thrones, Dominations*, his killer is likely to be someone who fears, envies, and/or hates him, or else someone who hoped to gain in some very concrete way from his death.

Lord Saint-George as Subplot

There is a sub-plot, apparently, in the matter of Lord Saint-George, whose father, the Duke of Denver, keeps him on a very short financial string: in a fragmentary summary of the plot, Lord Peter is seen "in a very human mood as an uncle" (TD 37A) and has evidently paid a rather large debt which his nephew has contracted. Denver persuades Wimsey to accept repayment and in another fragment threatens to withhold "every ha' penny" from Saint-George's already meager allowance. The youth makes several attempts to contact Lord Peter about the matter. We are not told the exact nature of this debt: is it for food and drink? For certain young or accommodating ladies? For gambling?

The matter of Saint-George's possible inheritance from Lord Peter, should Harriet remain childless, is raised in *Busman's Honeymoon* by the crusty Countess of Severn and Thames, who is Lord Peter's godmother: perhaps this sore point would have had some bearing on the subject of Saint-George's indebtedness. In "The Haunted Policeman," (1938) when Peter first takes up his own firstborn child in his arms, the attendant nurse notes that he "handled the child competently; as, in a man who was an experienced uncle, was not, after all, so very surprising" (LP 408). Sayers wrote three short stories in which the births of the Wimsey children are mentioned or germane: "The Haunted Policeman," the very latterly published "Talboys" (1972) in which the Wimseys have three sons, Bredon, Roger, and Paul, and the never-published fragment, "The Master Key," set in February 1936.[7] Peter and Harriet married on October 8, 1935 and their eldest son, Bredon, was born, probably, in November of 1936. This means that the child was conceived in February of 1936,[8] the month following the events recorded in *Thrones, Dominations*.

Perhaps *Thrones, Dominations* was to have culminated in the triumphant announcement of Harriet's first pregnancy: the subplot itself may have been intended simply as a secondary plotline against which Harriet's decision to have children could be played, but it may also have been intended to cast some suspicion upon Lord Saint-George in regard to the murder. Lord Peter's nephew as a suspect would echo his father, the Duke of Denver's role in *Clouds of Witness*.

Major Themes: Marriage and Mystery

I have written about the presumed murder mystery in *Thrones, Dominations* because I think there was intended to be one. I do not think that the author wrote these materials as a way of searching for a plot and then, failing to find one, abandoned the attempt. The manuscript, as it stands, contains at least two main themes, one clearly present—the working out of Lord and Lady Peter's marital relationship—and one absent but surely, in a Lord Peter novel, implicit—a mystery which is to be detected by Harriet and Peter. The conflict and atmosphere of sexual tension suggests more than the exploration of a marriage, not least in the teasing scene with which the manuscript concludes, and which Sayers has intriguingly crossed out:

> In the drawing room as they entered, there appeared to be a faint atmosphere of crisis. The ten figures, seated or standing politely about with coffee-cups had that air of centralized alertness by which a theatrical producer directs and maintains attention to an important announcement. There was just time to observe that Gaston Chapparelle was the arrangement's centre, before he broke [sic]. (TD 171)[9]

The reference to the "theatrical producer" reminds us that the "new" characters in the novel are most of them associated with the theater, the playwright Amery, the producer Harwell, and the director Mr. Warren. In particular, Rosamund Harwell is a former couturier's mannequin, and she is to be pictured by the portraitist Chapparelle with a mask and is thus associated also with the symbolism of the theater. It may be suggested that Sayers abandoned this manuscript because her attentions had become deeply absorbed in her actual participation in the theater as she had become an active playwright. She may have preferred to live out this theatrical role and lifestyle rather than to write about it.

The symbolism of the theater is certainly present, but there is another symbolic context which, as the manuscript stands, is far more powerful and is embodied first of all in the title: this is the death of King George V, which forms the focal point of the materials actually in existence and which has drawn much of the attention of critics. Sayers had used a specific event—Armistice Day—in *The Unpleasantness at the Bellona Club*, and in *Thrones, Dominations*, the death of the King is also likely to have been intended as more than a set-piece. Dawson Gaillard (1981) has called attention to Lord Peter's meditation, as he sits in Parker's office, upon the event:

> a scene near the end of [...] *Thrones, Dominations* leaves no doubt that Lord Peter is through. In that scene, he walks into Charles Parker's office, where they discuss the recent death of King George V (January 1936). Peter feels that with King George's death, he has lost a standard as well as his youth. He feels as though he has grown old in a moment, he tells Charles. And cryptically he remarks that King George stood "for something" that he shall miss [...] Perhaps it is the strength of King George's belief in himself that Lord Peter shall miss.[10]

The title and epigraph of the novel suggest rather more even than this, however. I have shown in my essay "Changing, Fearfully Changing,"[11] that the theme of mutability is already strongly present in *Strong Poison*, which stands but midway in the sequence of Sayers's detective novels.

In the manuscript as we have it, the title *Thrones, Dominations* must be taken together with the powerful sequence of the "village funeral" of the King as a symbolic system turning upon the meaning and role of hierarchy, rule, domination, submission, and allegiance. The monarchy is here a structure set together with its echo, the marriage relationship. These two august structures—monarchy and marriage—have been used as among the most resonant symbols of the relationship of the soul to God, and I think there may have been an intention by Sayers to use them so in this novel. Christ is called "the King of Kings," or referred to in that role, in Luke 23.2, I Timothy 1.17 and 6.15, and Revelation 15.3 and 17-14. Jesus referred repeatedly to the "Kingdom of God" (Matthew 6.33 and John 3.3), and the "Father's kingdom" (Matthew 26.29). The theme continues with reference to "the kingdom" in Colossians 1.13, James 2.5, II Peter 1.11, and Revelation 11.15. A consultation of any Concordance will show the frequency of this motif in both Testaments. In Revelation 19.7 and 9 we read of the "marriage of the Lamb," and although Jesus states in Matthew 22.30, Mark 12.25, and Luke 20.35 that there will be no human marriage in heaven, he used marriage and marriage feasts as a frequent motif in his parables. Christ himself is "the bridegroom" in Matthew 9.15 and 25.1-10, in Mark 2.19, in Luke 5.34, and in John 3.29. We read of the bridal relationship between Christ and his Church in Revelation 21.9, in which the heavenly guide invites St. John the seer to "Come hither, I will show thee the bride, the Lamb's wife," and presents him with a vision of the New Jerusalem, and in 22.17: "the Spirit and the bride say, 'Come.'"

The specific image chosen by Sayers for her royal symbolism is, however, none of these. The two words "Thrones" and "Dominations" are the names of the third and fourth highest choirs or orders of angels in the nine-fold hierarchy proposed by Dionysus the Areopagite in *The Mystical Theology and the Celestial Hierarchies*. The two highest are well-known: Cherubim and Seraphim. Anglicans are familiar with these figures from the first verse of the hymn by Athelstan Riley (1906), which lists all nine choirs of angels:

> Ye watchers and ye holy ones,
> Bright Seraphs, Cherubim and Thrones,
> Raise the glad strain, Alleluiaa!
> Cry out Dominions, Princedoms, Powers,
> Virtues, Archangels, Angels' choirs,
> Alleluia, alleluia, alleluia, alleluia, alleluia![12]

In his *Dictionary of Angels* (1967) Gustav Davidson quotes the Pseudo-Dionysus: "it is through the Thrones that [...] God brings his justice to bear upon us."[13] The Thrones derive from Jewish Throne mysticism, medieval speculative thought based upon visionary descriptions of the Throne of God in the Old Testament. The dominant characteristic of the Thrones is "steadfastness,"[14] and they are to be equated with the *Ofanim* or living Wheels of the Throne and with the Four Living Creatures "full of eyes round about" of Ezekiel 10.20, whose attribute is vigilance.[15]

Dominations (dominions, lords, lordships)[16] are derived from the *Hashmallim* of Jewish mysticism: "through them the majesty of God is manifested,"[17] and they are signified by their "Emblems of authority: sceptres, orbs." Lordship, majesty, and authority are here placed not at the top of the nine-fold hierarchy but only fourth, at the head of the second of three three-membered ranks. The order of the list is by no means universal, but Sayers's title is very evidently taken from the Pseudo-Dionsyian sequence.

In *Thrones, Dominations*, a parallel is drawn between the earthly Kingdom of Great Britain and the heavenly kingdom of God, with the former, fragile, mortal, and human, as an echo of the eternal, spiritual, and supernatural Kingdom of God. In the magnificent set piece of the King's funeral procession, as people on the street uncover their heads at the passing gun-carriage with its majestic but pathetic burden, "You knew where it was, seeing the dark crowd turn pink, as though a pale sun were following it westward" (TD 91). The gesture of homage is spontaneous and universal. Gaston Chapparelle, the artist, comments upon the physical exposure of the heir and his brothers as they walk through the crowd with only a few unarmed police. "This is just a village funeral," Peter tells him (TD 92).

The personal, local, humble, human relationships of the village, where hierarchy (in Sayers's always idealized depiction) is enacted on a face-to-face basis, are the paradigm for the Kingdom, and by extension for the relationship between God and humankind, in which humility and self-giving are practiced by both parties, divine as well as human. As the translation of the *Te Deum* in the Prayer Book so forthrightly puts it, "When thou tookest upon thee to deliver man, thou didst not abhor the Virgin's womb." A King's funeral is a village funeral: Lord and Lady Peter's wedding is a village wedding—this is the equation Sayers is suggesting. In her profoundly traditional worldview, the orderly structure of reality holds, from the humblest to the most exalted.

The specific application of Sayers's chosen symbolism is made clear in her epigraph:

> Thrones and Imperial Powers, off-spring of Heav'n,
> Etherial Virtues; or these Titles now
> Must we renounce, & changing stile be call'd
> Princes of Hell?

These lines from John Milton's *Paradise Lost* (Book II, lines 310-313) continue:

> for so the popular vote
> Inclines, here to continue and build up here
> A growing Empire; doubtless: while we dream,
> And know not that the King of Heav'n hath doom'd
> This place our dungeon (Book II, lines 313-314)

In these passages, Beëlzebub is speaking in response to a speech by Mammon at the gathering at Pandemonium chaired by Satan. In his remarks, Beëlzebub calls attention to the creation in "another world" of "some new Race call'd Man" (Book II, line 348), and Satan, *a propos* of the epigraph quoted above, declares

> I assume
> These Royalties, and not refuse to Reign.[18]

He decides to go to that world—Earth—with consequences of which, like all detective novelists, Sayers was deeply concerned.

The implication of these passages is that there is an inverse regnancy where those who could have reigned in heaven can choose to reign in hell, that "Empire" which is in fact a "dungeon." This polarity of heaven and hell are paralleled in *Thrones, Dominations* by the contrasted marriages. James Brabazon (1981) says that

> the writing is saturated with an awareness of sex and its potency. Between Wimsey and Harriet the attraction is controlled, held in a state of tension and all the more powerful for that. Between Laurence and Rosamund Harwell the passion spills

out, it is visible to everyone, uncontrolled, violent, and dangerous.[19]

But there is more to the matter than this. The sexual relationship of Harriet and Peter is one of mutual consent, a free offering of each to the other. The relationship of the Harwells is one of resistance overmastered. In an interview with Harriet, Lord Peter's Uncle Paul Delagardie says that Peter's sexual experience has been

> without that taint of cruelty which for so many men spices the dish of desire. He has never had to pursue, to overcome, to beat down a bodily resistance, to bruise and break before he enjoys. He does not like his kisses salted with angry tears. (TD 12)

In contrast, Laurence Harwell does not expect a woman to "come half-way to meet desire." His wife has never more than "reluctantly yielded" to passion.

> Since every act of love was an act of compliance, it was right to be grateful for it—her surrender was so beautiful—an intoxicating compliment. (TD 109)

In consequence, their marriage is one in which "the territory was never won."

Since the language of these passages is that of pursuit, resistance, compliance, surrender, and won territory, the ruler here is a conqueror, who builds up an empire which is a dungeon for ruler and ruled alike. In contrast, Sayers presents a conversation between the Wimseys in which Harriet asks her husband,

> "You said that if you chose you could make me love you—after a fashion. It was true, Peter. Why didn't you choose?"
>
> He said simply: "It would have given me no pleasure."
> (TD 14)

He does not choose to overmaster her. His rulership is one of perfect assent. "Ruler" and "ruled" are united: as C.S. Lewis makes Ransom say in *That Hideous Strength*, "obedience and rule are more like a dance than a drill—specially between man and woman where the roles are always changing."[20] It is to this stately dance in the lives of Peter and Harriet that we now turn.

Lord Peter as Lover and Husband

In Dale's interpretation,[21] the narrative sequence of *Thrones, Dominations* begins on page 61 of the manuscript, with a scene in which M. Paul Delagardie and his friend M. Théophile Daumier are admiring a "true red-blonde" representation of English beauty seated with a male companion at a nearby table. There is, it develops, another couple in the room who are, by their description, Lord Peter and Harriet Wimsey: "The fair-haired diplomat with the eyeglass and the decided looking brunette in orange taffeta" (TD 65). M. Daumier says of them:

> I perceive exactly the English married couple par excellence … he consults her about the menu, is particular that she has what she requires, and orders his own dinner to suit himself. If she drops her napkin, he picks it up. When she speaks, he attends … politely. (TD 65)

Delagardie explains: "My nephew is nervous, fastidious, and inhibited. My niece by marriage, obstinate, energetic and independent. They are both possessed of a truly diabolical pride. Mayfair is awaiting with interest the result of this curious matrimonial experiment" (TD 70).

This very human Lord Peter; as defined by his Uncle, is further defined by Margaret Hannay (1979):

> *Thrones, Dominations* […] continues the progression of Lord Peter from pasteboard paragon toward a full humanity. As we continue to see through Harriet's eyes, his personal vanity becomes increasingly clear—his interminable dawdling in the bathroom, his agonized fears over pimples, his terror that he will come to need false teeth.[22]

The portrait of Lord Peter as a human being is something of a foil for another view of him which is central to the theme of *Thrones, Dominations*: Harriet, meditating upon her husband, thinks

> There was a preposterous contrast between Peter's diffidence as a husband and his confidence as a lover, so that his bedside

> manner displayed no inhibitions but only an infinite series of courtesies ... (TD 83)

The phrase "bedside manner" echoes its use by the overwhelming Lady Severn, who, as she is ninety, can do as she likes, and in a humorous scene is depicted visiting the girl "young Peter" has married. After a series of personal but approving remarks, she asks how Harriet likes "being part of the Wimsey estate" (TD 25). Harriet replies that Peter does not treat her as such, which Lady Severn attributes to his good manners, adding: "An excellent bedside manner too, or so they tell me." In response, "Harriet said gravely: 'I don't think they ought to have told'" (TD 26). When the old lady is taken on a tour of the house we learn that there is a William and Mary bedstead placed upon a dais, "So that he can kiss the steps when he comes to bed" (TD 32), as Lady Severn tartly remarks.

A man whose success as a lover is based upon "an infinite series of courtesies" is a very distinctive sort of person, quite different from one who would "like his kisses salted with angry tears." Fortunately, the manuscript offers a very clear explanation for Lord Peter's proclivities, and several scenes in which he and his wife explore the subject.

On the first page of the manuscript as it is numbered in the Wade Collection, Harriet is talking to Peter's Uncle Paul Delagardie, who asks her if Peter has ever told her about the previous women in his life. She replies:

> "I know there have been women, of course. He's never made any secret of that. Why should he? But he never mentions names or details, thank goodness!" (TD 1)

In fact we have learned at least one detail in *Busman's Honeymoon*: A few nights before the wedding Lord Peter says suddenly to Harriet:

> "Tu m'enivres!"
> Language and voice together had been like a lightning-flash, showing up past and future in a single crack of fire [...]
> When his lips had reluctantly freed themselves, he had said:
> "I'm sorry. I didn't mean to wake the whole zoo." (BH 46; ch. 1)

And after a brief exchange on the subject of the "zoo", in which there is in fact a mention of "old Paul Delagardie, whose ironic eyes saw everything," Peter explains his francophone outburst (which can be translated "thou intoxicatest me!"):

> "I have now completely given myself away. No English vocabulary. No other Englishwoman. And that is the most I can say for myself." (BH 47; ch. 1)

In response to Harriet's disclaimer of detailed knowledge, Uncle Paul remarks that he has always thought her "a most unusual woman" (TD 1). She replies that "It's what we are now that matters, not what happened to either of us in the past." I once received a letter from a correspondent who asked me if I really believed it possible that Harriet and Peter stayed out of one another's bed until their wedding night: I do indeed believe it, partly because I have known another couple who expunged their past in the same way, so as to begin from the beginning on their wedding night, and partly because it makes perfect symbolic sense. Certainly Harriet's reply to Uncle Paul reinforces the meaning of this gesture.

M. Delagardie now proceeds to regale Harriet with the story of Peter's youthful love life. "The Peter of 1907 would have amused you, I think" (TD 3), the avuncular old voyeur begins. Peter had "a pleasant and lightly-veiled tenor with a promise of warmth" (TD 4). This appraisal combines images from the judgment of both music and wine, metaphors perhaps of his capabilities of sexual performance as well as of his speaking voice. The youth had come to consult his uncle and "the subject was that of sex" (TD 4). Asked what he had already done about it, Peter replied, "Nothing." Delagardie speculates that Peter had "escaped the grubbier manifestations of schoolboy sexuality" (TD 4). From my reading of British public school memoirs, I assume that these "grubbier aspects" would include masturbation and/or homosexual activity. We learn that Peter has been referred by his mother to M. Delagardie, her own brother, so we may infer that the boy had made very delicate inquiries of her as his budding sexuality began to manifest itself.

The old sage now describes the four options which he presented to his nephew:

1. To practice patience, marry early a girl of equal inexperience, and "inflict on one another a series of shocks from which you may never recover" (TD 6).
2. "You can, of course, assume the privilege of your position and debauch the under-housemaid" (TD 6).
3. "You may attach yourself to a discreet married woman" (TD 6). She will be experienced and know how to avoid pregnancy. On the other hand, there will be the problem of maintaining secrecy.
4. "You can put yourself into competent professional hands and learn your job properly" (TD 7).

The choice, it seems, is between "nice girls, good wives, bad wives, and courtesans" (TD 7). Delagardie expands upon the last category: "The great courtesan still existed; she was a specialist, and my God! She had style" (TD 7). On this basis, Peter's Uncle advised him to wait until Christmas and then travel with him to Paris where he would introduce him "to circles where you will be welcome for my sake and your own" (TD 8). Brabazon has pointed out that in all Sayers's books "a sane, practical and wholesomely sensual attitude to sex is invariably associated with the Continent, and particularly with France":[23] so here.

M. Delagardie explains to Harriet that he advised this course in order to

> "... see that no notion of fear, shame, guilt and so forth should attach itself to his own first personal encounter with passion. If it could not now be an idyll, it must at least be an adventure in the gallant manner." (TD 10)

So it was done: "I succeeded in commending him to the advice of a lady whose affections were at that time disengaged." Delagardie says of this lady, "She was no great beauty, but of singular charm and generosity of spirit. ... She had the art of awakening passion, and she found him an apt pupil." And this was his uncle's advice to Peter in undertaking this formal liaison: "Remember: it is your part to give pleasure as well as to receive it" (TD 10). This is very much to the point, for a lover who is capable of "An infinite series of courtesies." Delagardie sums up the relationship to Harriet: "It lasted, with perfect contentment on both sides, until Peter's last year at Oxford" (TD 11). And then, "he fell in love, and broke off the connection."

The love affair was with the infamous Barbara, an exquisitely beautiful young woman who became engaged to Peter when he went overseas and was submitted to the ordeal of the trenches; when he returned he found her married to a middle-aged army major and out of his reach forever. Delagardie says rather cruelly to Harriet that Peter "has never received unkindness except from the women he loved" (TD 11), and presses the point: "The first was unfaithful before he ever possessed her. The second—" (TD 11-12) Harriet finishes the sentence: "The second showed a great reluctance to be possessed" (TD 12). She acknowledges the pain she has caused her husband by making him wait five years before consenting to marry him after he has saved her from the gallows in *Strong Poison*.

In acknowledging her acknowledgement, Delagardie concludes her remarks by saying that none of Peter's partners have been unkind or unfaithful "after the act of possession" (TD 12), and he takes credit for this success, as being due to "my methods of education." Love to Peter, he says, is "an affair for mutual enjoyment." That is obviously the crux of this long passage—whether or not the services of an Edwardian courtesan, even over a four-year period, would actually have produced such a result.

In the manuscript a new scene begins immediately after the above conversation. This time Harriet is talking to Peter, asking him (as I quoted above) why he did not make her love him, and receiving the reply that it would have given him no pleasure. This is evidently literally, that is to say, physically, true:

> "Why not?"
> "You know why not. I can't face unwillingness." (TD 14)

Would he, in fact, have become impotent in the face of reluctance or resistance?

> "Peter, that's ridiculous. You can't seriously mean you're incapable of overcoming a little reluctance."
> His vanity shied at the word.
> "Incapable? Well, I suppose it would be silly to say that. But I should simply hate to try." (TD 14)

Harriet, intrigued, begins to probe:

She had found the blind spot in him. Where most people kept the lust to dominate, there was an almost inhuman blank. A goblin curiosity made her press on. (TD 15)

Has anybody in fact "Shown the faintest reluctance to go to bed with you?" No, but that is because he has never approached a reluctant partner, herself included, as he reminds her. In this response, "She caught a glimpse of a pride so colossal that it had a kind of innocence" (TD 15).

Harriet concludes that Peter is so certain of his power that he need not assert it. He, perhaps unnerved by her "goblin curiosity" (powerful phrase!) asks if she is somehow "losing any kick" through his *politesse*, but she replies forthrightly that she is "not a masochist" and concludes that it is a good thing the two of them have met and married: their "abnormalities" fit!

James Brabazon has said of Sayers's novel, *Busman's Honeymoon*, that "the striking thing is the depth with which she explores the passionate, unsentimental, but richly rewarding progress of their love."[24] Obviously *Thrones, Dominations* took, and was to have taken, this exploration still further. The central point, that true lovers must give and receive equal pleasure, was a matter of deep concern to Sayers. Brabazon discusses the subject of "Bedworthiness" as she explored it in her writings on Dante: in her essay "The 'Terrible Ode,'"

The case she makes for her hero as a passionate but perfectly normal lover is not only convincing in itself but also strong evidence […] as to where her own sexual preferences and sympathies lay.[25]

The same could surely be said for her portrayal of Lord Peter in *Thrones, Dominations*.

Sayers set forth in the clearest way her views upon this subject in a remarkable letter to Charles Williams dated October 18, 1944, in which she expatiated upon "the distinguishing marks of True Bedworthiness in the Male." She wrote in her most didactic tones (as was very much her wont in writings of the wartime era):

I find them to consist in the presence of Three Grand Assumptions […]

1. That the primary aim and object of Bed is that a good time should be had by *all*.
2. That (other things being equal) it is the business of the Male to make it so.
3. That he know his business.

The first Assumption rules out at once Satyromaniacs, sadists, connoisseurs in rape, egotists, and superstitious believers in female reluctance [...]

The second Assumption rules out the hasty, the clumsy, the lazy, the inconsiderate, the peremptory, the untimely, and (in most cases) the routinier [...]

The third Assumption rules out the tentative as well as the incompetent and inadequate ...[26]

All of this presents the image of a lover whose "bedside manner" consists of "an infinite series of courtesies."

Biographical Influences and Children

Did Sayers ever have personal knowledge of a lover like this? (I ask rhetorically because Brabazon has supplied an answer.) From his definitive biography, we learn that the last of her unconsummated love affairs was with the writer John Cournos. She would not use contraceptives, and hence would not have intercourse with him, since he wanted "neither marriage nor children."[27] (The combination of passion and perceived betrayal in her letters to Cournos parallels the powerful emotions of Harriet Vane toward her lover Philip in *Strong Poison*.) "What she wanted from sex," as Brabazon paraphrases her letter to Cournos of December 4, 1924, "was babies and 'bodily comfort,' decency, normality, social and physical 'wholeness.'"[28]

Babies, bodily comfort, decency, normality, social and physical wholesomeness: these are precisely the traits Sayers wished to embody in the relationship of Harriet and Lord Peter in *Thrones, Dominations*. As for John Cournos, "He can hardly have expected to find Dorothy claiming that if a man was entitled to physical fulfillment, so too was a woman; and that for her, fulfillment consisted in bearing a child, not simply in sexual intercourse [...]"[29] The matter of "bearing a child" is a central theme in *Thrones, Dominations*.

In her affair of the heart with Cournos, Sayers did not, by her own report, perfectly match the ideal female partner required by Lord

Peter in *Thrones, Dominations*. She admitted in a letter to him December 4, 1924, that "I wanted to be persuaded—and in the bigger matter as well—I longed to be overborne, like any Victorian fool—"[30] By April 23 of the previous year, at the latest, she had found herself pregnant by "the Beast,"[31] as she called her first physical lover, the father of her son and only child, Anthony Fleming, who was born January 3, 1924. In late January of 1925 she wrote to Cournos:

> Give me a man that's human and careless and loves life, and one that can enjoy the rough and tumble of passion. I like to die spitting and swearing, you know, and I am no mean wrestler. But there again, precautionary measures cramp the style.[32]

What Sayers wanted, Brabazon says, is "a man who was unromantic, unpretentious, lustful, friendly, comfortable—"[33] He concludes of her eventual husband, whether or not he possessed all of these qualities (and I would suggest that Oswald Atherton Fleming was in fact both romantic and pretentious), "that he was good in bed," and hence, I conclude, at least lustful, friendly, and comfortable. This is an attractive thought, though Brabazon suggests a deterioration of the relationship as alcoholism and latant shell-shock gradually took their toll.

There is much in these glimpses of Sayers as a "rough and tumble" lover which does not perfectly accord with the portrait of Harriet and Peter in *Thrones, Dominations*, but I do not require that life imitate art, and Dorothy was not in fact Harriet. Harriet comes from a wounding lover, with whom she has cohabited without wedlock but, I think, with the use of contraceptives, to the arms of Lord Peter as a wedded Lady, and within four months of their marriage she is pregnant.

In *Thrones, Dominations* the possible children of the Wimsey marriage are discussed in several passages. Lady Severn asks Harriet if she plans children as well as books, and Harriet replies that she knows she can write books but does not yet know if she can have children (TD 26). Again, Lady Severn asks Peter what he is going to call the children (presumably in order to find out if he plans to have any) and he replies without hesitation, "Matthew, Mark, Luke and John" (TD 35), and proceeds to "Keziah, Jemima, and Keren-happuch" (which are the names of Job's daughters), followed by the

Nine Muses, the Kings of Israel and Judah, "the Major and Minor Prophets and the eleven thousand Virgins of Cologne" (TD 35-36). This wonderful retort makes it clear that Lord Peter not only has no reservations about his ability to beget children, but plans an unlimited supply.

Peter's expectation of children is raised again in a conversation with his brother, the Duke of Denver, in the most elaborately developed version of Helen's dinner party. The brothers are discussing Lord Saint-George, and Denver wants to assure himself that Peter will have heirs, just in case Saint-George should be killed in a plane crash or an auto accident, in order to protect the family line. Peter's reply is this:

> "But the decision isn't in my hands and I don't intend that it shall be. If my wife has children, she shall have them for fun and not as a legal instrument for securing the orderly devolution of property." (TD 170)

And with that, Gerald has to be content. The scene concludes as the two men enter the drawing room.

Childbearing is thus a central element in the free and mutual relationship of Lord and Lady: she is to be his partner by her own free choice both in the conjugal act and in its consequences. There is an implication here that Lord Peter, unlike his author, would have tolerated contraception if his wife chose to practice it or even, perhaps, if she asked him to do so, although I suspect that in the latter case Harriet would have allowed him his own proper freedom in the matter too. As we know from the outcome of their marriage described in "The Haunted Policeman," Lady Peter was delivered of a son, and this child was not begotten on the wedding night. Presumably nature had been left to take its course and the conception of the child occurred in the due sequence of physiological possibility. It is possible that Harriet's remarks to Lady Severn simply mean that as the honeymoon has not produced a pregnancy (assuming that she has had time to find this out), she does not yet know if they will be able to have children but is waiting to see what will happen. I think this is enough obstetrical speculation for one study: my point is that this happy couple intend to have children and that they concur freely and independently in this desire.

The question of children in the Wimsey marriage has a related question, raised by Harriet herself when she tells Peter's godmother that she knows she can write books but does not know if she can have babies. Are Harriet's books in fact to continue? S.L. Clark (1978) has broached this question, and begins with a reference to a scene in *Gaudy Night*: "In the conversation which Harriet and Peter have in the deserted dining room of the Egotist's Club, it is almost as if Harriet wishes to cast up to him the danger of his position *vis a vis* the scholarly woman, of which she sees herself to be a type, almost as if she wishes to predicate the demise of her career as an author on her unlikely acceptance of his proposal."[34] Clark continues the argument in a note: "What proves telling is Harriet's subsequent fear in the unpublished novel fragment *Thrones, Dominations* [...] that this is precisely what is happening."[35]

In fact, the question is raised in *Thrones, Dominations*, but it is also answered. We learn that Harriet intends to go on writing from one of the versions of the dinner party: she tells a fellow guest to go on calling her "Miss Vane" as she will (like Sayers) continue to publish under that name and will use it as her own (TD 55). Peter adds that he was consulted and "agreed with alacrity" (TD 56). He explains:

> "It gives one the illusion that one has a mistress as well as a wife—which is obviously gratifying and less expensive than the reality." (TD 56)

We assume from what Harriet has learned about Peter's youth that he ought to know!

To plan to write after marriage and actually to do so are two different things, as Jane Studdock learns in C.S. Lewis's novel of the nuptial relationship, *That Hideous Strength*. Sayers devotes several passages to Harriet's confrontation with the question. In one, we find Harriet at her desk.

> Lady Peter Wimsey, thoughtfully chewing her cigarette-holder, paused in her writing and stared out of the window. She had begun to realize why marriage is sometimes a handicap to a novelist's career. The emotion of love—of fulfilled and satisfactory love at any rate—does not stimulate the creative imagination; but puts it to sleep. (TD 22)

At this point in her meditations she is interrupted by the arrival of Lady Severn. As this guest is taken on a tour of the house, we learn that Peter and Harriet share the Library but each have their own study and interview room, suggesting clearly that they both plan to engage in study and writing.

In another domestic scene, after a series of details about the household staff and various visitors, Harriet again engages in a reverie: is she really a writer?

> "If one is really a writer, then one must write, and write now, while the hand kept its cunning, while the technique was still in one's head, while one was still in touch with one's public." (TD 89)

This very concrete litany suggests a similar sequence of thoughts in the head of Sayers after her own marriage had begun. In the case of Harriet, as of Sayers, we find in *Thrones, Dominations* that not only does she continue to write, contrary to her fears, but that, because she is now happy, she begins to write a tragedy! "The immediate effect of physical and emotional satisfaction seemed to be to lift the lid off hell." This is a remarkably telling observation: the Jungian law of compensation is amusingly involved here. The novel, it emerges, concerns a corpse which has been found in the local water supply. After about a week, Harriet needs technical information and asks her husband's aid: together they "plunged eagerly ... into the statistics of putrefaction" (TD 90).

We need worry no more, I think, that Harriet's career will be interrupted by her domestic happiness. In what may have been intended as an addendum to Harriet's interview with Paul Delagardie, he says that he has spoken with her because he wants to be certain that they are happily married. That is why he has "offered his counsels" (TD 107). Marriage, he says, is "the perilous synthesis." *Thrones, Dominations* suggests that this particular perilous synthesis will succeed.

Rosamund and Harriet

But there is another marriage in *Thrones, Dominations*, in which the emphasis is upon the "perilous" rather than upon the "synthesis." In the same introductory scene which featured as onlookers M. Delagardie and his friend, M. Daumier, we learn what the Harwells did for the rest of their Parisian afternoon. They attended the Grand Guignol! This theatrical presentation, which always featured the graphic portrayals of murders, was found to be stimulating by the Harwells. M. Delagardie for his part attends the Folies Bergeres, which he, with his own proclivities, also finds stimulating.

The Harwells appear again as members of a group of people who are watching the progress of the dead King's body on its gun-carriage: present are Lord and Lady Peter Wimsey, the artist Gaston Chapparelle, Laurence and Rosamund, and the latter's father. The little party is invited to gather at the Wimsey house for drinks afterwards. Various portions of the conversation are recorded: there is a brief flare-up about the plan to have Harriet's portrait painted by Chapparelle, a man with "a certain reputation." When assured that he need not fear for his wife's virtue, Wimsey replies "I am quite aware of that, Chapparelle" (TD 94).

At the same time, Rosamund Harwell's father Mr. Warren discusses prison with Harriet. She was once imprisoned to await the outcome of her trial for the murder of her lover, and, as we learn, he has served a prison term as a "defaulting director" of a disastrous theatrical production. People who have shared the same kinds of suffering sometimes take a rueful pleasure in swapping remembrances of their ordeals. Meanwhile, Peter and a wealthy patron discuss a young playwright's works: the writer is Claude Amery.

The impromptu guests are invited to inspect the house and Harriet escorts Rosamund.

> "Are you domesticated?" inquired Rosamund, rather abruptly.
> "Not at all," said Harriet. (TD 98)

The house, she explains, is run by the housekeeper, Miss Trapp, a "domestic dragon" who was Lord Peter's "old nurse" and who had "housekept at Gerald's place in Hertfordshire for donkey's years" (TD 99); she has now joined the household along with the new butler Meredith Bunter (who is, deliciously, the brother of Lord Peter's long-term valet, Mervyn Bunter). Together, housekeeper and butler look after everything, Harriet says. One detects a hint of genuine satisfaction in her account of this arrangement, along with a dollop of self-confidence at her success at integrating herself into the deeply-rooted lifestyle, and even, perhaps, a whiff of annoyed retribution for a stupid or at least unwelcome question about her domesticity.

The conversation between the two women now turns to the subject of makeup, and Harriet remarks that her dressmaker forbids her to wear makeup (TD 100). Rosamund evidently strikes out for the second time in this exchange, since she does wear makeup. Either Harriet is cheerfully aware of being more advantaged and more sophisticated than her would-be adversary or she is innocently stepping upon the sensitive toes of her guest without being aware of it. One hopes it is the latter!

In any event, when Rosamund rejoins her husband she is furious, although the specific object of her rage has not been mentioned in the above-quoted sequence. What she dislikes about Peter and Harriet is, she says angrily, "his manners to her." Asked why these have offended her, she declares "I thought they were condescending and horrible" (TD 102). When her husband understandably asks why, she explains that it is because Lord Peter has referred, in the hearing of his guests, to Harriet's role as an "artist." He has done this, Rosamund says, "just to remind us all that she used to have to work for her living" (TD 102). As we recognize this as a charming compliment from Peter to the wife whose professional life he wholeheartedly admires, we do not know why it has aroused so much ire, though we are soon to learn the answer.

Meanwhile Peter and Harriet also talk together about their impromptu party. Peter explains that he wants her portrait painted in order to "show you to yourself" (TD 104). Harriet responds:

> "Does everything mean so much to you?"
> "No, not everything. Only everything to do with you."
> "You'll have to grow out of that, Peter."
> "Too late. I've stopped growing." (TD 104)

Each partner meticulously attends to the needs and feelings of the other. They meet as equals, individual people each of whom has the capacity to make the other happy. Despite Delagardie's concern, they are well-matched.

It is not so with the Harwells, whose relationship is decidedly one-sided. Laurence Harwell, a wealthy man who sponsors theatrical productions, meditates upon "the congruence of night and day on which all matrimonial law is founded." This thought is based upon the fact (mentioned earlier) that his wife never yields herself to him without reluctance. Rosamond has come to him as a kind of Cinderella, rescued after her father's imprisonment and given money and status along with marriage. It now emerges that she has worked as a mannequin at Fanfreluche's dressmaking establishment before her marriage. Harriet's remarks about dressmakers have indeed touched a sensitive spot; Sayers writes:

> Any Fanfreluche creation would always have a touch of the witch-broom and the pumpkin about it for Rosamund, who asked nothing better than to put the whole humiliating episode out of her life. (TD 111)

For "humiliating," Sayers first wrote "degrading" and then crossed it out. To be ashamed of one's work was, for this author, to take a view of it at the furthest possible distance from her own.

The mention of "the witch-broom and the pumpkin" with its hint of Hallowe'en is not accidental; in a separate episode, as Chapparelle prepares to portray Harriet, he tells her that he plans to paint Rosamond with a mask in her hands. She is like a girl shut up in a "black tower by a witch," the painter tells Harriet: a tower with an ivory gate. Rosamund is afraid, perhaps unaware, of reality, he says. We read in Virgil's *Aeneid* that false dreams come through a "gate of ivory," while true dreams come through a "gate of horn."[36] Sayers used masks as images of falsity and illusion in *Murder Must Advertise*. This concatenation of motifs—witch-broom, pumpkin, mask, black tower, witch, ivory gate—cannot be accidental. It points the way to the most telling motif in the manuscript, that of the Siren.

In drawing the figure of the Siren, of whom Rosamond is an embodiment, Sayers piles up layer upon layer of symbolism: it would be useful to explore the meaning of the motif before examining its use in *Thrones, Dominations*. Sayers has taken this figure from Homer's epic poem, *The Odyssey*, which describes the fabulous adventures of the hero Odysseus on his return home from the Trojan Wars. When translated from its metaphor-laden Greek, the *Odyssey* is as laconic as the Bible, and sets forth its wonders and horrors in a businesslike manner, but the words of its characters remain more colorful, and the role of the sirens is given its fullest expression in a speech of Circe (the archetypal Witch in Greek literature), who warns Odysseus of their danger:

> "First you will come to the Sirens, who bewitch everyone who comes near them. If any man draws near in his innocence and listens to their voice, he never sees home again, never again will wife and little children run to greet him with joy; but the Sirens bewitch him with their melodious song."[37]

A twentieth-century writer expatiates upon this theme as it is understood today: the sirens were "more seductive than any mortal woman, more murderous than any witch, thirstier of human blood than any poor shade."[38] As Circe bids him, Odysseus plugs the ears of his sailors with beeswax and has himself bound to the mast, albeit with his ears unstopped. His seamen see the bones of the sirens' victims and are immune to their song, but Odysseus, who hears their irresistible singing, disregards everything and would have perished had he not been held fast.

The Siren appears again in *The Divine Comedy of Dante Alighieri*, which Sayers spent the last part of her life translating and interpreting. This appearance is the passage she calls the "Dream of the Siren,"[39] which comes "at the dawn-hour,"[40] as Dante and Virgil pass through the Cornice of Sloth in the 19th Canto of the *Purgatorio*:

> Lo, the sweet Siren; yea, 'tis I, 'tis I
> Who lead the mariners in mid-sea astray,
> Such pleasures in my melting measures lie.[41]

Sayers points out in her essay that this self-announcement of the Siren—"*Io son*," cantava, "*io son dolce sirena*," forms an exact parallel, or more accurately a precise inversion of the famous greeting of Beatrice to Dante which is the culminating event of the *Purgatorio*: "*Guardaci ben; ben sem, ben sem Beatrice*." "Look well; I am, I am Beatrice." Sayers states that "The Siren is the false Beatrice"[42] and compares this figure to the false Adela who appears to Lawrence Wentworth in Charles Williams's novel *Descent into Hell*. She says of the Siren; "She is made by the Ego gazing upon itself, and it responds, seeming to woo [...] until the will that summoned it up is wholly subject to the thing it has summoned."[43]

Such a hellish relationship is portrayed in *Thrones, Dominations*, with wife and husband alike locked into a false and inverted
174

partnership. In a telling scene, Rosamund is depicted wearing her long hair in "two thick plaits" as she sits in her green and blue boudoir, the decor of which suggests "chilly depths" and "the embraces of the Siren, whose voice, mocking and caressing, was like a carillon of doomed bells" (TD 112). These bells are an echo of those on the towers of drowned buildings ringing from beneath the sea.

From Rosamund's point of view, it is "her husband's sheer, unmistakeable maleness that she at once adored and resented; he dominated her senses and at the same time infuriated her by his large masculine arrogance" (TD 115-116). At this moment, he is preoccupied; there is a crisis in the theatrical business because the death of the King will require the closing of theatres. When Laurence Harwell prepares to leave his wife alone while he addresses these difficulties, she remarks that she will call Claude Amery for companionship. Her husband offhandedly agrees, with a remark about the young man's evident desire to have his play produced. At this,

> The siren smiled a small, secret, and provocative smile. Unfortunately, it was wasted on Ulysses. (TD 117)

In the same scene, it emerges that Rosamund has refused to have children; this disclosure, placed at the end of its sequence, is given prominence as the culmination of Rosamund Harwell's disordered selfhood.

The contrast between Rosamund and Harriet is reiterated in a scene in which the latter walks down Oxford Street to visit her dressmaker, Alcibiade, with whom she is on the very best of terms. He is described as "a completely normal Englishman with an artistic eye ... and a wife and three children" (TD 120) whose real name is Hicks. The phrase "perfectly normal Englishman" means that contrary to stereotypes associated with his profession, he is not a homosexual, and contrary to his professional name, he is not Greek. Sayers was to make a reference to homosexuals in theatrical life in her play *Love All*, and used the motif there only to create a humorous effect.[44] In the use of stereotypes of race, religion, and sexual orientation, she was, like most popular writers of her period, perfectly unabashed. [45] Alcibiade has been recommended by Peter's mother, and has made the frocks forming Harriet's "wedding-outfit"; that is to say, the dresses which formed a new wardrobe to be worn after marriage.

This time, Harriet needs to obtain an appropriate mourning costume to wear, because the King has died. Her dressmaker prescribes a black dress with an "Elizabethan collar" and after a moment's worry about ironing this elaborately gauffred frill of white linen, she remembers her new status and only asks if her maid will be able to do it. Alcibiade replies that he will prepare "a dozen interchangeable collars" and keep them clean for her, a plan which will be not only convenient for Harriet but a great relief to the maid: Harriet muses that "One was in danger of forgetting the bad old times altogether, and if one did, what sort of books would one write?" (TD 122).

Peter for his part is seated on Parker's desk at Scotland Yard meditating upon the King's death. He announces that he may "renounce the merry murder-chase and abandon myself to the care of landed property and the supervision of a household" (TD 124). I take this juxtaposition of scenes, with Harriet wondering what sort of stories she will write, and Peter contemplating the end of his detective career, to mean that just as Harriet will continue to write, so Lord Peter will continue to detect. The finding of corpses in unexpected circumstances is an expected part of the detective novel: protestations to the contrary by the detective must signal to the habituated reader the inevitability of murder.

Outcomes

While the Wimseys press on toward their happy future, the Harwells press on toward their disastrous one. All the main characters begin to foregather in London for the King's funeral: Delagardie, who is in the French Riviera, receives Daumier, who offers sympathy on the monarch's death. After an attempt to ignore his own feelings, Delagardie decides to go to London. Old Mr. Warren is in town for the event too, staying at his daughter Rosamund's house. Laurence has postponed his new play because of the funeral, and Claude Amery is in eager attendance. The stage is, as it were, set for a fatal crisis among these various players.

Harriet, meanwhile, writes a letter suggesting that Claude Amery's play be produced at the Swan Theatre. Rosamund is exasperated: she herself had suggested the Swan but Laurence rejected it because another play he had refused to back had done very well there, and he was still angry about it. Rosamund does not know this, and now that Harriet has recommended it, she presses the matter with her husband. "To be asked and to give, even to the half of one's kingdom, should be accounted one of the seven joys of marriage" (TD 133), he thinks, reiterating the association of kingdom and marriage even in his disordered relationship, and with an inward sigh agrees to read the play again and perhaps even to produce it himself. He is not doing this for Claude, he tells Rosamund, but for her, because he loves her and in order that she shall not need the favors of the Wimseys.

As a result of this capitulation, the Harwells are about to make love, when an interruption breaks Rosamund's mood and she demurs. Restlessly, she tries and fails to reach Amery by phone to tell him the good news. In a repulsive but powerful scene, she lolls in the sight of her frustrated husband, playing with her little dog, calling herself its "Muzzer" in the stereotyped manner of a childless woman, and allowing the excited animal to kiss her on the mouth, to her husband's voiced objection (TD 138). In consequence, they quarrel over whether he is jealous of the dog, then over whether he is jealous of Claude Amery, and finally whether he is jealous of Gaston Chapparelle. The matter, bred of sexual arousal and denial, escalates into a full-scale quarrel in which Rosamund's refusal to have a child becomes a major element. He would be jealous of a child too, she retorts, or else it would grow up to be weak like her father. In the end her husband, touched, perhaps, by her weakness and childishness, relents, and the storm rumbles toward a quiet aftermath.

Later Rosamund writes to Harriet, to say that her husband has agreed to sponsor Amery's play, and to thank her for her help. "What it is to be able to twist one's husband round one's little finger!" (TD 143) thinks Harriet, as she reads the letter. Would Peter do a play for her just to please her? She asks him. No, he replies offhandedly, "Nothing would induce me to back a play. Whose play?" (TD 144). And they talk of other things. This delicious scene, intended as a healthy reversal of the sick scenario just portrayed, is genuinely funny, and it shows again, if we needed reminding, that Peter is a person in his own right and that his wife prefers him so.

The most elaborate version of Helen's dinner party is found at the end of the manuscript as it has been preserved. Its degree of elaboration suggests to me that Sayers may have intended it to supplant her other efforts. The rather urbane tone taken toward marriage and the sexual relationship in the version I quoted above is here replaced by a more subtle and complex exploration of the theme.

The sequence opens with the Duchess of Denver planning her entertainment, which is to be in honor of the newlyweds. The Duke for his part is concerned with his son's apparent indifference to the estate. He writes to Lord Saint-George, commanding him to come to dinner with his uncle and aunt. He and his wife discuss the seating arrangements, and it emerges that Gaston Chapparelle will be invited to attend because he will be engaged to paint Lord Saint-George.

As the party begins, everyone awaits the arrival of the Wimseys. When they appear, Harriet's dress is lavishly complimented in French by Chapparelle: "Robe exquise, goût parfait" (TD 157). (Exquisite gown, perfect taste.) Sayers's emphasis in this manuscript upon Harriet's wonderful post-marital wardrobe may suggest that the dressmakers are to play some role in the story, or perhaps is intended to underline the contrast between the happiness that Harriet receives and indeed gives through the possession and public display of this wardrobe and the unhappiness experienced by Rosamond in recalling her career as a dressmaker's mannequin adorned in wonderful clothing which was not her own.

Gerald is Harriet's partner at dinner. In the version which contained Lord Peter's facetious remark about the expense of keeping a mistress, the Duke was portrayed as matching the rather flip mood in a meditation upon Harriet:

> It occurred to him that if his fastidious brother took this person to bed with him it must be because he found pleasure in the experience; and he now perceived that she might be positively desirable. (TD 53)

In the version we are now discussing, however, we learn of Gerald that "He was exceedingly conscious that Oxford-trained female novelists were not in his line of country" (TD 157), a thought which is more in keeping with Sayers's portrayal of the Wimsey marriage and its meaning. Gerald asks his dinner partner about her marriage in this version of the sequence, and she says, frankly, "It's going to be all right, Gerald. Really and truly" (TD 159).

As conversation at the table continues, "Lord Saint-George sat in an uneasy silence, wondering whether he would be able to get a word in with his uncle before his father got hold of him" (TD 164). His anxiety lends suspense to the scene and whets our appetite to know what his trouble is. In this version of the dinner, at least three motifs are skillfully woven together: Lord Saint-George's money problems, the question of the Wimseys' relationship, and the role of Gaston Chapparelle. The artist is asked if he will paint the portrait of a female guest, and he refuses. Then, turning to Lord Peter, he says, "I should like to paint your wife" (TD 165). He explains:

> "She is not beautiful … But she is paintable. That is not the same thing. She has character. She has bones." (TC 165-66)

Saint-George, who is his father's son, makes an innuendo about the artist's intention, and Chapparelle retorts: "I do not care whom my sitter loves, provided she loves somebody" (TD 166). In fact, he continues, it is easier if her lover is her husband. Peter says he is "obliged" to hear it:

> "Your proposal is that my wife should provide the bones, you provide the paint, while I do my best (I hope I understand this part of it correctly) to provide the human interest." (TD 166)

This, surely, is a sweeter and more appropriate appraisal of their relationship than that he can imagine his wife to be his mistress. Finally, he adds that the artist must ask Harriet for her permission to allow herself to be painted, not merely consult him as her husband. The motif of their mutual freedom of choice is given here a very attractive application. As we know, Harriet accepts after Peter explains that he wants her to see herself, and the portrait is in fact painted.

It is the central theme of *Thrones, Dominations* as it stands that Peter and Harriet's married love is sacred. Their marriage is an "holy estate," valid and freely entered union which will fulfill its role as described in the Book of Common Prayer: "Matrimony was ordained for the hallowing of the union betwixt man and woman; for the procreation of children […]; and for the mutual society, help, and comfort, that one ought to have of the other." The marriage of the Harwells is profane: she has married in order to better herself and he has married in order to obtain (albeit with ever-renewed resistance) her sexual favors. Freedom, mutuality, and even true union are absent from their relationship. What ought to be a training ground for heaven is a rehearsal for hell.

Like all fragments, *Thrones, Dominations* must frustrate every attempt at a final interpretation. It is a torso, and the precise attitudes of its limbs, like those of the Venus de Milo, can only be guessed. Jung said somewhere that stage actors perform with their torsos. We can certainly say that Sayers has portrayed the heart of the story in her presentation of the two contrasted couples. Shadowed but not eclipsed by the unhappy Harwells, Peter and Harriet are shown as they were to continue, endlessly engaged in maintaining their perilous synthesis. It is a delicate, resonant, witty, and beautiful portrait, imbued with a fragrant sexuality that has lasted long enough to imbue with its redolent sweetness the Wimseys' golden anniversary.

Notes
[1] *Bulletin No. 62* (Sudbury, Suffolk: The Dorothy L. Sayers Historical and Literary Society, 1985) 2.
[2] Nancy M. Tischler, *Dorothy L. Sayers, A Pilgrim Soul* (Atlanta, GA: John Knox Press, 1980) 87.
[3] Alzina Stone Dale, "*Love All* and *Busman's Honeymoon*," Proceedings of the 1984 Seminar Held at Witham on Sunday 22 July (Witham: The Dorothy L. Sayers Historical and Literary Society, 1985) 19.
[4] Dale, "*Love All* and *Busman's Honeymoon*" 6.
[5] Alzina Stone Dale, "Fossils in Cloud-Cuckoo-Land," *The Sayers Review* 3.2 (December 1978): 9-10.
[6] Dorothy L. Sayers, *Thrones, Dominations*, unpublished manuscript in the Marion E. Wade Collection, Wheaton College, Wheaton, Illinois, 37A. Pages hereinafter cited will be included in the text. I would like to express my heartfelt thanks to Marjorie Lamp Mead and P. Allen Hargis for their very gracious assistance to me in the examination of this work.
[7] Editor's note: Most of the information given is also summarized in Geoffrey Lee, "Time and Dorothy L. Sayers," *The Chronology of Lord Peter Wimsey* (Witham: The Dorothy L. Sayers Historical and Literary Society, 1983) 29, 30.
[8] Lee, "Time and Dorothy L. Sayers" 13-14.

Notes

[9] It seems that the word "broke" should possibly be "spoke," but Laura Schmidt at the Marion E. Wade Center of Wheaton College, Illinois, confirmed the accuracy of the quotation in Patterson's manuscript relative to Sayers's original manuscript.

[10] Dawson Gaillard, *Dorothy L. Sayers* (New York: Frederick Ungar Publishing Co., 1981) 98.

[11] Nancy-Lou Patterson's "Changing, Fearfully Changing" (1985) is included in this volume.

[12] Athelstan Riley (1906) Dionysus the Areapogite in *The Mystical Theology and the Celestial Hierarchies.*

[13] Gustav Davidson, *A Dictionary of Angels* (New York: The Free Press, 1967) 289.

[14] Davidson 45.

[15] Davidson 183.

[16] Davidson 97.

[17] Davidson 97.

[18] John Milton, *Paradise Lost*, ed. Merrit Y. Hughes (Indianapolis: The Odyssey Press, 1962) Book II, lines 450-455.

[19] James Brabazon, *Dorothy L. Sayers: The Life of a Courageous Woman* (London: Victor Gollancz Ltd., 1981) 157.

[20] C.S. Lewis, *That Hideous Strength* (1945; Hammersmith, London: HarperCollinsPublishers, 2003) 247; ch. 7.

[21] Dale, "Fossils in Cloud-Cuckoo-Land" 5.

[22] Margaret P. Hannay, "Harriet's Influence on the Characterization of Lord Peter Wimsey," *As Her Whimsey Took Her*, ed. Margaret P. Hannay (Kent, OH: Kent State UP, 1979) 50.

[23] Brabazon 77.

[24] Brabazon 156.

[25] Brabazon 231.

[26] Brabazon 112.

[27] Brabazon 93.

[28] Brabazon 94.

[29] Brabazon 94.

[30] Brabazon 96.

[31] Brabazon 97.

[32] Brabazon 110.

Notes

[33] Brabazon 111.

[34] S.L. Clark, "Harriet Vane Goes to Oxford: *Gaudy Night* and the Academic Woman," *The Sayers Review* 2.3 (August 1978) 33.

[35] Clark 43, note 24.

[36] "Two gates has Slumber: the one [...] of horn, / And through it true visions may easily pass [...] / The other of gleaming ivory, wherethrough the spirits send earthward dreams that but lie." *Virgil's Aeneid,* trans. Michael Oakley (London: Everyman's Library, 1957) 139. The verses are among the last of Book VI.

[37] Homer, *The Odyssey,* trans. W.H.D. Rouse (New York: Mentor, 1937) 138; book xii.

[38] *Water Spirits* (Alexandria, Virginia: Time-Life Books, 1985) 49.

[39] Dorothy L. Sayers, "The Cornice of Sloth," *Further Papers on Dante: His Heirs and His Ancestors,* volume 2 (London: Methuen and Co., 1957) 135.

[40] Sayers, "The Cornice of Sloth" 136.

[41] Sayers, "The Cornice of Sloth" 137.

[42] Sayers, "The Cornice of Sloth" 139.

[43] Sayers, "The Cornice of Sloth" 143.

[44] The Lord Chamberlain did not approve of the joke and it was cut from the production. *Dorothy L. Sayers, Love All and Busman's Honeymoon,* ed. Alzina Stone Dale (Kent, OH: Kent State UP, 1984) xxviii.

[45] See Nancy-Lou Patterson's "Images of Judaism and Anti-Semitism in the Novels of Dorothy L. Sayers" (1978) included in this volume.

Nancy-Lou Patterson, Illustration for the Mythcon 24 Program.
Conference held at the University of Minnesota, 1993.
Further reproduction prohibited.

9. Even the Parrot Knows Better Than to Eat the Peel: Dorothy L. Sayers (1893–1957) Writes for Children

> To postpone the acceptance of responsibility to a late date brings with it a number of psychological complications which, while they may interest the psychiatrist, are scarcely beneficial either to the individual or to society.

——Dorothy L. Sayer, *The Lost Tools of Learning* (1948)

In this brief paper, Patterson reviews some of Dorothy L. Sayers's publications for and about children and education.

"Even the Parrot Knows Better Than to Eat the Peel" was first published as part of the Mythcon 24 program, a conference held at the University of Minnesota in 1993.

In a paper delivered at Oxford in 1947, Dorothy L. Sayers described herself as a child:

> My views about child-psychology are, I admit, neither orthodox nor enlightened. Looking back upon myself (since I am the child I know best and the only child I can pretend to know from inside) I recognize three states of development. These, in a rough-and-ready fashion, I will call the Poll-parrot, the Pert, and the Poetic—the latter coinciding, approximately, with the onset of puberty.[1]

She explains that "the Poll-parrot stage is the one in which learning by heart is easy." "The Pert Age [...] is characterized by contradicting, answering-back, and the propounding of conundrums." And "the Poetic Age" "yearns to express itself" and "should show the beginnings of creativeness." For these three stages, she recommends "Grammar to the Poll-parrot, Dialectic to the Pert, and Rhetoric to the Poetic age." Since rhetoric is back in fashion, we may consider the works Sayers herself wrote with children in mind.

In his literary biography, *Dorothy L. Sayers* (1979), Ralph E. Hone discusses her children's stories. Her book, *Even the Parrot: Exemplary Conversations for Enlightened Children* (1944) takes its title from her Nurse's saying, "Even the parrot ... knows better than to eat the peel." It includes five essays, "The Canary or Healthful Slumbers," "The Cat or Family Affections," "The Bee-Hive or the Perfect Society," "The Boa-Constrictor and the Rules of Diet," and "The Rabbit or Town-Planning." These chapters, ranging widely over scientific and technical subjects, seem especially aimed at the Pert Age, and the book was suffuciently successful to go into "additional printings."[2]

During her last five years, Sayers wrote a series of short children's works. Those published include *The Days of Christ's Coming* (1953), *The Story of Adam and Eve* (1955), and *The Story of Noah's Ark* (1956). Unpublished are "The Story of Easter" and "The Enchanted Garden" (an adaptation of Boiardo's *Orlando Innamorato*).[3] *The Days of Christ's Coming* is that rare achievement, a work perfect for children and adults alike; it begins:

> When God the eternal Son of God the Eternal Father willed to be born as a Man among men by the power of God the Spirit, there was great joy and wonder in Heaven. But on earth every one was busy with his or her own affairs—making money, making war, making merry, eating and drinking or looking after the household.[4]

In this jewel-like work, the sacred infuses and illuminates the secular, as it does the best and most frequently published of her writings for adults.

Notes
[1] Dorothy L. Sayers, Paper delivered at Oxford, 1947. Editor's note: This short paper was published in *The Lost Tools of Learning* (1948) and is now available as an inexpensive unpaginated ebook and online at < http://www.gbt.org/text/sayers.html>.
[2] Ralph E. Hone, *Dorothy L. Sayers, A Literary Biography* (Kent, OH: Kent State UP, 1979) 141, 173.
[3] Hone 177-78.
[4] Dorothy L. Sayers, *The Days of Christ's Coming* (New York: Harper, 1960, n.p.).

10.   "A Bloomsbury Blue-Stocking": Dorothy L. Sayers's Bloomsbury Years in Their Spatial and Temporal Context

It's no affair of mine how you behave in Bloomsbury [...]

——Dorothy L. Sayer, *Gaudy Night* (1935)

In "A Bloomsbury Blue-Stocking" Patterson traces the influence of Sayers's Bloomsbury years on her detective fiction. She describes the origins of the literary Bloomsbury group, which was long established by the time Sayers moved to Bloomsbury, and compares Sayers's early life with that of Virginia Woolf (née Stephen), while also pointing out how specific real life events and locations influenced Sayers's novels.

Patterson raises the subject of influences from the author's own life on her fiction in several other papers, including "'The Perilous Synthesis': Sacred and Profane Love in Dorothy L. Sayers's Thrones, Dominations." *She specifically addresses the relevance of sin, as discussed by Sayers herself in "The Other Six Deadly Sins" (1941), in Sayers's own life here and in "'Cat o' Mary': The Spirituality of Dorothy L. Sayers," and in more detail with reference to her novels in "'Eve's Sharp Apple': Five Transgressing Women in the Novels of Dorothy L. Sayers."*

"A Bloomsbury Blue-Stocking" was first published in Mythlore *19.3 (Summer 1993): 6-15.*

In the last to be published of Dorothy L. Sayers's detective novels, the Countess of Severn and Thames writes to Lord Peter's mother, the Dowager Duchess of Denver, that

> to see your amorous sweet devil of a son wedded to an Oxford-Bloomsbury blue-stocking should add considerably to the gaiety of the season. (BH 15; Prothalamion)

The soubriquet "blue-stocking," which she applies to Harriet Vane—defined as "a woman with intellectual or literary interests,"[1]—could equally be applied to Sayers herself; both she and her creation had attended Oxford and lived in Bloomsbury. These facts are by no means co-incidental or without significance in Sayers's life and work. It is my thesis that her Bloomsbury years formed a significant source for and influence upon her detective fiction. S.P. Rosenbaum (1987), a specialist in Bloomsbury studies, states that while modern literary study dislikes the use of "spatial and temporal context"[2] in the interpretation of literature, he uses this mode in his discussion of Bloomsbury, and so shall I.

Bloomsbury

The extreme cachet of Bloomsbury has been characterized variously by Sayers's biographers; Alzina Stone Dale (1978; 1992) calls it "the part of London [...] where young intellectuals lived and worked and talked about art and love and politics,"[3] while Nancy M. Tischler (1980) styles it "Vanity Fair," defining "Bloomsbury women" as "flamboyant, iconoclastic, and independent career women who rejected the Victorian rules of decorum and domesticity for a new freedom."[4] The reality behind these colorful impressions will be discussed below. That Sayers herself knew what a reference to Bloomsbury meant is made clear in *Gaudy Night* when Harriet Vane returns from the results of a disastrous sojourn in Bloomsbury to the apparent sanctuary of Oxford. She is confronted by Shrewsbury College's Miss Hillyard, who demands to know what her relations are with Lord Peter, a man she calls "notorious all over Europe" (GN 427; ch. 20), and declares: "It's no affair of mine how you behave in Bloomsbury. But if you bring your lovers here—" (GN 427; ch. 20). She is clearly implying Bloomsbury's reputation for sexual liberty. What that liberty actually meant for Dorothy and for her alter ego Harriet, as well as for the women whose lives in part gave that reputation to Bloomsbury, is attributed with terrible accuracy by Louise de Salvo (1992) to "Bloomsbury's virulent if unconscious misogyny, masquerading beneath the veneer of a sexually liberated, enlightened humanism."[5]

What, then, is Bloomsbury? As a geographical location, Bloomsbury remains, even today, a "partly residential" district located between the West End and "the City." The site of both the British Museum and the University of London, it is distinguished by a series of beautiful, tree-surrounded squares, the earliest of which—

Bloomsbury Square—was created in 1660, lined with seventeenth-and eighteenth-century houses,[6] many of them already broken up into flats in Sayers's day. Into this physical setting, the Bloomsbury of "modern English fiction, biography, economics, aesthetics, painting and decoration," and "models of modern living" ("for good or ill"),[7] came into being in 1904, when, following the death of the eminent Victorian biographer Leslie Stephen, his four children moved to 46 Gordon Square, Bloomsbury.[8] Vanessa Bell, elder of his two daughters, destined to become an artist, explained this move in a memoir written in 1951:

> We knew no one living in Bloomsbury then and that I think was one of its attractions [...] It seemed as if in every way we were making a new beginning in the tall clean rather frigid rooms, heated only by coal fires in the old-fashioned fireplaces.[9]

Her younger sister, Virginia Stephen (whom the world knows by her married name Virginia Woolf), wrote of the house as it looked in 1908:

> The drawing room had greatly changed its character since 1904 [...] The age of Augustus John was dawning. His Pyramus filled one entire wall. The Watts portraits of my father and my mother were hung downstairs [...] Clive had hidden all the match boxes because their blue and yellow swore with the prevailing colour scheme.[10]

In this setting, the four young people held an impromptu salon every Thursday evening; one of its number, Clive Bell, who married Vanessa in 1907, recorded that the "set of friends" thus formed was first given a name "by Lady MacCarthy [...] in a letter: she calls them 'the Bloomsberries.'"[11]

The Bloomsbury Group that developed from this beginning consisted in part of Virginia and Leonard Woolf, Vanessa and Clive Bell, Lytton Strachey, E.M. Forster, John Maynard Keynes, Roger Fry, Duncan Grant, and Desmond MacCarthy. Rosenbaum (1987) describes them as "a collectivity of friends and relations who knew and loved one another for a period of time extending over two generations."[12]

Nigel Nicholson, a son of Virginia Woolf's most famous lover, Vita Sackville-West, characterized these relationships succinctly: "They were all in love, man with girl, man with man, girl with man, girl with girl."[13] The fact that even on the occasion of the centenary of Virginia Woolf's birth (she was born in 1882), he could characterize these distinguished women as "girls"—while calling their partners, also young at the time—"men," carries a lingering whiff of "unconscious misogyny." Many of the "men" (unlike Virginia Woolf) had attended university, and unlike Dorothy L. Sayers, the "Oxford-Bloomsbury blue-stocking," they had experienced a "shared education at Cambridge."[14] The difference, in Sayers's case, is significant.

Leonard Woolf attributed "the colour of our minds and thought" to "the climate of Cambridge and Moore's philosophy";[15] Virginia Woolf had not escaped this influence. Her father, Leslie Stephen, had emerged from the cultural milieu that characterized Cambridge in the early nineteenth century, including the "Clapham Sect," a major center of Anglican Evangelicalism, whose major moral focus was the abolition of slavery. The revolt of its Bloomsbury descendants was not against this moral mandate, but against evangelical restraints upon "the senses […], the intellect […], amusement, enjoyment, art; on curiosity, on criticism, on science."[16]

Although the Bloomsbury Group, unlike their forebears, "sought a secular salvation,"[17] Sayers did not. The point is not that the Bloomsbury Group lacked a recognizable religious source and element. They were, in terms of their "intuitive awareness of a unanalysable good,"[18] Platonists, or rather Neo-Platonist. Even Bloomsbury's aestheticism was Romantic, formalist, and Platonic, in its emphasis upon "significant form."[19] Virginia Woolf wrote (inaccurately, I suspect) that "human character changed" in December, 1910, when Roger Fry's first exhibition of postimpressionist art opened.[20] This remarkable statement can be better understood by noting that the second postimpressionist show, organized by Fry in 1912, included "Van Gogh, Gauguin, Vlaminck, Derain, Rouault, Picasso, and Cezanne."[21]

The Bloomsbury Group survived a move to Fitzroy Square, which occurred after Thoby Stephen died (1906) and Vanessa Stephen married Clive Bell (1907). Virginia and her surviving brother Adrian moved to this address, also in Bloomsbury, and the Thursday evening gatherings continued.[22] The year that Sayers first went to live in Bloomsbury, 1920, a "Memoir Club" was founded by members of the Bloomsbury Group to "commemorate Old Bloomsbury."[23] This Club met on "a continuing basis for the New Bloomsbury"[24] until 1956. Sayers's Bloomsbury years thus took place in an environment already firmly identified with Bloomsbury arts and letters, displayed and published there and forming a vital part of the environment in which Lord Peter had his birth.

Dorothy L. Sayers and Virginia Stephen/Woolf

Sayers, born in 1893, was eleven years younger than Virginia Woolf, her most obvious Bloomsbury parallel, and not, like Virginia Stephen, in 22 Hyde Park Gate, London, but in the "old" Choir House in Brewer Street near the entrance to Christ Church College in Oxford. Her father, the Reverend Henry Sayers, a far less eminent man than Leslie Stephen, nevertheless enjoyed some significance in Oxford. He was Chaplain of the College and Headmaster of the Choir School of Christ Church Cathedral,[25] actually the College chapel, where Dorothy was baptized on July 26, 1893,[26] in an exquisite setting known for its fine Pre-Raphaelite stained glass. One result of her birth was that the family moved to a "new" Choir House on Brewster Street, itself a thoroughfare so old it still possessed its cobbles.[27] Here she spent four years, followed by a more radical move in 1898 to Bluntisham-Earith in Huntingdonshire (a "living" which was "in the gift" of Christ Church).[28] It was a country rectory where her father enjoyed having time for his books, and his wife experienced the life of a rural rector's spouse. Also unlike Virginia Stephen, who grew up in a complexly mixed household of the children of current and previous spouses, including the half-brother who inflicted his sexual desires upon her, Dorothy was and remained an only child. Considering her conviction as an adult that birth control was forbidden to Anglicans, one can only speculate how this singularity came about. Her household was not empty of companionship, however, because a collection of aunts took an active part in her early life, and she acquired a very close friend in her cousin Ivy Shrimpton, whose friendship was to play a pivotal role in her Bloomsbury years.

From all accounts including her own unpublished autobiographical fragments, she flourished in this setting, the center of attention for the next nine years, until she was sent (again unlike the young

Virginia Stephen, who was entirely educated at home) to the Godolphin School, Salisbury, in January 1908. Here her "Edwardian Childhood," as she called it, effectively ended, and her adolescence began. By the Christmas of 1911 her public school experience had culminated in a "nervous breakdown"[29]—a parallel, probably, though no one has sufficiently penetrated to its source, with breakdowns suffered by Virginia Stephen—and did not return to the school after Christmas. There, safe from whatever psychological or physical distress had troubled her, she prepared for University, and won the Gilchrist Scholarship to Somerville College at Oxford, where she began her studies in 1912. Virginia Stephen, as has been said, did not attend University.

Mitzi Brunsdale (1990) says that Dorothy

> came out of Godolphin so angry at its Low Church practice, [and] its emotionalism and its furtive references to "Gawd" that she might have abandoned Christianity wholesale, as do many young people. Fortunately for her faith, Oxford at this time was in the grip of a modish Anglo-Catholicism.[30]

Indeed, Sayers found that her undergraduate years at Oxford gave her, by all accounts, true delight. She took a first class degree in 1915. Deciding to become a teacher, she taught at the Hull School for Girls in 1916. While living at Hull, she saw a selection of her poems published in *Op. I* (1916) by Blackwell in Oxford. These poems, strongly medievalizing and Anglo-Catholic in content and aesthetic, show vividly the difference between her Oxford mentality and that of the Cambridge-bred Bloomsberries. Interestingly, this first of her books foreshadows elements of her future writings: in "Lay" she writes, "I shall sing of thee in antique rime, / ... And intricate as bells rung down in time,"[31] introducing the theme of the bell-ringing central to *The Nine Tailors* (1934). And in "The Gates of Paradise" she describes how "Judas' soul went through the night," introducing a figure she was to explore deeply in *The Man Born to Be King* (broadcast 1941-42).

She followed this triumph in the same year by securing a job at Blackwell's (with her father's help), returning to live in Oxford in 1917. This time her parents had moved yet again, to a small and even more remote parish, Christ Church, in the Cambridgeshire Fens.

Along with her publishing job, Dorothy began to translate the *Tristan* of Thomas, a twelfth-century French poet.[32] This indicates that she intended to be a scholar as well as a poet (an ambition realized later in her life as a major translator and interpreter of Dante). She put together the manuscript of a second book of poetry, *Catholic Tales and Christian Songs* (published in 1918). These poems contain precursors as well: "I make the wonderful carven beams / [...] And the gilded, wide-winged cherubims,"[33] another motif to appear later in *The Nine Tailors*; and her first tiny play, "The Mocking of Christ," whose characters include "Persona Dei," Emperor, Pope, Chorus, King, Preacher, Bishop, Cathedral Organist, First Curate, Second Curate, Respectable Gentleman, Patriot, Patriot of Another Nationality, Sentimental Person, A Mummer, Dionysus, Osiris, Elijah, Joshua, Gautama, Mithra, Priest of the Grove of Nerni, Green Person, Bacchae, Balder, Prometheus, Adonis, Plato, Socrates, and a Captain, in the space of eleven pages. Knowing what her lifetime career would bring, one sees here that she was to go on, ultimately, as she had begun.

Sayers left this still somewhat sheltered setting and went, with the man who won her totally unrequited love, Eric Whelpton, to France in 1919, to teach there for a year at L'Ecole des Roches in Verneuil-sur-Avre, near Paris. Illness again intervened, in the form of mumps, and she returned to England in September, 1920, where she was able at least to take formally her long deferred degree at Oxford, a BA and MA, on October 14, 1920.[34] At this point she began her Bloomsbury years, still a virgin and twenty-seven years old. After a brief sojourn in St. George's Square, she moved into a tiny flat in No. 44 Mecklenburgh Square. This brief first stay and subsequent move are echoed in *Strong Poison*, where Harriet Vane stays at first with Sybil Marriott and Eiluned Price, until she "left Miss Marriott's house and took a small flat of her own in Doughty street (SP 12; ch. 1). On this model, Sayers's short stay in St. George's Square may have been spent in a place of the utmost austerity: "The door opened upon a small bed-sitting room, furnished with the severest simplicity" (SP 105; ch. 8), so limited in space and facilities that the occupants resort to "a tap in the landing" in order to fill a kettle (SP 106; ch. 8), and share a telephone which is also "somewhere outside" (SP 109; ch. 8).

Settled in No. 44 Mecklenburgh Square, and firmly ensconced in Bloomsbury sixteen years after the surviving Stephens settled there and began their weekly meetings in Gordon Square, Dorothy found herself forced to prepare her own meals for the first time in her life, buying her first frying pan and doing without curtains.[35] She was being supported by her parents, both similarly and differently to Virginia Stephen, who with her siblings lived upon an inheritance. Interestingly, the Rev. Mr. Sayers chose November 20, 1920 (when his daughter was first living in Bloomsbury) to change his will in order to leave his estate exclusively to his wife.[36] This is unlikely to have been totally coincidental. It may be that her choice of Bloomsbury seemed to him an augury against her future stability. He was mistaken, in that case, but neither he nor Dorothy could have known that for sure in 1920, although in that year she was working on the manuscript for *Whose Body?*, the first of what were to become her twelve immensely successful detective novels.

In accordance with the conventional (and accurate) wisdom that the writer should write what she knows, the fledgling novelist placed several of the characters in this first novel in Bloomsbury: Mr. Parker [the policeman who later becomes Lord Peter's brother-in-law] "was a bachelor, and occupied a Georgian but inconvenient flat at No. 12A Great Ormond Street, for which he paid a pound a week" (WB 102; ch. 5). This flat contains a sitting-room, "where Mrs. Munns, who did for him by the day, was laying the table" referring to a servant, a luxury Dorothy was not able at that time to enjoy for herself. Parker awakens "to the smell of burnt porridge," perhaps inspired by Dorothy's fledgling efforts as a cook, while "a raw fog was rolling slowly in" through the "hygienically open" window of his bedroom (WB 102; ch. 5). Later in the novel, Sir Julian Freke asks to share a cab with Parker, who is on the point of "returning to Bloomsbury" (WB 232; ch. 10), and Parker generously gives up his cab to Freke, who orders the driver to take him to "24 Russell Square [...] and look sharp" (WB 233; ch. 10).

By the end of 1921 Sayers had moved. "In November her land lady gave her notice to be out of her room by December 5."[37] Happily, her friend Murial Jaeger had located a new flat for her, in Great James Street, not far away.[38] Dorothy wrote to her parents on November 24, 1921, that her new flat was "quite small but very pretty."[39] This is the flat that she continued to own, by most accounts, until the end of her life, though it had long since ceased by that time to form the center of her existence:

Beginning with her settlement in Great James Street, Sayers engaged in intense relationships with three men. The first, John Cournos, whom she had perhaps already met in Oxford, became "part of her quasi-bohemian lifestyle in London."[40] By May of 1922, she had found long-term and solid employment, going to work as a copy-writer at S.H. Benson's advertising agency, where she remained until 1930. By October of 1922, Cournos had abruptly left England (and Dorothy) without a word. A Russian Jewish author some twelve years her senior, he had been raised as a stepson in a Hasidic family,[41] whose community, even more enclosed than an Anglican country rec-tory, he had obviously abandoned before he met Sayers. During the period of their relationship (1921-1922) they never lived together, though she did leave him "to keep the flat warm in my absence,"[42] as she somewhat suggestively put it in a letter to her parents, February 14, 1922. Her biographers conclude that Sayers ended her relationship with Cournos while still a virgin. She wanted to marry him and bear his children; from her church rectory-based view, the physical expres-sion of her love for him could only take place inside a marriage, and (or at the very least) without the use of contraceptive devices. He, on the contrary, was willing to become her lover but determined to pre-vent the birth of children from such a relationship. Dorothy portrayed her dilemma fictionally in *Strong Poison* (1930): the judge in Harriet Vane's trial for the murder of her lover says

> that she was angry with [him …] because, after persuading her against her will to adapt her principles of conduct, he then re-nounced those principles and so, as she says, "made a fool of her." (SP 11; ch. 1)

In reality, Cournos had married Sybil Norton in 1924, and Sayers wrote to him in bitter terms:

> I dare say I wanted too much—I could not be content with less than your love and your children and our happy acknowl-edgement of each other to the world. You now say you would have given me all those, but at the time you went out of your way to insist you would give me none of them.[43]

Clearly, she saw the demeaning and humiliating side of this relationship, in which the male partner agrees to share sexual experiences with the female partner, but insists upon denying her both marriage and childbirth, thus deciding for her how, in what circumstances, and to what issue her sexuality is to be expressed. He remains dominant, choosing to give and to withhold. She must submit, and in a way doubly, perhaps triply submissive, for her sexual activity, her social status, and her capacity for procreation are all placed in his control alone. The bitterness of her letters to Cournos is a bitterness compounded, for by this time her immediate response to his departure in 1922 had led to an even more disastrous result. By April of 1923 she had become pregnant, reportedly because of an affair with a racing motorcyclist, which, entered on the rebound, had presumably been consummated without the protection of any form of birth control. In this circumstance her pregnancy can hardly be described as an "accident,"[44] unless she had—as may well be—trusted her partner to be more experienced in such matters than she. Clearly she had so far let down the bars of her conventions as to undergo her sexual initiation, but it seems quite likely that she had kept her second provision—that the prevention of children was wrong—in place, probably in the naive expectation that if she became pregnant, her man of the people would marry her. He did not; firmly in control of the situation, he had met her sexual needs but refused, when their son Anthony appeared, to become his legal father, thus exercising his power not only over the inexperienced Dorothy but over the infant issue of his sexual pleasure as well.

By the time the new mother did become married in 1926, to Oswald Atherton Fleming, she may have abandoned her refusal of birth control too. Certainly she never bore Fleming any children, or perhaps this divorced man, already a father, was sufficiently sophisticated to prevent any further children by means he controlled himself. He never accepted Anthony into their home, although when Dorothy's son became old enough to go away to school, Fleming gave the boy his surname, without formal adoption. "Mac" Fleming, like Cournos and "Bill," used or withheld his capacity to procreate or acknowledge children as he chose, though he did grant Sayers the marriage and, in its context, the licit sexual expression she had sought (at least in accordance with secular law).

Their marriage coincided with the publication of *Clouds of Witness*, which had been three years in the making, and which contains an unflattering portrait of the Marxist motorcyclist Goyles whose shabby desertion of Lady Mary (Lord Peter's sister) leads her mother, the Dowager Duchess, to exclaim:

> Mary […] was so crazy to get to London—I shall always say it was the fault of that ridiculous club—what could you expect of a place where you ate such horrible food, all packed into an underground cellar painted pink and talking away at the tops of their voices, and never any evening dress—only Soviet jumpers and side-whiskers? (CW 142; ch. 6)

This fictional depiction of a relationship across the lines of class had expressed itself in the reality of Sayers's life by visits to West End dance halls. But she had indeed, like Lady Mary, developed a temporary sympathy with people who got their hands dirty for a living. She wrote of

> Howard roasting his posterior before the fire and looking all sleek and oily, saying in a haw-haw voice that it really was horrid out of doors—this to Bill, who had been testing motorcycles all day in fog and rain and inches deep in liquid mud.[45]

And she had, indeed, been "crazy to get to London."

When the child of her liaison was born, she resorted to her cousin Ivy Shrimpton, who cared for children for a living in her little cottage, and took Anthony to Ivy to be reared, as she and Ivy had been, in a remote and rural setting, having borne him in secret. He remained unknown, according to most of her biographers, even to her own parents, who would certainly have disapproved, though they might not have been surprised.

Unlike Dorothy L. Sayers, Virginia Stephen married her own "penniless Jew,"[46] Leonard Woolf, on August 10, 1912; she was some thirty years old at the time, about the same age as Sayers when Cournos left her in 1922. Virginia Woolf's marriage lasted until her suicide in 1941; Dorothy L. Sayers's marriage to Oswald Atherton Fleming lasted until he died in 1950. In the particular of a long-term marriage terminated only by death, both these marriages followed the Victorian ideal. On the other hand, both marriages were childless. Rosenbaum says that the hand of Victoria lay heavily upon the

Bloomsbury Group: they "were preoccupied with Victorianism throughout their careers."[47] In this preoccupation they contrasted "reality" (their own life vision, presumably) with "the unreality of Victorian life."[48] This "unreality" refers to the role of denial in the lives of Victorian families, where what "really" happened—including psychological, physical, and sexual abuse, in the case of the Leslie Stephen household—was smothered by efforts at maintaining "appearances," a pattern identified in the late twentieth century as a major characteristic of dysfunctional families.

Virginia Woolf had lost her mother at the age of thirteen and her father at twenty-two. The result was that her mother became "unreal" to her.[49] "Unreality shadows life throughout Bloomsbury's Victorian preoccupation, but no more so than in the death-ridden Stephens family,"[50] Rosenbaum says. This unreal mother obsessed Virginia at least until she wrote *To the Lighthouse*, which contains a portrait of her.[51] As for Virginia's father, she felt towards him a profound ambivalence.[52] This father-dominated household was the same place where the two sisters' half-brother George had made them victims of his developing sexuality, and which they were so glad to exchange for their new, self-chosen house in Bloomsbury.

Was Dorothy's life in complete contrast to all this? If her fiction reflects her true life, just possibly. She always depicted clergy in a warm light, along with their spouses: the picture of the Rev. and Mrs. Venables in *The Nine Tailors* is often cited as an example. And certainly her parents supported her financially in her efforts at independence. But she, the daughter of Victorian parents, vigorously maintained a Victorian silence to bridge the gap between "reality"— her illegitimate child—and appearances, whether or not she ever told her parents (or they ever suspected) what had happened. Certainly her son was kept aside and only very late and slightly acknowledged, well after her parents had died. For his part, Anthony maintained his personal silence to the end of life as well. After Janet Hitchman revealed the secret of his existence and relationship to Sayers in her biography *Such a Strange Lady* (1975), he gave permission to James Brabazon to produce her "authorized" biography, upon which most subsequent biographers have depended. It describes touchingly how he made himself known to his mother's closest friends after she died. Interestingly, Sayers never erected a tombstone to either parent, though she provided her mother with a house in Witham during her brief widow-hood after the Rev. Mr. Sayers died in 1928. Perhaps Dorothy's silence about these deaths was a continuation of the silence she maintained about her child. Or perhaps it was, in some way, an unspoken retribution—say, rather, an unspoken equivalent—for the silence she had felt obliged, by what she understood to be their view, to maintain about her child.

Some hint of Sayers's attitude toward her parents can be seen in the way she dealt with them in regard to her marriage to a divorced man (another major affront, certainly, to their values). Without any forewarning, she wrote to them on April 8, 1926:

> I am getting married on Tuesday (weather permitting!) to a man named Fleming, who is at the moment motoring corre-spondent to the *News of the World*. [...] I didn't mention this before, because it's our own business and I don't want an ava-lanche of interrogation from all sorts of people.[53]

Presumably these interrogators would have included her parents. Writing again to her now forewarned mother, April 14, 1926, in a jaunty, facetious, and perhaps defensive (not to say ironic) tone, she reported that "we were 'turned off' as the hangman says, in the salu-brious purlieux of the registrar's office in the Clerkenwell Road,"[54] a far cry from the cathedral wedding she well knew her parents hoped to see.

Sayers and her husband, whose name she never used publicly, settled down in her flat in 24 Great James Street. It was "cramped for space, so Sayers accepted that they would have to move before John Anthony could join them," according to David Coomes (1992).[55] In this small space they began "to get on each other's nerves,"[56] and when in August of 1928 a second flat on the floor above became available, the two facilities were joined. Sayers began to press for An-thony's inclusion, as she wrote to Ivy, but it was not to be. By Sep-tember of the same year the death of her father presaged a still greater spatial expansion in the marriage. "Mac" Fleming himself located a house for his mother-in-law, "Sunnyside, Newland Street, Witham, Essex," which he told her was "a pleasant, old fashioned town on the main road between Chelmsford and Colchester."[57] In August of 1929, his wife became sufficiently stablized in her writing career and its income to leave Benson's and the Witham house, by that time vacated through the death of Dorothy's mother, became "their principal dwelling place, with the flat in town kept simply as a pied-à-terre."[58] Perhaps this address aided Mac in his campaign to keep his marriage childless; there is so likely to be gossip in a village, if mysteries set in English villages are to be believed. In any event, this new address effectively ended Sayers's Bloomsbury years.

It did not, however, end her inclusion of Bloomsbury references in her fiction, or her habit of giving her characters residences there.[59] Of her twelve novels, only *The Five Red Herrings* lacks a Bloomsbury reference; instead it imagines a death in the Scottish setting of the Sayers-Fleming holidays. Although Dorothy L. Sayers and Virginia Woolf alike drew upon their own lives in their art, it would be shallow to explain their genius in terms of their variant sufferings alone. But an extensive literature has in fact explored Virginia Woolf's life and its relationship to her art. Sayers's life and art too have been much discussed, but little has been said about the relationship of her Bloomsbury experiences to her writings beyond the outlining of biographical events and the cataloguing of Bloomsbury references.

The character of Lord Peter (who does not live in Bloomsbury) may have emerged briefly before she settled there, but she wrote her first novel, *Whose Body?*, during her first full year of Bloomsbury residence, and this book shows him at his most jaunty and artificial. Here, even before she has taken up the anti-classical labors of an advertising copywriter, we hear an adopted sophistication and a commercial voice. Of course, Barbara Reynolds points out that Sayers first mentioned Dante in *Whose Body?*, written between the summer and autumn of 1921—a year which was significant for interest in Dante, both for a display of early editions of his works at University College in London, and for a sixteen-page Dante supplement to the *Times* of September 14, 1921.[60] This interest first evinced in the context of Sayers's residing in London, flowered two decades later in her well-known translation of the *Commedia* for Penguin. Clearly, living in Bloomsbury furthered Sayers's intellectual development as well as her affairs of the heart.

Bloomsbury in Sayers's Detective Novels and Stories

A review of the eleven novels that do mention Bloomsbury must begin with *Whose Body?*, where, as we have already seen, both the villainous Sir Julian Freke and the blameless Parker reside in very different addresses. Freke lives in Russell Square, "one of the largest squares in central London's Bloomsbury district," which "is bordered on the west by the University of London and the British Museum."[61] Parker, as we have also seen, occupies his humble flat at No. 12A Great Ormond Street, where he lives as a bachelor. I have suggested above that Sayers's emphasis upon details of his modest existence there may have been humorously based upon her own experience.

Clouds of Witness (1926) contains only one specific reference to Bloomsbury; the object of desire for the Duke of Denver (on trial for his life before the House of Lords with only his brother, Lord Peter, between him and the noose)—the beautiful Mrs. Grimthorpe— stays there briefly after being rescued from her abusive husband: "Peter saw her home to a respectable little hotel in Bloomsbury" (CW 317; ch. 19). The book treats illicit love in melodramatic terms—the time of its writing parallels without mimicking the very chancy romantic career of its author, and was published in the year that she married.

Unnatural Death (1927), like *Whose Body?*, places a villainous character in Bloomsbury: "Miss Whittaker knew London, of course. She had trained at the Royal Free [Hospital]. That meant she would know Bloomsbury better than any other district" (UD 197; ch. 17). Sayers, stating the premise of my essay, says "nobody knew better than Parker [who also lives in Bloomsbury] how rarely Londoners move out of their own particular little orbit" (UD 197; ch. 17). Basing his police procedure upon this principle, Parker centers his search for a solicitor that Miss Whittaker may have visited, in Bloomsbury: he "crossed the road towards Bedford Row" and "started at the first solicitor's he came to, which happened to be the office of one J.F. Trigg" (UD 198; ch. 17). Trigg has a very significant story to tell: he once interviewed Mary Whittaker under the name of "Miss Grant," and "She said she was staying at the Peveril Hotel in Bloomsbury" (UD 204; ch. 18). These passages are more than coincidental: it was true that Bloomsbury, as Sayers said, was "a quarter which swarms with solicitors" (UD 197-98; ch. 17), being located adjacent to London's legal district, and equally true that the Royal Free Hospital did indeed train nurses like (or, one hopes, unlike) Mary Whittaker. However, the likely meaning of London in general, and almost certainly the meaning of Bloomsbury in particular, for Sayers herself in her own life and choice to live there, is expressed explicitly and tellingly in this poignant observation about "London, whose rather untidy and grubby bosom is the repository of so many odd secrets. Discreet, in-curious, and all-enfolding London" (UD 197; ch. 17). London is a mother in whose bosom secrets may safely be deposited, as Sayers's own mother evidently was not. Indiscreet, incurious, and all-enfolding London, where young Dorothy could explore (whether safely or not, certainly secretly) her own sexuality and her own penchant for popu-lar art. One notes that when her widowed mother was provided with a domicile, it was not located conveniently near to the Bloomsbury flat of the Sayers-Fleming ménage, but well out of London in a village cottage.

Three of the short stories published in *Lord Peter Views the Body* (1928) contain references to Bloomsbury. In "The Abominable History of the Man with Copper Fingers," a Dr. Pettifer tells how "a totally unknown man had led him to a house in Bloomsbury where there was a woman suffering from strychnine poisoning" (PVB 6-7). This tale is told as an example of how "The more secluded London squares teemed with subjects for a writer" (PVB 6), a statement not only about Sayers's use of Bloomsbury as a writer's source, but again, as a reference to the seclusion, with all that could mean for good or ill, of the "London squares" for which Bloomsbury was especially well known. This seclusion, like the maternal capacity of London to keep secrets, is a part of the Bloomsbury Sayers may have sought as well as found.

The medical aspect of Bloomsbury appears again in "The Vindictive Story of the Footsteps that Ran," where Dr. Hartman, a "young physician" (PVB 161), says that "A struggling G.P. can't af-ford to let his practice go, even in Bloomsbury" (PVB 162). The phrase "even in Bloomsbury," emphasizes its reputation, perhaps, as a place where other things are indeed "let go." Lord Peter recalls addi-tional Bloomsbury residents in the same story: he says he

> "Frightened the postman into a fit the other day by askin' him
> how his young lady at Croydon was. He's a married man, livin'

in Great Ormond Street." Indeed, 'he lives just opposite to a friend of mine—Inspector Parker." (PVB 163)

We assume that the postman has a young lady and a wife at the same time, an arrangement not appropriately engaged in while living opposite a policeman. Parker at this time is not yet married, although his inventor was. The changes he made to his flat after marriage will, as we shall see, parallel those she had made to her own flat.

The third story, "The Entertaining Episode of the Article in Question," again touches upon domicile, neither secluded and macabre, as in "The Abominable History," nor referring to marriage and the residential element in the "The Vindictive Story," but lurid and *outré*. Lord Peter, sitting "in his book-lined sitting-room at 110A Piccadilly" (PVB 31), and hence very definitely not in Bloomsbury, receives a request from Bunter about a man "domiciled [...] in Guilford Street, Bloomsbury" (PVB 31), who turns out to be Jacques Lerouge, the female impersonator who is a thief, a safe-cracker, and a would-be diamond-snatcher, thus perpetuating the motif of the villain who resides in Bloomsbury already seen in *Whose Body?* and *Unnatural Death*. Sexual misbehavior and disorder were associated by Sayers not only with Bloomsbury, but with France, where her own desire for Eric Whelpton had been utterly disregarded. This motif appears strongly in *Clouds of Witness*, written early in her Bloomsbury period.

But Parker is not a villain, nor is Sir James Lubbock. In *The Unpleasantness at the Bellona Club* (1928), published in the same year as *Lord Peter Views the Body*, we see Lord Peter hailing a cab and driving to the residence of Sir James Lubbock, the "well-known analyst" (UBC 72; ch. 7). We learn in *The Documents in the Case* (1930), Sayers's only detective novel without Lord Peter, that Lubbock resides in Bloomsbury. John Munting, one of many informants whose testimony appears in this epistolary work, describes his discovery of the fact:

> "Dr. Waters," I said.
> "Yes?" [...]
> "May I have a word with you?"
> "By all means. Which way do you go?"
> "Bloomsbury," said I, desperately hoping that he lived at Hindon or Harringay. [...]

203

"Excellent, I am going that way myself." (DC 270; ch. 52)

In the cab, Dr. Waters "gave an address in Woburn Square," and soon after, Munting reports, "we were standing on Sir James Lubbock's doorstep, ringing the bell" (DC 271-72; ch. 52). Munting himself as he has explained earlier, "was then living in Bloomsbury— in fact, in my present house—and my wife [Elizabeth Drake, a character that some observers relate to Harriet Vane and hence to Sayers herself] was away with her people" (DC 141; ch. 45). He explains that he had been at that time writing "An introduction to an anthology," which had "a great deal of work at the British Museum" (DC 141; ch. 45), conveniently for him since it is located in Bloomsbury where he and the author who invented him had lived. This reference to "an" Introduction to an anthology accords with the fact that Sayers had published an anthology with a very significant Introduction herself, *Great Short Stories of Detection, Mystery and Horror*, in 1928. Here is the scholarly and editorial side of her life that Sayers reflects in her depiction of a completely sympathetic character. One other Bloomsbury reference in *The Documents in the Case* is to the "Redgauntlet Hotel, Bloomsbury, W.C." (DC 7; Intro.), where Paul Harrison, the son of the murdered man in this mystery, resides while the matter is investigated. He too is a character of the utmost respectability.

Sayers continued her custom of locating villainous characters in Bloomsbury, however. In *Strong Poison* (1930), having learned of Harriet's taking a "small flat of her own," we learn that Philip Boyes, "finding his solitary life depressing, has accepted the invitation of his cousin, Mr. Norman Urquhart, to stay at the latter's house in Woburn Square" (SP 12; ch. 1). Boyes is the victim, but certainly not the hero, in this detective tale; Urquhart is something worse. This novel gives a series of vivid portraits of Bohemian Bloomsbury. It is true that Marjorie Phelps, Lord Peter's artist friend, who plays Virgil to his Dante in their little excursion, has her own studio in Chelsea, but the motifs accord closely with Bloomsbury. Sayers makes her narrator note that Harriet and her former lover Philip Boyes are still "living in the same quarter of London" (SP 12; ch. 1); that is to say, in Bloomsbury. Harriet has left Sylvia Marriott's flat, which Philip L. Scowcroft (1991) says is "possibly in Bloomsbury,"[62] and moved to a flat in Doughty Street, where the narrator-judge places her. Later, in *Gaudy Night*, she lives in Mecklenburgh Square, where her author lived. Harriet is the heroine of both *Strong Poison* and *Gaudy Night*, and, similar to Sayers in many ways, is precisely like her in this.

The underworld journey of *Strong Poison* across Bloomsbury gives a sharply-observed series of vignettes of Bloomsbury life. Marjorie Phelps tells Lord Peter "You'll like Eiluned Price, I think. She scorns everything in trousers, but she's a good friend at a pinch" (SP 94; ch. 8). Eiluned lives with Sylvia Marriott in a "small bed-sitting room." I have suggested it is a picture of Sayers's first brief Bloomsbury residence; it is here "inhabited by a pale, spectacled young woman in a Morris chair" (SP 105; ch. 8). The portrayal of the two women, which might read today like a depiction of a lesbian couple, is charming, amusing, and perfectly sympathetic to both of their deftly drawn personalities. Marjorie identifies these friends of Harriet's to Lord Peter as "the rival gang" (SP 94; ch. 8), in opposition to Philip Boyes's friends, and offers to introduce him to these others.

Off they go "headed for a round of the studios" (SP 94; ch. 8). This is the Bloomsbury based upon a milieu begun when the Omega Workshop opened in 1913. Its pottery and furniture (made or designed by members and associates of the Bloomsbury Group) were displayed and made their appearance in popular magazines of the day as exemplars of contemporary interior decorating. The Workshop served as a precursor for the superb decoration by Duncan Grant of his own home, Charleston, and as an accompaniment to the home of Adrian and Virginia Stephen on "the north side of Brunswick Square," where the "ground-floor dining room" had its wall painted "with a continuous London street scene" by Duncan Grant and a friend," as David Garnett recalled in *The Golden Echo* (1953).[63] Such settings, of course, were created by and for people in social and financial circumstances far more elevated than those of Sayers's Bloomsbury, but they formed the matrix of this setting.

In the first studio, inhabited by "the Kropotkys," who are "pro-Boyes, Bolshevik, and musical" (SP 94; ch. 8), Lord Peter and his guide, stumbling "up a narrow and encumbered" stair, encountered "heat, sound, smoke, and the smell of frying" in a room "dimly lit by a single electric bulb, smothered in a lantern of painted glass"; there is "a vast and steaming kettle" on the stove and "a vast and steaming samovar" on the side-table, as well as a piano being played by a "young man with bushy red hair" (SP 95; ch. 8). Members of the Russian expatriate community are suggested here: John Cournos might have taken Dorothy to such a gathering. Next the searchers "try Joey Trimbles'" (SP 102; ch. 8) in "a studio over a mews," equally smoky, hot, and crowded, but adding "a strong smell of oil-paints" (SP 102; ch. 8), which do have a distinctive odor, much increased by the turpentine, linseed oil, damar varnish, and other volatile substances generally used with them. Finally, they locate Sylvia, at home with her friend Eiluned.

Still other aspects of Bloomsbury are mentioned in *Have His Carcase* (1932), as Olga Kohn writes to Lord Peter from "159 Regent Square, Bloomsbury," in a "very pretty hand" (HHC 295; ch. 22). Despite her refined handwriting, the author wryly and frankly tells us that Regent Square is anything but a high-class locality, being chiefly populated by grubby infants and ladies of doubtful calling, but its rents are comparatively cheap for so central a situation. At the "top of a rather dark and dirty stair," Lord Peter is "surprised to discover a freshly painted green door [...] opened at once by a handsome young woman" (HHC 297; ch. 22). In keeping with this depiction of Bloomsbury's less affluent addresses, we also learn how the long suffering "Mr. Mervyn Bunter sat in the bedroom of a cheap hotel in Bloomsbury, keeping his eye on a rather dusty window, adorned with a rather grubby curtain, which he could just see across a very dingy courtyard" (HHC 390; ch. 30).

Murder Must Advertise (1933) contains interesting information not only about Sayers's sojourn at Benson's, but intriguing details suggestive of the flat she occupied with her husband, in its enlarged form. These elements appear in connection with the arrival of Lord Peter, disguised as Death Bredon (a soubriquet composed of his own middle names), at Pym's advertising agency, where she has portrayed herself as one of the other employees—"Miss Meteyard—of Somerville [Sayers's own college]. One of the brighter ornaments of our department. She makes the vulgarest limericks ever recited within these chaste walls"; to Mr. Bredon's prompt response: "then we shall be friends" (MMA 12; ch. 1).

In his disguise, Lord Peter has apparently taken up residence in 12A, Great Ormond Street, a Bloomsbury address (MMA 24; ch. 1). Another resident of that quarter, also at Pym's, is Mr. Ingleby, who "lived in Bloomsbury, was communistic in a literary way, and dressed almost exclusively in pull-overs and grey flannels. He was completely and precociously disillusioned," as, indeed, is Miss Meteyard, who had "a somewhat similar mental makeup" (MMA 39; ch. 3).

As it emerges, Parker's flat and Mr. Bredon's flat combine to resemble the two-storey structure of Sayers's own flat in its nuptial phase. First we read that

> Lord Peter Wimsey had paid a call upon Chief-Inspector Parker of Scotland Yard, who was his brother-in-law.
> He occupied a large and comfortable arm-chair in the Chief-Inspector's Bloomsbury flat. [...] (MMA 78; ch. 5)

The author comments that "the scene was almost ostentatiously peaceful and domestic" (MMA 78; ch. 5) with Lady Mary knitting "upon the chesterfield" and "Parker himself" on "the window-seat"; a vision completed by "a couple of decanters and a soda siphon" on "a convenient table" and "a large tabby cat" on "the hearth rug" (MMA 78; ch. 5). In this cheerful vision we note the presence of alcohol (Fleming was an alcoholic) and the cat (Sayers was a life-long cat-fancier); a middle-class ambience is clearly sketched in these passages.

Later on, Parker goes to Great Ormond Street as the observer rather than observed:

> He opened the front door with his latch-key and stepped inside. It was the same house in which he had long occupied a modest bachelor flat, but on his marriage he had taken, in addition, the flat above his own, and thus possessed what was, in effect, a seven-roomed maisonette. (MMA 112; ch. 7)

Here, we read, in "the front hall, common to all the tenants," are mailboxes which include "Flat 3—Parker," along with "Flat 4," obviously the second and upper part of Parker's maisonette, now being used as a mailing address for "Bredon," who, since he is really Lord Peter Wimsey, actually lives in Picadilly. Flat 3, the lower flat, contains Parker's "living-room, dining-room and kitchen" (MMA 112-113; ch. 7), and Flat 4 the bedrooms. As Parker goes up the shared stairs between the two flats, he is attacked, and is later discovered by his wife, who has emerged from the upper level, which contains "the nursery" and "the bedroom" (MMA 114; ch. 7). Poignantly, Sayers has assigned one of the bedrooms to be a nursery, the usage she probably imagined for herself, her husband, and her son, when she added a similarly expanded facility to her own flat.

Bloomsbury references also appear in *The Nine Tailors* (1934), as a wire from Superintendent Blundell to Lord Peter locates a missing couple: "Vicar St. Andrews Bloomsbury says asked perform marriage by licence William Thoday Mary Deacon both of that parish" (NT 270; ch. 3; part 1), and Frank Jenkins explains that "He had been hanging around a garridge in Bloomsbury [...] when he saw a bloke coming along on this here bike" (NT 307; ch. 3, part 4). The bloke is James Thoday, the brother of Will Thoday, and the "garridge" ambience, a motif appearing in several other parts of Sayers's imagined world, derived perhaps, from her relationship with "Bill," whom she may have met because she, too, possessed a motorcycle, "which she rode with dignity, sitting bolt upright as if driving a chariot."[64]

In *Gaudy Night* (1935), Sayers gives Harriet Vane her own Bloomsbury address, the one she occupied when she wrote *Whose Body?*:

> Harriet Vane sat at her writing-table and stared out into Mecklenburgh Square. The late tulips made a brave show in the Square garden, and a quartet of early tennis-players were energetically calling the score of a rather erratic and unpractised game. (GN 7; ch. 1)

After her trial and acquittal in the murder of Philip Boyes, Harriet traveled on the continent with a woman friend, and "As soon as she got back to London, she moved to a new flat in Mecklenburgh Square, and settled down to work" (GN 64; ch. 3). Here Lord Peter takes her, after their first contact in several years, and leaves her as she is "mounting the stone staircase" (GN 68; ch. 3). During the cab ride "he was babbling pleasantly about the Georgian architecture of London. It was only as they were running along Guilford Street that" (GN 67; ch. 3) he brought up the subject of marriage; he had never, Harriet muses, "violated the seclusion of Mecklenburgh Square" (GN 68; ch. 3). Inside, "on the mantelpiece of her sitting-room stood a note, in Peter's small and rather difficult writing" (GN 69; ch. 3): he is going away to the North and she will not see him again for a time. These passages, besides offering a glimpse of the flat and its environment, drop a hint that Harriet may yet find a relationship with Peter, so delicate is he in his approach, so diffident and so careful of her feelings, not to say her reputation; and indeed at the end of this book, she has agreed to marry him. This address, where Sayers lived before she moved to Great James Street and began her relationship with John Cournos, may have suggested itself as neutral ground for the moment of renewal in Lord Peter's relationship with Harriet Vane.

The final mention of Bloomsbury in the novels comes in *Busman's Honeymoon* (1937), published nine years after Sayers's own marriage, as we are told about the wedding and honeymoon of Lord Peter and Harriet (Lady Peter). It contains the telling characterization from which I have taken my title: "an Oxford-Bloomsbury bluestocking" (BH 15; Prothalamion). Here, most clearly, Dorothy L. Sayers not only identifies Harriet with herself, but identifies herself as a product of those distinctive contexts, Oxford and Bloomsbury. Her Oxford origins and her Oxford University and Somerville College education between them made her an orthodox, high church Anglican, one who found her religious identity in the Prayer Book's sonorous Creeds, her aesthetics in the majestic ceremonies and architectural settings of the established church, and her moral certainties in a rural Anglican rectory.

Conclusions

Life-long marriage between never-married virgins, and childbearing within this context and without artificial intervention: these were the standards she had imbibed and attempted to maintain. Certainly she kept her delight in the intellectual intricacies of the Creeds; certainly she drew upon a rich liturgical heritage in her plays, written in many cases for presentation in medieval cathedrals. As for her received mores in regard to sexuality, relationship, and procreation: she was to violate all except fidelity. She engaged in an active sexual liaison before marriage; she bore a child out of wedlock; she married a divorced man. How did all this come about? Like the Bloomsbury Group members before her, she went to Bloomsbury to find freedom. Her choice of Bloomsbury, with its widely-known reputation, expressed vividly in the quotations we have examined from all but one of her twelve novels—as a place to live when she went, finally, to seek her fortune in London, where she began to write her novels, where she found long-term employment at Benson's, and where she undertook three affairs of the heart with such various and in many ways emotionally disastrous results—suggests that she had, in some way, looked for the anonymity, liberality, and freedom of the Bloomsbury ambience.

Did she actually know what this might mean and where it might lead? Almost certainly not. The innocence of a sexually inexperienced woman, even in her late twenties, and despite her apparent sophistication, can be, and was in this case, profound. In her relationship with Cournos her expectations of him were, to say the least, naive. But then, she was naive, as well as obdurate, more obdurate than he, who despite his amoral intentions toward her, could not break down her defenses and, perhaps in frustration at this affront, removed himself from London. Bloodied by this rejection, herself frustrated by his refusal to love her in her necessary context, she dropped her objections to premarital sex in her democratic relationship with Bill, with lifetime consequences to herself and to her resulting child. Even in her lifelong relationship with Fleming she was forced to marry outside the church.

Did she change her mind about the sinfulness of these activities? Perhaps; her treatment of sexual behaviors in her novels is focused far less upon the technical status of the lovers than upon the misuse of one person by another in these relationships, a region of human behavior of which she had gained genuine and bitter experience. And her categorization of "Lust" as one of the warm-hearted—as opposed to cold-hearted—sins, in her essay "The Other Six Deadly Sins,"[65] suggests latitude and toleration of the means, though not the intentions, of what had been in her life unequal contests between woman and man.

The Bloomsbury references in Sayers's novels and short stories contain two main categories, expressed in a variety of ways. Bloomsbury functions as a place of residence, whether long-term or transient, and at the same time, houses a host of offices, studios, and other facilities where professionals engage in their professions: doctors, lawyers, policemen, artists, and writers significantly among them. Bloomsbury is portrayed as a place of freedom, autonomy, independence, and self-determination. This is so in part because it is a place of privacy, secrecy, anonymity, and disguise. Bloomsbury, despite its elegant squares and historic houses, can be a place of humility, poverty, illegality, and other forms of liminality. Its position on the borderline between worlds makes it a place for bohemianism, political and sexual license and experimentation, and alternative literature and art, including popular forms.

The poles of personal freedom and professional empowerment are not, and in Sayers's Bloomsbury, were not, very far apart. She went to live there to pursue her self-chosen profession, writing, and to explore the combination of freedom and privacy Bloomsbury promised, not only for her own sexuality, but for all the other aspects of a free person's selfhood, capability, and identity. That she found them all, not only pain and failure, but joy and success, is indicated by the rich range of good and evil characters, and by the locations, respectable and disreputable, that she wove with such verve and skill into what she wrote. Bloomsbury continued to mean throughout her career a liberating delight in common life as well as high life, a willingness to enjoy and engage in popular culture with the same zest she used to pursue her art, her scholarship and her religion.

Dorothy L. Sayers had a genius for the popular, for motorcycles as well as for bell-towers, for advertising as well as for medieval translations, for mystery novels as well as Mystery plays. That is why her art still lives, when many works of greater moment in their own time have been relegated to esoterica. Her Bloomsbury years, with their intense personal experiences, gave her the grasp upon human realities that make her writings not only witty and accessible, but wise, humane, and, despite their deliberate and self-reflexive artificiality, true.

Notes

[1] Stephan P. Clarke, *The Lord Peter Wimsey Companion* (New York: The Mysterious Press, 1985) 49. This, along with Philip L. Scowcroft's essay (see below) was an indispensable aid in the preparation of my paper.

Notes

[2] S.P. Rosenbaum, *Victorian Bloomsbury: The Early Literary History of the Bloomsbury Group*, Part I (New York: St. Martin's Press, 1987) 16.

[3] Alzina Stone Dale, *Maker and Craftsman: the Story of Dorothy L. Sayers* (1978; revised ed. Wheaton IL: Harold Shaw Publishers, 1992) 60.

[4] Nancy M. Tischler, *Dorothy L. Sayers: A Pilgrim Soul* (Atlanta, GA: John Knox Press, 1980) 27.

[5] Louise DeSalvo, *Virginia Woolf: The Impact of Childhood Sexual Abuse on Her Life and Work* (New York: Fodor's Travel Publications, 1992) 92.

[6] *Fodor's London* (New York: Fodor's Travel Publications, 1992) 116

[7] S.P. Rosenbaum, ed., *The Bloomsbury Group: A Collection of Memoirs, Commentary and Criticism* (Toronto, ON: University of Toronto Press, 1975) 1

[8] Rosenbaum, ed., *The Bloomsbury Group* 2.

[9] Rosenbaum, "Vanessa Bell: Notes on Bloomsbury," *The Bloomsbury Group* 75-76.

[10] Rosenbaum, "Virginia Woolf: Sex Talk in Bloomsbury," *The Bloomsbury Group* 22.

[11] Gillian Naylor, ed., *Bloomsbury: Its Artists, Authors, and Designers* (Boston, MA: Little, Brown and Co., 1990) 24.

[12] Rosenbaum, *Victorian Bloomsbury* 3-4 (quote p. 3).

[13] Nigel Nicholson, "Bloomsbury: the Myth and the Reality," *Virginia Woolf and Bloomsbury*, ed. Jane Marcus (Bloomington, IN: Indiana UP, 1987) 16.

[14] Rosenbaum, *Victorian Bloomsbury* 3.

[15] Rosenbaum, *Victorian Bloomsbury* 6.

[16] Quoted from G.M. Young, *Victorian England: Portrait of an Age* (Oxford: Oxford UP, 1936) in Rosenbaum, *Victorian Bloomsbury* 22.

[17] Rosenbaum, *Victorian Bloomsbury* 23.

[18] Rosenbaum, *Victorian Bloomsbury* 26.

[19] Rosenbaum, *Victorian Bloomsbury* 29.

[20] Rosenbaum, *Victorian Bloomsbury* 29.

[21] Naylor 14.

[22] Rosenbaum, ed., "Introduction," *The Bloomsbury Group* 2.

Notes

[23] Rosenbaum, *Victorian Bloomsbury* 4.
[24] Rosenbaum, *Victorian Bloomsbury* 4.
[25] James Brabazon, *Dorothy L. Sayers: the Life of a Courageous Woman* (London: Victory Gollancz, 1981) 2.
[26] Brabazon 3.
[27] Brabazon 6.
[28] Brabazon 7.
[29] Brabazon 41.
[30] Mitzi Brunsdale, *Dorothy L. Sayers: Solving the Mystery of Wickedness* (New York: Berg, 1990) 57.
[31] Dorothy L. Sayers, *OP. I* (Oxford: B.H. Blackwell, 1916) 22.
[32] Brabazon 64.
[33] Dorothy L. Sayers, "The Carpenter's Son," *Catholic Tales and Christian Songs* (Oxford: B.H. Blackwell, 1918) 17.
[34] Brabazon 84-85.
[35] Brabazon 85.
[36] Brunsdale 9.
[37] Brabazon 88.
[38] Brabazon 88.
[39] Brabazon 88.
[40] Brunsdale 89-90.
[41] Brabazon 89-90.
[42] Brabazon 91.
[43] Letter to John Cournos, dated October 27, 1925, quoted in Brabazon 95.
[44] Brunsdale 91.
[45] Letter to Sayers's parents, dated February 15, 1923, quoted in Brabazon 98.
[46] Quentin Bell, *Virginia Woolf* vol. II (London: Paladin, 1987) 2, quoted from a letter of Virginia Stephen to Violet Dickinson, June 4, 1912.
[47] Rosenbaum, *Victorian Bloomsbury* 58.
[48] Rosenbaum, *Victorian Bloomsbury* 68.
[49] Rosenbaum, *Victorian Bloomsbury* 78.
[50] Rosenbaum, *Victorian Bloomsbury* 78.
[51] Rosenbaum, *Victorian Bloomsbury* 81.

Notes

[52] Rosenbaum, *Victorian Bloomsbury* 85.

[53] Quoted in Brabazon 116.

[54] Brabazon 117.

[55] David Coomes, *Dorothy L. Sayers: A Careless Rage for Life* (Oxford: Lion, 1992) 105.

[56] Brabazon 140.

[57] Brabazon 141.

[58] Brabazon 142.

[59] See Philip L. Scowcroft, "Some Bloomsbury Residents," *Sidelights on Sayers*, 36 (July 1991): 4-6 (Witham, Essex, England: The Dorothy L. Sayers Historical and Literary Society, 1991) for a survey of the characters who shared Sayers's chosen neighborhood. This little essay, impeccably researched as always by its author, has been absolutely indispensable in the creation of my present study.

[60] Barbara Reynolds, *The Passionate Intellect: Dorothy L. Sayers' Encounter with Dante* (Kent, OH: Kent State UP, 1989) 2.

[61] Clarke 414.

[62] Scowcroft 12.

[63] Quoted in Naylor 47.

[64] Janet Hitchman, *Such a Strange Lady: An Introduction to Dorothy L. Sayers (1893–1957)* (Holborn: New English Library, 1975) 55.

[65] Dorothy L. Sayers, "The Other Six Deadly Sins" (1941), *Christian Letters to a Post-Christian World*, ed. Roderick Jellema (Grand Rapids, MI: Wm. B. Eerdmans, 1969) 138-155.

11. Images of Judaism and Anti-Semitism in the Novels of Dorothy L. Sayers

"Light reading for the masses," said Parker.

——Dorothy L. Sayers, *Unnatural Death*

In "Images of Judaism" Patterson reviews Sayers's references to Jews in Whose Body?, Unnatural Death, Murder Must Advertise, Have His Carcase, Clouds of Witness, Five Red Herrings, The Man Born to Be King, *and* Busman's Honeymoon. *She then considers G.K. Chesterton, the widely known author of the Father Brown mysteries, as a possible source for Sayers's use of anti-Semitic motifs.*

Patterson took up this difficult subject in relation to Charles Williams's work in a paper titled "The Jewels of Messias: Images of Judaism and Anti-Semitism in the Novels of Charles Williams" (1979), available in Divining Tarot: Papers on Charles Williams's The Greater Trumps *and Other Works by Nancy-Lou Patterson.*

"Images of Judaism and Anti-Semitism in the Novels of Dorothy L. Sayers" was first published in The Sayers Review *2 (June 1978): 17-24.*

In her introduction to a recent edition of some of Dorothy L. Sayers's short stories, Janet Hitchman (1972) states that "in the context of present day thought, some of her remarks about 'Jewboys' and 'niggers' are hard to take."[1] The thought is echoed by Peter Green (1975) in his review of Hitchman's biography of Sayers: "Her mildly offensive anti-Semitism did not prevent her having a flamboyantly Jewish publisher all her life."[2] Hitchman states in *Such a Strange Lady* that "only *The Unpleasantness at the Bellona Club* and *The Nine Tailors* have no pejorative remarks about Jews."[3] She points out that Sayers was "insufferably rude" about "niggers," "servants and the working class," and "the Soviet menace" indiscriminately. As Hitchman's is the only examination of this subject beyond occasional casual references, I will try to draw together the major examples of Sayers's writings in which Jews or Judaism are mentioned.

The first of Sayers's detective novels, *Whose Body?* deals with the murder of Sir Reuben Levy. It begins with the discovery of what Inspector Parker describes as "the Semitic-looking stranger in Mr. Thipps's bath"—a nude dead body which is not, in fact, Sir Reuben's, though "he would be really extraordinarily like Sir Reuben if he had a beard." His most "Semitic" trait, of course, though it is not actually mentioned, would be the fact that the corpse, naked, is manifestly circumcised. Parker refers to the body as belonging to "a tall and sturdy Semite" (WB 46; ch. 2), and the narrator describes him thus:

> The features were thick, fleshy and strongly marked, with prominent dark eyes, and a long nose curving down to a heavy chin. The clean-shaven lips were full and sensual. (WB 31; ch. 1)

The hair is described as "thick and black and naturally curly" (WB 31; ch. 1).

The widow of the victim, Lady Levy—formerly Christine Ford—was a school chum of the Dowager Duchess of Denver (Lord Peter's mother), whose family, the Duchess says, made "dreadful trouble" "about her marrying a Jew," before Levy "made his money [...] in that oil business out in America." She had been engaged to Julian Freke (a distinguished doctor) but "she fell in love with Mr. Levy and eloped with him. He was very handsome, then, you know, dear, in a foreign-looking way, but he hadn't any means, and the Fords didn't like his religion." The Duchess is not, apparently concerned: "Of course, we're all Jews nowadays," she says, and "I'm sure some Jews are very good people, and personally I'd much rather they believed something, though of course it may be very inconvenient, what with not working on Saturdays and circumcising the poor little babies and everything depending on the new moon and that funny kind of meat they have with such a long-sounding name, and never being able to have bacon for breakfast" (WB 70; ch. 3).

The characters introduced in this story reappear in later novels. In *Strong Poison*, Freddy Arbuthnot confides in Lord Peter, in a discussion about a mutual acquaintance:

> I've got an idea [...] that the chappie is rather up against it, as you might say [...] and if I was to put him in touch with Goldberg [...] it might get him out of a hole and so on. And Gold-

berg will be all right, because don't you see, he's a cousin of old Levy's, who was murdered, you know, and all these Jews stick together like leeches, and, as a matter of fact, I think it's very fine of them. (SP 152; ch. 12)

This remark is expanded when he tells Lord Peter that "Rachel Levy is—er—in fact—going to become Mrs. Freddy" (SP 152; ch. 12). Arbuthnot explains that the family didn't mind his being a Christian so much as his being a Gentile, and that he didn't mind what they counted his future children as, because "it would be all to the little beggars' advantage to be in with the Levy and Goldberg crowd, especially if the boys turn out to be anything in the financial way" (SP 153; ch. 12). They are to be married at the Synagogue and he invites Lord Peter to be his best man. Wimsey, unboggled, agrees, saying, "Bunter will explain the procedure to me. He's bound to know. He knows everything" (SP 153; ch. 12).

As has become apparent, Jews are equated in this series of quotations with high finance and stable family life. But not all of Sayers's Jews are wealthy. In *Unnatural Death*, Parker and Wimsey, investigating the site of Vera Findlater's murder, discover "a man's mauve-grey cap" (UD 235; ch. 20), which is "stained with brilliantine" (UD 248; ch. 21), a "large linen handkerchief, very grubby and with no initials or laundry-mark," and "foot-marks—two men's and a woman's" (UD 237; ch. 20). Parker examines these marks ruminatively, trying to reconstruct the scene. He muses—there are no quotation marks in the original—"the second man, who seemed to possess rather narrow feet and to wear the long-toed boots affected by Jew boys of the louder sort—had come after her from the car—" (UD 237-38; ch. 20).

The much-quoted epithet is thus Parker's; the killer does not, in fact, turn out to be a Jew, or for that matter, a man. Lord Peter examines the cap. He remarks: "I imagine we may put down this elegant bit of purple headgear to the gentleman in the slim boots. Bright yellow, I fancy, with buttons. He must be lamenting his beautiful cap" (UD 238; ch. 20). Another piece of evidence is "that monthly collection of mystery and sensational fiction published under the name of *The Black Mask*."

"Light reading for the masses," said Parker.

"Brought by the gentleman in the yellow boots, perhaps," suggested the Chief Constable. (UD 238-39; ch. 20)

Wimsey makes an accurate guess at this point, attributing the magazine to "a boyish taste in fiction" (UD 239; ch. 20). But Parker is not to be deterred. Following Sir Charles's suggestion that the magazine might be a clue to the killer—"The Black"—he says, "Perhaps the long-toed gentleman was a nigger [...] Nigger taste rather runs to boots and hair-oil. Or possibly a Hindu or Parsee of sorts" (UD 239; ch. 20). Parker has a catholic set of prejudices which Sir Charles—who expostulates "an English girl in the hands of a nigger. How abominable!"—obviously shares (UD 239; ch. 20). Lord Peter makes no contribution to this disagreeable exchange.

There is, in fact, a Black character in the story, a West Indian clergyman who is distantly related to one of the victims. Sayers (or rather Lord Peter) arranges matters so that "this innocent, decent old creature" (UD 246; ch. 21),[4] whom the real murderer had attempted to implicate, inherits £10,000. Lord Peter is not innocent of racist language himself, however, for in *Murder Must Advertise*, under the guise of "Mr. Bredon," he is working at Pym's advertising agency. He finds that the name "Green Pastures Margarine" suggests "niggers" to him—"The play, you know." His superior, Mr. Ingleby, retorts, "You mustn't mention niggers in the copy" (MMA 17; ch.1). Mr. Bredon spends some time as a new copy-writer, during which he learns that one of his copy-chiefs, Mr. Armstrong, "disliked any lay-out which involved a picture of a judge or a Jew" (MMA 38; ch.3). Bredon (Lord Peter in disguise) has been brought into the case "through Freddy Arbuthnot's wife—Rachel Levy that was, you know. She knows old Pym" (MMA 79; ch. 5), who owns the agency where murder has been done.

Sayers's most common stereotypic depiction of Jewish characters was as minor business-men who were inclined to be overweight. In *Have His Carcase*, Lord Peter visits a theatrical agency: the agents wonder if he would not himself be a good box office draw. One of them, Mr. Rosencrantz, described as "slightly less bulky but also inclined to embonpoint" (HHC 304; ch. 23) says, in a passage quoted by Hitchman: "it ud go vell, eh? Lord Peter Vimsey in the title-rôle? [...] Nowadays, they all vant somebody as does somethings" (HHC 306; ch. 23). In *Clouds of Witness*, a French salesgirl interviewed by Par-

ker in a Parisian jewellery shop, "had just finished selling an engagement ring to an obese and elderly Jew" (CW 129; ch. 5), a passage
also recorded by Hitchman. In the chapter "Graham's Story" in *Five
Red Herrings*, "Clarenth Gordon," a commercial traveler (in North
American terms, a traveling salesman), is interviewed by Lord Peter
and Inspector Macpherson. He is described as "a stout little gentleman
with a pronounced facial angle" (FRH 250; ch. 22). Hitchman objects
to this passage, though she does not mention the reference to the
salesman's profile. She says "there is no reason why he should be
Jewish, or why we should be treated to a page or more written in
listhps."[5] This particular book has page after page of Scottish dialect;
Sayers followed the common practice of using dialect to give color to
her characterizations, including Cockney accents, Scots accents, and,
in the "listhps," what she apparently perceived as "Jewish" accents.
British culture makes much of being able to place people by their dia-
lects: witness Professor Higgins in *Pygmalion*. When Sayers wrote for
radio in the series of plays on the life of Christ, *The Man Born to Be
King*, she gave particular attention to the use of such conventions to
distinguish characters: in her most egregious display of snobbery
(whether or not it was anti-Semitism), she wrote of St. Matthew in her
notes to "A Certain Nobleman": "He is as vulgar a little commercial
Jew as ever walked Whitechapel, and I should play him with a frank
Cockney accent" (MK 113; Third Play).

The last of the Lord Peter novels is *Busman's Honeymoon*.
Lord Peter and his bride Harriet Vane are trying, "with detective interruptions," to enjoy a honeymoon in a country cottage, "Talboys," near
Harriet's girlhood village. The major interruption is the discovery that
the body of the man from whom the cottage has been purchased is in
fact lying dead in the cellar. A minor interruption occurs when the
dead man's creditors arrive to repossess the furniture. Bunter (Wimsey's valet) introduces the first arrival by announcing that an "individual" is at the door. Lord Peter's question "What sort of individual?"
elicits the response that it is a "A financial individual, my lord, to
judge by appearances." This causes Lord Peter to ask, "Name of Moses?" When told that the name is MacBride, Wimsey remarks, "A dis-
tinction without a difference." When the "financial Scotsman" (BH
124; ch. 5) is admitted, Lord Peter is all graciousness, but Bunter con-

tinues to think of the visitor as an "inquisitive Hebrew" (BH 106; ch. 5).

MacBride turns out to be "a brisk young man, bowler-hatted, with sharp black eyes that seemed to inventory everything they encountered, and a highly regrettable tie" (BH 126; ch. 6). He is "from Town," as revealed by his "native accents" which "were, indeed—apart from a trifling difficulty with his sibilants—pure Whitechapel" (BH 126-27; ch. 6). Sayers no doubt had similar men in mind when she gave him her own highly regrettable description of St. Matthew quoted above. The young man represents "Macdonald and Abrahams" (BH 128; ch. 6), and Lord Peter persuades him, despite the debt to "Levy, Levy & Levy. Running five years" (BH 130; ch. 6), to wait until the honeymoon is over to take his due.

Several chapters later the debt is under discussion by Lord Peter and the policeman Kirk, who refers to "this Jew-bird, MacBride" (BH 177; ch. 8). When MacBride returns to complete his task he has a competitor, "a stout, elderly Hebrew"—these are the narrator's own words, echoing those used in *Clouds of Witness*, quoted above. The newcomer has "a breathless and hasty manner" and a lisp; he too has a financial claim to press. He has been running and is out of breath. "He mopped his forehead with his handkerchief." An argument ensues, during which Mr. Solomons—that is his name—utters "a loud expostulatory howl," at which point Lord Peter invites both men to supper. It is a pleasant meal with "Mr. Solomons on the right" and Mr. MacBride on the left." Mollified, and with arrangements amicably completed, the men depart "fraternally," and play no further part in the story.

Even the last, and hitherto unpublished story about Lord Peter, "Talboys," which is very much a whimsy, shows us Lord Peter regaling his son Bredon with the fragment, "Nebuchadnezzar, the King of the Jews"—[6] a purely nonsensical interpolation which is, as Hitchman says of some of the above quotations, quite unnecessary.[7]

G.K. Chesterton has been suggested as a source for Sayers's use of these motifs.[8] His *Autobiography* (1937) contains items indexed as "Jewish friendships," which include the following revealing passage:

> I remember once extricating a strange swarthy little
> creature with a hooked nose from being bullied [...] being

lightly tossed from one boy to another amid wild stares of wide-eyed scientific curiosity and questions like "What is it?" and "Is it alive" Thirty years afterwards, when that little goblin was a great grown bearded man [...] he had a sort of permanent fountain of thanks for that trifling incident, which was quite embarrassing.[9]

Chesterton, who praised the "loyalty of the Jewish family"—a motif appearing in Sayers's novels—assigned anti-Semitism to the position of Jews as "foreigners; only foreigners that were not called foreigners." In a more extreme version of this idea, G.K. Chesterton's brother, Cecil Chesterton, was "convinced as any fanatic that there was a Jewish conspiracy for the overthrow of Christian civilization."[10] These variant positions led to the Chesterton brothers' involvement in the Marconi case, which some writers have equated with Sayers's Megatherium scandal (HHC 78; ch. 6). The British Cabinet took over a company formed to use the new invention of telegraphy; it was then announced that the Attorney General, Rufus Isaacs, Lloyd George, and the Liberal Whip, had all received at the hands of Rufus Isaacs's brother Godfrey, of the same company, shares in its American branch. Cecil Chesterton took a strong stand against all this, with the result that he was sued for criminal libel and fined £100. G.K. Chesterton was horrified. To him, the Isaacs brothers had preferred their family interest to that of the country, and this he saw as a peculiarly Jewish vice. Within a month after the Armistice of 1918, Cecil Chesterton died. In a paroxysm of anger, G.K. Chesterton learned that Rufus Isaacs had accompanied Lloyd George to the Paris Peace Conference. His private sorrow became a projected public menace. He wrote to Isaacs: "Is there any man who doubts that you will be sympathetic with the Jewish International?"[11] Defending himself against the role of "Anti-Semite," he said, "I allow for your position more than most men will allow for it; more, most assuredly than most men *will* allow for it in the darker days that yet may come [...] I wish you no such ghastly retribution."[12]

As a background to understanding Chesterton and Sayers, a brief history of Jewish life in England may help. Even in Hellenistic times Jews were regarded as "misanthropic."[13] The Jewish communities scattered about the Roman Empire experienced sporadic disparagement. Christianity was first fostered in this diasporic setting—

witness Acts—but Christians came to regard the continuing existence of the Jews as God's punishment on the one hand and a perplexing challenge on the other. Jews too struggled with the mystery of their dispersal and perpetuity. Arnold Ages (1973) says that Anti-Semitism always claims "that Jews are unassimilable, a foreign element in the life of nation states."[14] This is exactly how Chesterton saw the Jew, and one recalls the Duchess of Denver finding Sir Reuben Levy handsome "in a foreign-looking way."

One of the outposts to which Jews had come was Britain. There, "Jewish merchants and middlemen,"[15] because they were not prevented, as Christians were, from lending money at interest, began to "finance trade, provision armies and act as [...] bankers," until by the twelfth century there were comfortable communities in London, Oxford, Cambridge, and elsewhere. During the thirteenth century, however, increasing discrimination as well as outright massacre culminated in 1290 with the banishment of all 16,000 Jews from England. They were not to return until Cromwell invited them back in the middle of the seventeenth century, in hopes that "their ingenuity and international contacts would increase the flow of trade."[16]

By the end of the eighteenth century there were some twelve to twenty thousand Jews in England, mostly in London. Some found employment as pedlars and haberdashers, dealing in second-hand clothes, with "a thin upper crust of the very rich," and at the bottom a few who "turned to crime."[17] In 1831 the restrictions preventing Jews from trading in the City were removed; in 1858 Baron Lionel de Rothschild was permitted to sit in parliament; by 1880 there were 60,000 English Jews, a "small, compact community."[18] In 1881, however, there began the terrible persecutions of Jews in Russia and Poland; by 1914 nearly 150,000 Eastern European Jews had come to Britain. These new arrivals were dumped into the employment market where they took their turn as "dealers in old clothes," works in tenement sweat shops, and "rogues, filchers, counterfeiters and receivers."[19] In this setting, "Immigrant Jewry formed a society apart."[20] We have here the foundation of the negative stereotypes projected against Jews from Fagin in *Oliver Twist* to Parker's imaginary mauve-capped "Jew boy."

Despite her extraordinary achievements, Dorothy L. Sayers had her ordinary side; she had not rid herself entirely of her parsonage snobberies. To those who love Sayers's writings, it gives no pleasure to perceive her fault. Certainly, the Jewish stereotypes in her novels have their origins in the realities of British history, and it can be said in her defense that of all her Jewish characters not one is a villain or a rogue. But the fault was there. It was the very casualness with which it was done that made it so culpable. A novel frequently carries a resonance derived from the thinking of its readers. In doing so it may take on a moral or ethical quality. If it does, both writer and reader must be sensitive to the implications of what is being said. If we assign moral responsibility we cannot say, "but everybody did it." C.S. Lewis (1958) wrote of "the temptation […] to condone, to connive at; by our words, looks and laughter, to 'consent.'"[21] What is asked is a standard of self-examination beyond that used by Sayers in her treatment of Jews.

Notes
[1] Janet Hitchman, introduction, Dorothy L. Sayers, *Striding Folly* (London: New English Library, 1972) 22.
[2] Peter Breen, "A Clergyman's Daughter," *Times Literary Supplement* 28 Feb. 1975: 224. For this paper, "anti-Semite" means "anti-Jewish."
[3] Janet Hitchman, *Such a Strange Lady* (London: New English Library, 1975) 123.
[4] Lord Peter's words.
[5] Hitchman, *Such A Strange Lady* 124.
[6] Dorothy Sayers, "Talboys," *Striding Folly* (London: New English Library, 1972) 97.
[7] Hitchman, *Such a Strange Lady* 124.
[8] I am indebted to George Colvin for suggesting that I study the example of G.K. Chesterton as an anti-Semitic model for Dorothy L. Sayers.
[9] G.K. Chesterton, *Autobiography* (London: Hutchison and Co., 1937) 75; ch. 3.
[10] Christopher Hollis, *The Mind of Chesterton* (London: Hollis and Carter, 1970) 132-33.
[11] Chesterton, quoted in Maisie Ward, *Gilbert Keith Chesterton*, new edition (Lanham, MD: Rowman & Littlefield Publishers, 2006) 360.

Notes

[Editor's note: The source for this quotation has been added to the original paper.]

[12] Chesterton, quoted in Ward, *Gilbert Keith Chesterton* 362. [Editor's note: The source for this quotation has been added to the original paper.]

[13] Arnold Ages, *The Diaspora Dimension* (The Hague: Martinus, 1973) 4.

[14] Ages 19.

[15] Chaim Bermant, *Troubled Eden—An Anatomy of British Jewry* (London: Vallentin, Mitchell, 1969) 6.

[16] Bermant 8.

[17] Bermant 12.

[18] Bermant 21.

[19] Fernand Braudel, *Capitalism and the Material Life, 1400–1800* (Glasgow: Fontana, 1974) 436.

[20] Lloyd P. Gartner, *The Jewish Immigrant in England, 1870–1914* (London: George Allen and Unwin, Ltd., 1960) 166.

[21] C.S. Lewis, *Reflections on the Psalms* (London: Geoffrey Bles, 1958) 71.

12.   "Cat o' Mary": The Spirituality of Dorothy L. Sayers

[I]n the old days, [the] religious were perceived as spiritual and lay people as pious. Now the playing field is level and all are perceived the same.

———Fr. Philip Sheldrake, S.J. (1993)[1]

In this short paper, Patterson considers Sayers's self-identification— indicated by the title of her autobiographical novel fragment Cat o' Mary (c. 1934)—with Mary the contemplative, rather than Martha, who represented an active life, with reference to The Man Born to Be King *(1943) and her other writings, James Brabazon's (1981) and Barbara Reynolds's (1989 and 1993) studies of Sayers's life, and Anglicanism in general. Not surprisingly, the subject of sin, discussed by Sayers in "The Other Six Deadly Sins" (1941), is introduced here, as it is in "'Eve's Sharp Apple': Five Transgressing Women in the Novels of Dorothy L. Sayers" and "'A Bloomsbury Blue-Stocking': Dorothy L. Sayers's Bloomsbury years in Their Spatial and Temporal Context."*

"Cat o' Mary" was first published in Studies in Sayers Essays Presented to Dr. Barbara Reynolds on her 80th Birthday, *ed. Christopher Dean (Hurstpierpoint, West Sussex: The Dorothy L. Sayers Society, 1994) 28-32.*

———————

In his biography of Dorothy L. Sayers, James Brabazon (1981) says that she identified herself with the heroine of her unpublished fragment, Cat o' Mary (1934), whose title refers to the biblical story of Martha and Mary. In doing so, he asserts, she portrayed herself as "a woman whose true life was bound up not with religion but with the intellect," and as one "in whom religion was an aspect of the intellect, not one of personal devotion."[2] In a standard interpretation of Luke 10.38-42, where Jesus tells the busy Martha that "Mary has chosen the better part" because she sits at his feet and hears his word, Mary represents the contemplative life, and Martha represents the active life, so one may ask why the very active Sayers identified herself with Mary.

Interestingly, in the place where she explicitly treats Mary and Martha, *The Man Born to Be King* (1943), she identifies "Mary Magdalene with Mary of Bethany and the unnamed 'Woman who was a Sinner' of Luke VII [verses 37-38]" (MK Intro. 32). That suggests that when she viewed the Mary of Bethany who sat at the feet of Jesus in Luke 10.38, the Mary Magdalene who sat at the tomb in Matthew 27.61, and the woman to whom Jesus says "Thy faith hath saved thee; go in peace" in Luke 7.50, as all being the same woman, she identified herself strongly with this listening, anointing, forgiven woman. If that is so, her concept of Cat o' Mary was a great deal more complex than Brabazon suggested.

Barbara Reynolds, in her biography of Sayers (1993), describes her as possessing a "combination of intellectual light and spiritual ardour,"[3] adding to this characterization her friend's traits of "kindness" and "friendship."[4] Following her lead, it will be my thesis that Sayers exemplified a sanctity of doing as well as being, and that she showed as well as taught a way of friendship not only with her fellow humans but with God. Hers was a way based upon mutual meeting, shared intellectuality, and collaborative work. Was she, then, not a contemplative? That is, was she a Martha rather than a Mary (in all the complex meaning of that name)? P.D. James (1981), in her somewhat subversive introduction to Brabazon's biography of Sayers, points to "the unifying theme in all her work of the almost sacramental importance of man's creative activity."[5] Exactly so: Sayers herself wrote in her essay "Why Work?" (1942) that "the secular vocation is sacred."[6]

Indeed, she insisted that

> It is not right for her [the Church] to acquiesce in the notion that a man's life is divided into the time he spends on his work and the time he spends in serving God. He must be able to serve God *in* his work, and the work itself must be accepted and respected as the medium of divine creation.[7]

In this she was in accord with Evelyn Underhill (1959), an Anglican scholar readily recognizable as a mystic, who wrote that "acknowledgement of the sacred character of the normal, is based on that fact—the central Christian fact—of the humble entrance of God into our common human life."[8] This profoundly incarnational viewpoint is characteristic of Anglicanism, and the life of Dorothy L. Sayers presents a model of Anglican spirituality, a life lived in accordance with the Affirmative Way, whose hallmarks are the incarnational ones of concreteness and engagement.

She exemplifies "the Anglican style of gradual growth rather than sudden conversion, love of tradition, and emphasis on codes of courtesy and ethical behavior,"[9] to the degree that C.S. Lewis scholar Doris T. Myers (1984) recommends her novels and essays as guides to the "Anglican attitude."[10] Because Anglican spirituality usually takes place in the context of a fully lived life rather than in the crisis of conversion, Sayers has been misunderstood, all her writings to the contrary, perhaps because of a single letter, in which she said, "I am quite without the thing known as 'inner light' or 'spiritual experience.' I have never undergone conversion."[11] She continued, "But since I cannot come at God through intuition, or through my emotions, [...] there is only the intellect left [...] It is the only point at which ecstasy can enter."[12] On the basis of this confession, she has been seen to be characterizing herself as she did Salome and Mary Cleophas, whom she described on their way to the tomb of Christ in the final play of *The Man Born to Be King:* "These two are typical of a rather matter-of-fact, exterior kind of faith, without intimate religious experience," she wrote, "the sort that reads its Bible and gets on with its work, and yet is, just occasionally, 'visited'" (MK 321).

This combination of "getting on with its work," and yet being "visited" does describe the Anglican life, and certainly describes Sayers. It may also help to explain why, despite her declaration of the sacrality of secular work, she reluctantly agreed to write specifically upon, and in terms of, Christianity, first in a series of plays, and additionally in various essays. Four years after her death, Bishop W.C. Wand (1961) wrote that the "comprehensiveness" of Anglicanism, which prevents its faith from forming a "strait-jacket of spiritual and intellectual authority,"[13] makes it "a field for the amateur, rather than a bastion for the professional theologian."[14] Clearly conscious of her amateur role, Sayers wrote that "The position of people like Eliot and Lewis and me is rather more complicated than people quite realise."[15] In undertaking to write specifically as an amateur, she felt, as she put it forcefully, "a violent inner reluctance and a strong sense of guilt."[16] Her reluctance arose from her recognition that she was not a professional theologian, but once having been asked, she put her hand to the plough and carried out the work of the Christian apologist with all her skills, not only setting forth the faith, but writing in the prophetic voice. She did this despite her sense of having failed to live in accordance with Christian propriety, when as a young woman she engaged in a series of unhappy love affairs and gave birth to a child outside of wedlock. It was of this rocky life-road with its painful, humiliating, and costly experiences that she wrote, "of all the presuppositions of Christianity, the only one I really have and can swear to from personal inward conviction is sin."[17]

What, then, of the "ecstasy", which for Sayers could only enter through the intellect? Reynolds has documented, in *The Passionate Intellect* (1989), Sayers's encounter with Dante, and her richly interpreted, strongly felt translation of *The Divine Comedy*.[18] I experienced (in my way and at my own level) a similar encounter, when, as an Anglican confirmand at the age of twenty-four, the first book pressed into my hand was not the Bible or the Book of Common Prayer, but Sayers's little book of essays, *Creed or Chaos,* where she proclaims that Christ "was not merely a man so good as to be 'like God'—He *was* God."[19] The Creeds, which are recited in connection with nearly every service in the Prayer Book, form for the Anglican a kind of intellectual music, sonorously repeated day by day, week by week, and year by year. They form, too, the heart and soul of Sayers's spirituality: she meant what she said when she wrote that "The Christian faith is the most exciting drama that ever staggered the imagination of man—and the dogma *is* the drama."[20]

But for many readers, myself included, her spirituality breathes just as deeply from her secular writings, most especially her twelve detective novels, which she wrote as a job, in order to support herself, her son, and her husband. C.S. Lewis (1959) said that "real honest-to-God work, so far as the arts are concerned, now appears chiefly in low-brow art; in the film, the detective story, the children's story. These are often sound structures; seasoned wood, accurately dovetailed, the stresses all calculated; skill and labour successfully used to do what is intended."[21] In just this workmanlike way, her novels depict the reality of sin, concrete and cruel; they also depict a stable world where values are expressed in the actions of people, both ordinary and extraordinary. There is a robust appreciation of life's pleasures and responsibilities. This is how she lived, following her friendships, her motherhood, her marriage, and her intellectual endeavors to their utmost conclusions.

Her most important spiritual teaching, perhaps, is her understanding that friendship forms a model for the relationship of the soul to God. A decade before her death she wrote that "God wants to call us His friends [...] we are privileged to stand with Him on terms of mutuality and exchange."[22] John 15.14-15 clearly forms the fiery kernel of her spirituality: both Mary and Martha were, after all, personal friends of Jesus, and the Cat o' Mary can teach us to be His friends too.

Notes
[1] Fr. Philip Sheldrake S.J., quoted in "Religious Life—A Common Language?" St. Paul's Printer (Summer 1993) 4.
[2] James Brabazon, *Dorothy L. Sayers, The Life of a Courageous Woman* (London: Victor Gollancz, 1981) 15.
[3] Barbara Reynolds, *Dorothy L. Sayers: Her Life and Soul* (London: Hodder and Stoughton, 1993) 368.
[4] Reynolds 369-70.
[5] P.D. James, Foreword to James Brabazon's *Dorothy L. Sayers, The Life of a Courageous Woman* (London: Victor Gollancz, 1981) xvi.
[6] Dorothy L. Sayers, *Creed or Chaos* (London: Methuen, 1947) 59.
[7] Sayers, *Creed or Chaos* 58.
[8] Evelyn Underhill, *Concerning the Inner Life with The House of the Soul* (London: Methuen, 1959) 90-91.
[9] Doris T. Myers, "The Compleat Anglican: Spiritual Style in The Chronicles of Narnia," *Anglican Theological Review* 66.2 (April 1984): 158.
[10] Myers 159 note 4.
[11] Brabazon 262,
[12] Brabazon 263.
[13] The Rt. Rev. W.C. Wand, *Anglicanism in History and Today* (London: Weidenfeld and Nicholson, 1961) 48.
[14] Wand 47.
[15] Brabazon 262.
[16] Brabazon 262.

Notes

[17] Brabazon 263.

[18] Barbara Reynolds, *The Passionate Intellect: Dorothy L. Sayers' Encounter with Dante* (Eugene, OR: Wipf and Stock Publishers, 1989).

[19] Sayers, *Creed or Chaos* 2.

[20] Sayers, *Creed or Chaos* 1.

[21] C.S. Lewis, "Good Work and Good Works" (1959), *The World's Last Night* (New York: Harcourt, Brace, and Co., 1960) 80.

[22] Reynolds, *Dorothy L. Sayers: Her Life and Soul* 369.

13. Why We Honor the Centenary of Dorothy L. Sayers (1893–1957)

The theme of the comic is the integration of society.

——Northrop Frye, *Anatomy of Criticism*

Patterson reviews the relevance of Sayers to Mythlore, *which is dedicated to the Inklings, particularly C.S. Lewis, J.R.R. Tolkien, and Charles Williams. She notes the parallels between Sayers's work and that of these authors, some of their correspondence, and their observations about each other in their publications.*

"Why We Honor the Centenary of Dorothy L. Sayers (1893–1957)" was first published in Mythlore *19.3 (Summer 1993): 4-5.*

When Dorothy L. Sayers died in 1957, C.S. Lewis wrote a vivid and affectionate panegyric to be delivered at a memorial service held at the Athaeneum Club. The Very Reverend George Bell, Bishop of Chichester, read it aloud to her mourners, and Lewis gave a copy to her son, Anthony Fleming. He in turn eventually gave it to Walter Hooper, who published it (and deserves much thanks for doing so) in C.S. Lewis's *Of This and Other Worlds* (1982). People who wonder why Sayers's centenary is being honored by *Mythlore* are urged to read Lewis's pungent and entrancing tribute, which makes clear her relationship to the sphere of literature occupied by Lewis himself, as well as Charles Williams and J.R.R. Tolkien. Those coming late to this triumvirate, or lacking access to a good library, can read on, as I endeavor to explain the matter. Those who can think of still more reasons are invited to send letters to *Mythlore*, thus keeping Glen Good-Knight happy because its Letters column will be well filled for years to come.

Mythlore is devoted, not to all Inklings, but to three of them in particular, and in general to other writers who influenced the three or were influenced by them. In his pioneering work on Lewis, *C.S. Lewis: Apostle to the Skeptics* (1949), Chad Walsh (1949) spoke of "a few of the writers who have left the greatest imprint on Lewis,"[1] and puts George MacDonald at the head of the list, followed immediately by

Charles Williams, who was, he says, "avidly read and ardently admired by a small circle of Christian intellectuals, including T.S. Eliot and Dorothy Sayers."[2] He adds a few other names, but of all these, only Charles Williams was an Inkling. Again, stating that Lewis's literary appeal may "simply be variety," he calls Lewis "well nigh unique among modern religious writers," and adds, "I can think of only three rivals: G.K. Chesterton, Charles Williams, and Dorothy Sayers."[3]

Sayers's works closely parallel those of Lewis without in the least degree imitating them: she and he both wrote works in a popular genre: his were science fiction and hers were detective novels. She and he both wrote poetry, each of them first appearing in print with slim volumes of poetry in 1916 (Sayers) and 1919 (Lewis) respectively. Both were pressed into writing apologetics, and produced vigorous defenses and explications of Christianity, expressing themselves as members of the one, holy, catholic, and apostolic church, who happened to be Anglicans. Both wrote significant works of scholarship regarding major works of medieval literature. Readers of *Mythlore* will note that so far, the same could be said for J.R.R. Tolkien (with the exception of apologetics), though I think his essay "On Fairy-Stories" (to which I shall return) contains the single most perfect defense of Christian thought in the twentieth century: see below.

In adding the name of Charles Williams we can increase this list of parallels. Williams and Sayers (along with T.S. Eliot) wrote significant Christian plays. These, in particular, qualify Sayers most obviously, as a mythopoeic writer. The characters in her plays, as in Lewis's novels, include angels; and as in Williams's novels, they include both the living and the dead. And, since the definition of the category in Colin Manlove's indispensable study, *Christian Fantasy from 1200 to the Present* (1992), Sayers would qualify by the fact of her bravura translation of Dante's *Divine Comedy*. Her translation, in the Penguin edition, which for about thirty years was surely the most widely read version of the *Commedia* in history, Lewis (1966) found to be full of "audacities in both language and rhythm."[4] As for her radio play cycle, *The Man Born to Be King* (1941–1942), Lewis wrote, "I have re-read it in every Holy Week since it first appeared, and never re-read it without being deeply moved."[5] The two of them exchanged letters regularly. Some of these appear in *Letters of C.S.*

Lewis (1966). In a letter of the 10th of December, 1945, he told Sayers "you are one of the great English letter writers."[6] It was to her (probably because she was a fellow apologist and would understand), on the 2nd of August, 1946, that he wrote his famous admission that "a doctrine never seems dimmer to me than when I have just successfully defended it."[7] And, in 1956, he wrote to her about his marriage to Joy Davidman, at a time when he expected her to die immediately. In fact, Joy Lewis lived long enough to ask Sayers in person if it were true that she hated to hear her detective works mentioned, and "was relieved to hear her deny it."[8] Indeed, in his panegyric, Lewis explains very accurately and perceptively the process of development in the character of Lord Peter Wimsey, through his relationship with Harriet Vane. He quotes "a better critic" (than those who thought Sayers was "falling in love with her hero") on the matter. This critic, who may have been his wife, says "It would be truer to say she was falling out of love with him; and ceased fondling a girl's dream—if she has ever done so—and begun inventing a man."[9] Lewis had a circle of intellectual friends outside of the Inklings; this included most especially his wife, but it obviously included Dorothy L. Sayers.

As for Charles Williams, Sayers addressed her translations of *The Divine Comedy* "To the Dead Master of the Affirmations, Charles Williams."[10] Lewis says that in her essay in the volume he edited, *Essays Presented to Charles Williams* (1947), "...'And Telling You a Story': A Note on The Divine Comedy," you get the first impact of Dante on a mature, a scholarly, and an extremely independent mind."[11] In this breath-taking essay, which as Lewis says, gives her whole method in approaching Dante, she says, "While I still knew Dante chiefly by his repute, *The Figure of Beatrice* [by Charles Williams] was published [in 1943], and I read it—not because it was about Dante, but because it was by Charles Williams. It became immediately evident that here was an Image, and here an Image-maker, with whom one had to reckon."[12] Here Sayers is writing precisely in terms of Williams's own theological language—the "Affirmations" of which she deemed him the "Master" were those of which he speaks in his often used phrase, "The Affirmation of Images," and he follows this affirmation in his own spirituality, keeping it in balance with the more widely documented Via Negativa (Way of Negation) of the best-known Christian mystics. This affirmative way, Sayers saw and celebrated in Williams and Dante alike. It is the Way she followed in her own spirituality, which has been, I think, much misunderstood.

She and Williams engaged in a lively exchange of letters; since neither hers nor Williams's letters have been published in collections (more's the pity), one turns to James Brabazon's fine biography, *Dorothy L. Sayers: A Biography* (1981) for a few snippets of the letters she wrote to Williams about Dante. These "range over every kind of topic, whether the historical background of the poem, its theology, its style, its humanity, or the character and personality of Dante himself."[13] Most potently, in regard to the last, is the letter she wrote on Dante's "bedworthiness." This means exactly what you think. Dante, "she adjudged, from the evidence of his poetry, to have been a passionate and satisfying lover."[14] Look it up in the source I have cited, (recently republished in paperback), if you think that Christian writers cannot celebrate human sexuality.

It is impossible in this brief format to explore further the deep debt of mutual exchange among Sayers and the two Inklings who enjoyed her friendship. One must remember that while she was never part of that entirely male group, the Inklings, she had herself a close circle of female friends (they called themselves the Mutual Admiration Society) with whom she enjoyed a rewarding intellectual relationship over the whole of her adult life. But *Mythlore*, a journal that focuses upon C.S. Lewis, Charles Williams, and J.R.R. Tolkien, must take account of this major contemporary of theirs.

The mention of Tolkien leads me to my final point in considering the mythopoeic bona fides of Sayers as a writer of mystery novels. The mystery is quintessentially a comedy, as defined by Northrop Frye. In discussing "Comic Fictional Modes" (which include *The Divine Comedy*), Frye says "in some religious poetry, for example at the end of the *Paradiso*, we can see that literature has an upper limit, a point at which an imaginative vision of an eternal world becomes an experience of it."[15] For Frye, "the theme of the comic is the integration of society."[16] He explains that the detective story is a form of comedy, in a sequence that passes through melodrama to myth, and finally to science fiction, "a mode of romance with a strong inherent tendency to myth."[17] All the genres along this continuum are in their degree forms of mythopoeic fantasy whose realistic and ironic garb conceal a romantic core. And what, most especially in detective fiction, is that core? In the detective novel, a wrongful death or other extreme crime disrupts Frye's "integration of society," and at the moment when the killer (disrupter) is identified, that integration begins to be restored. There is always, in a true detective novel, a happy ending, as Tolkien says there must be in the true fairy tale.

In "On Fairy-Stories" J.R.R. Tolkien (1964), speaks of "the consolation of the Happy Ending."[18] Of this, he says, "I will call it Eucatastrophe." He continues, "It does not deny the existence of dyscatastrophe, of sorrow and failure: [...] it denies (in the face of much evidence, if you will) universal final defeat, and in so far is *evangelium*, giving a fleeting glimpse of Joy, Joy beyond the wall of the world, poignant as grief."[19] The structuring of her art in terms of the "pre-eminently [...] high and joyous"[20] Christian story of the Birth of Christ ("the Eucatastrophe of Man's history") and the Resurrection ("the Eucatastrophe of the story of the Incarnation,") which is present in every one of Sayers's detective novels, surely entitles her to be placed upon the shelf reserved for masterpieces (after their kind) of mythopoeic fiction.

As C.S. Lewis said, "For all she did and was, for delight and instruction, for her militant loyalty as a friend, for courage and honesty [...]—let us thank the Author who invented her."[21] This present issue of *Mythlore* is dedicated to Dorothy L. Sayers's Centenary in order to do just that.

Notes
[1] Chad Walsh, *C.S. Lewis: Apostle to the Skeptics* (New York: Macmillian, 1949) 134.
[2] Walsh 136.
[3] Walsh 156.
[4] C.S. Lewis, "A Panegyric for Dorothy L. Sayers," *Of This and Other Worlds*, ed. Walter Hooper (London: Collins Fount Paperbacks, 1982) 124.
[5] C.S. Lewis, "A Panegyric for Dorothy L. Sayers" 125.
[6] *Letters of C.S. Lewis,* ed. with a memoir by W.H. Lewis (London: Collins Fount Paperbacks, 1966) 208.
[7] *Letters of C.S. Lewis* 209.
[8] C.S. Lewis, "A Panegyric for Dorothy L. Sayers" 122.

Notes

[9] C.S. Lewis, "A Panegyric for Dorothy L. Sayers" 122-23.

[10] Dante Alighieri, *The Divine Comedy of Dante Alighieri, The Florentine,* trans. Dorothy L. Sayers *Cantica I, Hell* (Harmondsworth, UK: Penguin, 1949); and Cantica II *Purgatory* (Harmondsworth, UK: Penguin, 1955).

[11] C.S. Lewis, "A Panegyric for Dorothy L. Sayers" 125.

[12] Dorothy L. Sayers, "… 'And Telling You a Story': A Note on the Divine Comedy," *Essays Presented to Charles Williams,* ed. C.S. Lewis (1947; Grand Rapids, MI: Eerdmans, 1966) 1.

[13] James Brabazon, *Dorothy L. Sayers, A Biography* (New York: Charles Scribner's Sons, London: Charles Scribner's Sons, 1981) 231.

[14] Brabazon 112.

[15] Northrop Frye, *Anatomy of Criticism* (1957; Princeton, NJ: Princeton UP, 1971) 45.

[16] Frye 43.

[17] Frye 49.

[18] J.R.R. Tolkien, "On Fairy-Stories," *Tree and Leaf* (London: George Allen and Unwin, 1964) 60.

[19] Tolkien, "On Fairy-Stories" 60.

[20] Tolkien, "On Fairy-Stories" 63.

[21] C.S. Lewis, "A Panegyric for Dorothy L. Sayers" 127.

Bibliography

Achen, Sven Tito. *Symbols Around Us.* New York: Van Nostrand Reinhold, 1978.

Ages, Arnold. *The Diaspora Dimension.* The Hague: Martinus Nijhoff, 1973.

Anonymous. "Rev. of *Maker and Craftsman* by Alzina Stone Dale. Grand Rapids, MI: Eerdmans, 1978." *Dorothy L. Sayers Society Bulletin* No. 22 (1979) 1.

Bachelard, Gaston. *The Poetics of Space*, trans. Maria Jolas. 1958. Boston, MA: Beacon Press, 1969.

Baring-Gould, William S. and Cecil Baring-Gould. *The Annotated Mother Goose.* New York: Bramhall House, 1962.

Basney, Lionel. "The Nine Tailors and the Complexity of Innocence." *As Her Whimsey Took Her.* Ed. Margaret P. Hannay. Kent, OH: Kent State UP, 1979. 23-35.

Beaumont, Cyril W. *The History of Harlequin.* 1926. New York: Benjamin Blom, 1967

Bell, Quentin. *Virginia Woolf.* Vol. II. London: Paladin, 1987.

Bell, Vanessa. "Notes on Bloomsbury." *The Bloomsbury Group: A Collection of Memoirs, Commentary and Criticism.* Ed. S.P. Rosenbaum. Toronto, ON: University of Toronto Press, 1975. 73-84.

Bermant, Chaim. *Troubled Eden—An Anatomy of British Jewry.* London: Vallentin, Mitchell, 1969.

Book of the British Villages. Basingstoke, Hampshire: Drive Publications, 1980.

Brabazon, James. *Dorothy L. Sayers, The Life of a Courageous Woman.* Preface by Anthony Fleming. Foreword by P.D. James. London: Victor Gollancz, 1981. [Reviewed by Patterson in *Mythlore* 8.4 (#30) (1982): 22-23.]

—— *Dorothy L. Sayers, A Biography*. Preface by Anthony Fleming. Foreword by P.D. James. London: Victor Gollancz, 1988. [Reviewed by Patterson in *Mythlore* 16.1 (#59) (1989): 46-49.]

Braudel, Fernand. *Capitalism and the Material Life, 1400–1800*. Glasgow: Fontana, 1974.

Breen, Peter. "A Clergyman's Daughter." *Times Literary Supplement* 28 Feb. 1975: 223-24.

Browne, E. Martin. Introduction, *Religious Drama 2 Mystery and Morality Plays*. New York: Meridian Books, 1958.

Brunsdale, Mitzi. *Dorothy L. Sayers, Solving the Mystery of Wickedness*. New York: Berg, 1990. [Reviewed by Patterson in *Mythlore* 17.4 (#66) (1991): 53.]

Bulletin No. 62. Sudbury, Suffolk: The Dorothy L. Sayers Historical and Literary Society, 1985.

Burnett, Frances Hodgson. *A Little Princess* (1905). Gutenberg Ebook #146.

Cawley, A.C., ed. *Everyman and Medieval Miracle Plays*. London: J.M. Dent and Sons Ltd., 1956.

Chesterton, G.K. *Autobiography*. London: Hutchison and Co., 1937.

—— "The Flying Stars." *The Innocence of Father Brown*. 1911. Harmondsworth, UK: Penguin Books, 1950. 55-66.

Christie, Agatha. "The Affair at the Victory Ball." *Poirot's Early Cases*. London: Collins, 1974. 9-24.

—— *An Autobiography*. 1977. New York: HarperCollins, 2011.

Christopher, Joe. "An Inklings Bibliography." *Mythlore* 9.3 (Autumn 1981): 43-44.

—— *A Private Celebration of Dorothy L. Sayers' Centenary*. Stephenville, TX: The Carrollian Press, 1993. [Reviewed by Patterson in *Mythlore* 20.2 (#76) (1994): 40-41.]

—— Rev. of *Dorothy L. Sayers: A Pilgrim Soul*. Atlanta, GA: John Knox Press, 1980. *Mythlore* 8.4 (Winter 1982): 46-47.

—— "Works in Progress on Dorothy L. Sayers." *The Sayers Review* 2.1 (May 1978): 22-33.

Cirlot, J.E. *A Dictionary of Symbols.* New York: Philosophical Library, 1962.

Clarke, Stephan P. *The Lord Peter Wimsey Companion.* New York: The Mysterious Press, 1985. [Reviewed by Patterson in *Mythlore* 13.1 (#47) (1987): 47-48.]

Clark, S.L. "Harriet Vane Goes to Oxford: Gaudy Night and the Academic Woman." *The Sayers Review* 2.3 (August 1978): 22-44.

Coomes, David. *Dorothy L. Sayers: A Careless Rage for Life.* Oxford: Lion Publishing, 1992. [Reviewed by Patterson in *Mythlore* 19.2 (#72) (1993): 37-38.]

Dale, Alzina Stone. "Fossils in Cloud-Cuckoo-Land." *The Sayers Review* 3.2 (December 1978): 1-13.

—— *Maker and Craftsman: the Story of Dorothy L. Sayers.* Grand Rapids, MI: William B. Eerdman's, 1978. Revised ed. Wheaton IL: Harold Shaw Publishers, 1992. [Reviewed by Patterson in *Mythlore* 6.3 (#21) (1979): 16-17.]

Dale, Alzina Stone, *ed. Dorothy L. Sayers: The Centenary Celebration.* New York: Walker and Co., 1993. [Reviewed by Patterson in *Mythlore* 20.1 (#75) (1994): 57-58.]

—— ed. and Introduction. *Love All* [by Dorothy L. Sayers] *and Busman's Honeymoon* [by Dorothy L. Sayers and Muriel St. Clare Byrne.] Kent, OH: Kent State UP, 1984. [Reviewed by Patterson in *Mythlore* 11.3 (#41) (1985): 39-40.]

Dante Alighieri. *The Divine Comedy of Dante Alighieri, The Florentine, Cantica I, Hell.* Trans. Dorothy L. Sayers. Harmondsworth, UK: Penguin, 1949.

—— *The Comedy of Dante Alighieri, The Florentine, Cantica II Purgatory.* Trans. Dorothy L. Sayers. Harmondsworth, UK: Penguin, 1955.

—— *The Divine Comedy of Dante Alighieri, The Florentine, Cantica III Paradise.* Trans. Dorothy L. Sayers and Barbara Reynolds. Harmondsworth, UK: Penguin, 1962.

Davidson, Gustav. *A Dictionary of Angels.* New York: The Free Press, 1967.

DeSalvo, Louise. *Virginia Woolf: The Impact of Childhood Sexual Abuse on Her Life and Work*. New York: Fodor's Travel Publications, 1992.

Durkin, Mary Brian. *Dorothy L. Sayers*. Boston, MA: Twayne Publishers, 1980. [Reviewed by Patterson in *Mythlore* 8.3 (#29) (1981): 31-32.]

Eliot, T.S. *Murder in the Cathedral*. 1935. New York: Harvest Book, Harcourt Brace & Co, 1963.

Fleming, Anthony. Preface to *Dorothy L. Sayers, A Biography* by James Brabazon. Foreword by P.D. James. London: Victor Gollancz, 1988. xi-xii.

Fodor's London. New York: Fodor's Travel Publications, 1992.

Frye, Northrop. *Anatomy of Criticism*. 1957. Princeton, NJ: Princeton UP, 1971.

Gaillard, Dawson. *Dorothy L. Sayers*. New York: Frederick Ungar, 1981. [Reviewed by Patterson in *Mythlore* 9.4 (#34) (1983): 43-44.]

Gardiner, Stephen. *Evolution of the House*. Frogmore, St. Albans: Paladin, 1976.

Gardner, A. H. *Outline of English Architecture*. Third edition. London: B.T. Basford, 1948.

Garner, Alan. *The Guizer: A Book of Fools*. London: Hamish Hamilton, 1975.

Gartner, Lloyd P. *The Jewish Immigrant in England, 1870–1914*. London: George Allen and Unwin, 1960.

Graves, Robert. *Greek Myths*. 1955. Combined edition. London: Penguin, 1992.

Halifax, Joan. *Shaman: The Wounded Healer*. London: Thames and Hudson, 1981.

Hall, Trevor H. "Atherton Fleming: A Literary Puzzle." *Dorothy L. Sayers: Nine Literary Studies*. London: Duckworth, 1980. 40-61.

—— "Dorothy L. Sayers and Psychical Research." *Dorothy L. Sayers: Nine Literary Studies*. London: Duckworth, 1980. 114-23.

—— *Dorothy L. Sayers: Nine Literary Studies*. London: Duckworth, 1980. [Reviewed by Patterson in *Mythlore* 8.2 (#28) (1981): 17.]

Hannay, Margaret P. "Harriet's Influence on the Characterization of Lord Peter Wimsey." *As Her Whimsey Took Her*. Ed. Margaret P. Hannay. Kent, OH: Kent State UP, 1979. 36-50.

Hannay, Margaret P., ed. *As Her Whimsey Took Her*. Kent, OH: Kent State UP, 1979. [Reviewed by Patterson in *Mythlore* 6.4 (#22) (1979): 25.]

Hartley, Dorothy. *Lost Country Life*. New York: Pantheon Books, 1979.

Hitchman, Janet. Introduction. *Striding Folly* by Dorothy L. Sayers. London: New English Library, 1972. 9-31.

—— *Such a Strange Lady, A Biography of Dorothy L. Sayers (1893–1957)*. London: New English Library, 1975. [Reviewed by Patterson in *Mythprint* 12.5 (November 1975): 4.]

Hollis, Christopher. *The Mind of Chesterton*. London: Hollis and Carter, 1970.

Homer. *The Odyssey*. Trans. W.H.D. Rouse. 1937. New York: New American Library, 1960.

Hone, Ralph E. *Dorothy L. Sayers, A Literary Biography*. Kent, OH: Kent State UP, 1979. [Reviewed by Patterson in *Mythlore* 6.4 (#22) (1979): 26-27.]

Hone, Ralph E., ed. *Poetry of Dorothy L. Sayers* by Dorothy L. Sayers. Cambridge, England: The Dorothy L. Sayers Society in association with The Marion E. Wade Center, 1996. [Reviewed by Patterson in *Mythlore* 22.1 (#83) (1997): 63-64.]

James, P.D. Foreword. *Dorothy L. Sayers, The Life of a Courageous Woman* by James Brabazon. Preface by Anthony Fleming. London: Victor Gollancz, 1981. xiii-xvi.

Julian of Norwich, *Showings*. Trans. Edmund Colledge O.S.A. and James Walsh, S.J. New York Paulist Press, 1978.

—— Julian of Norwich, *A Book of Showings to the Anchoress of Norwich Part Two*. Eds. Edmund Colledge and James Walsh. Toronto, ON: Pontifical Institute of Mediaeval Studies, 1978.

Jung, C.G. *Aion: Researches into the Phenomenology of the Self.* 1959. Second edition. Princeton, NJ: Princeton UP, 1969.

—— "On the Psychology of the Trickster Figure." In Paul Radin's *The Trickster.* New York: Schocken Books, 1972. 195-211.

—— "The Philosophical Tree," *Alchemical Studies.* Princeton, NJ: Princeton UP, 1967.

—— *Symbols of Transformation.* 1956. Princeton, NJ: Princeton UP, 1967.

Kenney, Catherine. *The Remarkable Case of Dorothy L Sayers.* Kent, OH: Kent State UP, 1990.

Kereny, Karl. "The Trickster in Relation to Greek Mythology." In Paul Radin's *The Trickster.* New York: Schocken Books, 1972. 173-191.

Lee, Geoffrey Alan. *Lord Peter Rings the Changes: A Study of Change Ringing in The Nine Tailors.* Hurstpierpoint, West Sussex: The Dorothy L. Sayers Historical and Literary Society, 1987.

—— Rev. of *The Life of a Courageous Woman* by James Brabazon. London: Victor Gollancz, 1981. *The Dorothy L. Sayers Society Bulletin,* No. 34 (1981) no page nos.

—— "Time and Dorothy L. Sayers," *The Chronology of Lord Peter Wimsey.* Witham: The Dorothy L. Sayers Historical and Literary Society, 1983. 1-14.

Leonardi, Susan J. *Dangerous by Degrees: Women at Oxford and the Somerville Novelists.* New Brunswick and London: Rutgers UP, 1989. [Reviewed by Patterson in *Mythlore* 17.2 (1990): 55.]

Lewis, C.S. "Answers to Questions on Christianity." 1944. *God in the Dock: Essays on Theology and Ethics.* Ed. Walter Hooper. Eerdmans, 1970. 48-62.

—— "A Panagyric for Dorothy L. Sayers." *Of This and Other Worlds.* Ed. Walter Hooper. 1966. London: Collins Fount Paperback Books, 1982. 122-27.

—— *Essays Presented to Charles Williams.* 1947. Grand Rapids, MI: Eerdmans, 1966.

—— "Good Work and Good Works" (1959). *The World's Last Night.* New York: Harcourt, Brace, and Co., 1960. 71- 81.

—— *Letters of C.S. Lewis.* Ed. with a Memoir by W.H. Lewis. London: Collins Fount Paperbacks, 1966.

—— *Mere Christianity.* New York: Harper Collins, 2000.

—— "Must Our Image of God Go?" 1944. *God in the Dock: Essays on Theology and Ethics.* Ed. Walter Hooper. Eerdmans, 1970. 184-85.

—— *Reflections on the Psalms.* London: Geoffrey Bles, 1958.

—— *Surprised by Joy: The Shape of My Early Life.* 1955. New York: Harcourt, Brace Jovanovich, 1966.

—— *The Voyage of the Dawn Treader.* 1952. Collector's Edition with Illustrations by Pauline Baynes. New York: Harper Collins, 2010.

Loades, Ann, ed. *Dorothy L. Sayers, Spiritual Writings.* London: Society for Promoting Christian Knowledge [SPCK], 1993. [Reviewed by Patterson in *Mythlore* 20.1 (#75) (1994): 56-57.]

Macoy, Robert. *A Dictionary of Freemasonry.* 1869. Brattleboro, VT: Echo Point Books & Media, 1989.

Madden, David. *Harlequin's Stick—Charlie's Cane: A Comparative Study of Commedia Dell'arte and Silent Slapstick Comedy.* Bowling Green, OH: Popular Press, 1975.

Malefijt, Annemarie de Waal. "Homo monstrosus." *Scientific American* 219.4 (October 1968): 113-118.

Manlove, Colin. *Christian Fantasy from 1200 to the Present.* Notre Dame, IN: Notre Dame UP, 1992.

Marc, Olivier. *Psychology of the House.* Trans. Jessie Wood. London: Thames and Hudson, 1977.

Mayer III, David. *Harlequin in His Element: The English Pantomime 1806–1836.* Cambridge, MA: Harvard UP, 1969.

McCrumb, Sharyn. "Where the Bodies are Buried: the Real Murder Case in the Crime Novels of Dorothy L Sayers." *Dorothy L Sayers: The Centenary Celebration.* Ed. Alzina Stone Dale New York: Walker and Company, 1993. 87-98.

McMenomy, Christie. Rev. of *Maker and Craftsman: The Story of Dorothy L. Sayers* by Alzina Stone Dale. Grand Rapids, MI: William B. Eeerdmans, 1978. *The Sayers Review* 4.1 (September 1980): 26-27.

—— Rev. of *Dorothy L. Sayers: A Literary Biography* by Ralph E. Hone. Kent, OH: Kent State UP, 1979. *The Sayers Review* 4.2 (January 1981): 12-13.

Milton, John. *Paradise Lost*. Ed. Merrit Y. Hughes. 1935. Indianapolis, IN: The Odyssey Press, 1962.

Myers, Doris T. "The Compleat Anglican: Spiritual Style in The Chronicles of Narnia," *Anglican Theological Review* 66.2 (April 1984): 148-60.

Naylor, Gillian, ed. *Bloomsbury: Its Artists, Authors, and Designers*. Boston, MA: Little, Brown and Co., 1990.

Newall, Venetia. *An Egg at Easter: A Folklore Study*. London: Routledge and Kegan Paul, 1971.

Nicholson, Nigel. "Bloomsbury: the Myth and the Reality." *Virginia Woolf and Bloomsbury*. Ed. Jane Marcus. Bloomington, IN: Indiana UP, 1987. 7-22.

Niklaus, Thelma. *Harlequin Phoenix*. London: The Bodley Head, 1956.

Oreglia, Giacomo. *The Commedia dell' Arte*. 1961. London: Methuen, 1968.

Panek, Leroy Lad. Watteau's Shepherds: The Detective Novel in Britain 1914–1940. Bowling Green, OH: Bowling Green University Popular Press, 1979. [Reviewed by Patterson in *Mythlore* 9.4 (#34) (1983): 43-44.]

Patterson, Nancy-Lou. [Including her major *Mythlore* papers and other major papers that specifically address the work of the Inklings and Inklings-related authors, as well as some minor papers identified in her citations. These papers are included in this multi-volume anthology of Patterson's Inklings and Inklings-related work.]

—— "'A Bloomsbury Blue-Stocking': Dorothy L. Sayers' Bloomsbury Years in Their Spatial and Temporal Context." *Mythlore* 19.3 (1993): 6-15.

—— "'A Comedy of Masks': Lord Peter as Harlequin in *Murder Must Advertise.*" *Mythlore* 15.3 (1989): 22-28.

—— "'All Nerves and Nose': Lord Peter Wimsey as Wounded Healer in the Novels of Dorothy L. Sayers." *Mythlore* 14.4 (1988): 13-16.

—— "'Always Winter and Never Christmas': Symbols of Time in Lewis's Chronicles of Narnia." *Mythlore* 18.1 (Autumn 1991): 10-14. [See *Ransoming the Waste Land Volume II.*]

—— "An Appreciation of Pauline Baynes." *Mythlore* (Autumn 1980): 3-5.

—— "Angel and Psychopomp in Madeleine L'Engle's 'Wind' Trilogy." *Children's Literature in Education* 14.1 (1983): 195-203.

—— "Anti-Babels: Images of the Divine Centre in *That Hideous Strength.*" *Mythcon II, Francisco Torres, Santa Barbara, CA, 1971.* Ed. Glen Good Knight. Los Angeles: The Mythopoeic Society, 1971. 6-11. [See *Ransoming the Waste Land Volume I.*]

—— "Archetypes of the Mother in the Fantasies of George MacDonald." *Mythcon I, Harvey Mudd College, Claremont, Ca., 1970.* Glen GoodKnight. Los Angeles: The Mythopoeic Society, 1970. 14-20.

—— "'A Ring of Good Bells': Providence and Judgement in Dorothy L. Sayers' *The Nine Tailors.*" *Mythlore* 16.1 (1989): 50-52.

—— "Art in the English Classroom: An Interdisciplinary Approach." *English Quarterly* 6.4 (Winter 1973): 345-49.

—— "Artist's Statement about the Cover: The Merry Party." *The Lamp-Post of the Southern California C.S. Lewis Society* 19.4 (Winter 1995-96): 4-6.

—— "Artist's Statement on This Month's Cover." *The Lamp-Post of the Southern California C.S. Lewis Society* 8.4 (December 1994): 4.

—— "'Banquet at Belbury': Festival and Horror in *That Hideous Strength.*" *Mythlore* (Autumn, 1981): 7-14, 42. [See *Ransoming the Waste Land Volume I.*]

—— "Beneath That Ancient Roof: The House as Symbol in Dorothy L. Sayers' Busman's Honeymoon." *Mythlore* 10.3 (1984): 39-46.

—— "'The Bolt of Tash': the Figure of Satan in C.S. Lewis's *The Horse and His Boy* and *The Last Battle*." *Mythlore* 16.4 (Summer 1990): 23-26. [See *Ransoming the Waste Land Volume II*.]

—— "Bright-Eyed Beauty: Celtic Elements in Charles Williams, J.R.R. Tolkien, and C.S. Lewis." *Mythlore* 10.1 (Spring 1983): 5-10.

—— "Cat o' Mary: The Spirituality of Dorothy L. Sayers." *Studies in Sayers: Essays Presented to Dr. Barbara Reynolds on her 80th Birthday*. Dorothy L. Sayers Society, 1994. 28-32.

—— "'Changing, Fearfully Changing' [Polarization and Transformation in Dorothy L. Sayers's Strong Poison]." *University of Waterloo Courier* (Sept. 1985): 11-17.

—— "Charles Williams." *Modern British Essayists. Second Series*. Ed. and Foreword Robert Beum. Detroit, MI: Gale, 1990. 316-25.

—— "C.S. Lewis and the Dragon." *The Lamp-Post of the Southern California C.S. Lewis Society* 27.1 (Spring 2003): 21-25.

—— "Death by Landscape." *Niekas* 45 (July 1998): 22-25.

—— "'Eve's Sharp Apple': Five Transgressing Women in the Novels of Dorothy L. Sayers." *The Sayers Review* III.3 (April 1980): 1-24.

—— "'The Glorious Impossible': Mystery and Metaphor in the Fantasies of Madeleine L'Engle." Archives, University of Waterloo.

—— "The Green Lewis: Inklings of Environmentalism in the Writing of C.S. Lewis." *The Lamp-Post of the Southern California C.S. Lewis Society* 18.1 (Mar. 1994): 4-14. [See *Ransoming the Waste Land Volume II*.]

—— "Guardaci Ben: The Visionary Woman in C.S. Lewis' Chronicles of Narnia and *That Hideous Strength*." *Mythlore* in 6.3 (Summer; 1979): 6-10; and 6.4 (Autumn 1979): 20-24. [See *Ransoming the Waste Land Volume I*.]

—— "'Halfe Like a Serpent': The Green Witch in *The Silver Chair*." *Mythlore* 11.2 (Autumn 1984): 37-47. [See *Ransoming the Waste Land Volume II.*]

—— "The Holy House of Ungit." *Mythlore* 21.4 (Winter 1997): 4-15. [See *Ransoming the Waste Land Volume II.*]

—— "*Homo Monstrosus*: Lloyd Alexander's Gurgi and the Shadow Figures of Fantastic Literature." *Mythlore* 3.3 (1976) / *Tolkien Journal* (1976): 24-8.

—— "The Host of Heaven: Astrological and Other Images of Divinity in the Fantasies of C.S. Lewis. Part I. The Fields of Arbol." *Mythlore* 7.3 (Autumn 1980): 19-29. "Part II." *Mythlore* 7.4 (Winter 1981): 13-21. [See *Ransoming the Waste Land Volume I.*]

—— "Images of Judaism and Anti-Semitism in the Novels of Dorothy L. Sayers." *The Sayers Review* II.2 (June 1978): 17-24.

—— "The 'Jasper-Lucent Landscapes' of C.S. Lewis." *The Lamp-Post of the Southern California C.S. Lewis Society.* Part I. 22.1 (1999): 6-24. "Part II." 23.2 (1999): 16-32. Part III 23.4 (1999): 7-16. [See *Ransoming the Waste Land Volume II.*]

—— "The Jewels of Messias: Images of Judaism and Antisemitism in the Novels of Charles Williams." *Mythlore* 6.2 (Spring 1979): 27-31.

—— "Kore Motifs in *The Princess and the Goblin*." *For the Childlike: George MacDonald's Fantasies for Children*. Ed. Roderick McGillis. Metuchen, NJ: Scarecrow, 1992. 169-82.

—— "Letters from Hell: the Symbolism of Evil in *The Screwtape Letters*." *Mythlore* 12.1 (Autumn 1985): 47-57. [See *Ransoming the Waste Land Volume II.*]

—— "Lord of the Beasts: Animal Archetypes in C.S. Lewis." *Narnia Conference, Palms Park, West Los Angeles, 1969*. Ed. Glen GoodKnight. Los Angeles: The Mythopoeic Society, 1970. 24-32. [See *Ransoming the Waste Land Volume II.*]

—— "'Miraculous Bread … Miraculous Wine': Eucharistic Motifs in the Fantasies of C.S. Lewis." *Mythlore* 22.2 (Summer 1998): 28-46. [See *Ransoming the Waste Land Volume I.*]

—— "Narnia and the North: The Symbolism of Northerness in the Fantasies of C.S. Lewis." *Mythlore* 4.2 (1976): 9-16. [See *Ransoming the Waste Land Volume II.*]

—— "On The 'Lady Alice' Quadrangle in *That Hideous Strength.*" *The Lamp-Post of the Southern California C.S. Lewis Society* 9.4 (1986): 22. [See *Ransoming the Waste Land Volume I.*]

—— "Ransoming the Wasteland: Arthurian Themes in C.S. Lewis's Interplanetary Trilogy, Part I." *The Lamp-Post of the Southern California C.S. Lewis Society* 8.2-3 (November 1984): 16-26. "Part II." 8.4 (December 1985): 3-15. [See *Ransoming the Waste Land Volume I.*]

—— "'Some Kind of Company': The Sacred Community in *That Hideous Strength.*" *Mythcon XVI, Wheaton College, Wheaton, Ill., 1985.* Ed. Diana Pavlac. The Mythopoeic Society, 1985. 247-70. Rpt. in *Mythlore* 13.1 (1986): 8-19. [See *Ransoming the Waste Land Volume I.*]

—— "Some Women in C.S. Lewis's *That Hideous Strength.*" *The Toronto Pilgrimage C.S. Lewis Society* 1.1 (Jan.1994): 1-7. [See *Ransoming the Waste Land Volume I.*]

—— "Thesis, Antithesis, Synthesis: The Interplanetary Trilogy of C.S. Lewis." *CSL: The Bulletin of the New York C.S. Lewis Society* 16.8 (June 1985): 1-6. [See *Ransoming the Waste Land Volume I.*]

—— "'This Equivocal Being': The Un-Man in C.S. Lewis's *Perelandra.*" *The Lamp-Post of the Southern California C.S. Lewis Society* 19.3 (Fall 1995): 6-24; 19.4 (Winter 1996) 7-19. [See *Ransoming the Waste Land Volume I.*]

—— "Trained Habit: The Spirituality of C.S. Lewis." *The Canadian C.S. Lewis Journal* 87 (Spring 1995): 37-53.

—— "Tree and Leaf: J.R.R. Tolkien and the Visual Image." *English Quarterly* 6.4 (Spring 1974): 10-26.

—— "The Triumph of Love: Interpretations of the Tarot in Charles Williams' *The Greater Trumps.*" *Mythcon III, Regency Hyatt House, Long Beach, Ca., 1972.* Ed. Glen GoodKnight. Los Angeles, CA: The Mythopoeic Society, 1974. 12-32.

—— "The Unfathomable Feminine Principle: Images of Wholeness in *That Hideous Strength*." *The Lamp-Post of the Southern California C.S. Lewis Society* 9.1-3 (1986): 3-38. [See *Ransoming the Waste Land Volume I.*]

—— "Why We Honor the Centenary of Dorothy L. Sayers (1893–1957)." *Mythlore* 19.3 (1993): 4-5.

Pickering Kenneth W. *Drama in the Cathedral: The Canterbury Festival Plays 1928–1948*. Worthing, West Sussex: Churchman Publishing, 1985. [Reviewed by Patterson in *Mythlore* 12.4 (1986): 41.]

Pinsent, John. *Greek Mythology*. London: Paul Hamlyn, 1967.

Reaves, R.B. "Crime and Punishment in the Detective Fiction of Dorothy L. Sayers." *As Her Whimsey Took Her*. Ed. Margaret P. Hannay. Kent, OH: Kent State UP, 1979.

Reynolds, Barbara. *Dorothy L Sayers: Her Life and Soul*. London: Hodder and Stoughton, 1993. [Reviewed by Patterson in *Mythlore* 19.4 (#74) (1993): 33-34, 45.]

—— "G.K. Chesterton and Dorothy L. Sayers." *The Chesterton Review* 10.2 (May 1984): 136-57.

—— *The Passionate Intellect: Dorothy L. Sayers' Encounter with Dante*. Kent, OH: Kent State UP, 1989.

Reynolds, Barbara, ed. *The Letters of Dorothy L. Sayers, 1899–1936: The Making of a Detective Novelist*. Preface by P.D. James. 1995. New York: St. Martin's Press, 1996. [Reviewed by Patterson in *Mythlore* 21.3 (#81) (1996): 56-57.]

—— *The Letters of Dorothy L. Sayers, Volume 2, 1937–1943: From Novelist to Playwright*. Cambridge: Carol Green Publishing [The Dorothy L. Sayers Society], 1997. [Reviewed by Patterson in *Mythlore* 22.2 (#84) (1998): 51-52.]

—— *The Letters of Dorothy L. Sayers, Volume 3: 1944–1950: A Noble Daring*. Cambridge: The Dorothy L. Sayers Society, 1998. [Reviewed by Patterson in *Mythlore* 23.1 (#87) (2000): 72–74.]

Reynolds, William. "Dorothy Sayers and the Drama of Orthodoxy." *The Sayers Review* 3.1 (October, 1978): 32-45.

Riley, Athelstan. "Ye Watchers and Ye Holy Ones" (1906). *The Mystical Theology and the Celestial Hierarchies* by Dionysus the Areapogite. Publishing information unknown.

Rose, Martial, ed. *The Wakefield Mystery Plays.* New York: WW. Norton & Co., 1961. 372-84.

Rosenbaum, S.P. ed. *The Bloomsbury Group: A Collection of Memoirs, Commentary and Criticism.* Toronto, ON: University of Toronto Press, 1975.

—— *Victorian Bloomsbury: The Early Literary History of the Bloomsbury Group.* Part I. New York: St. Martin's Press, 1987.

Sayers, Dorothy L. "The Abominable History of the Man with Copper Fingers." *Lord Peter Views the Body.* 1928. London: Victor Gollancz Ltd., 1976.

—— "… 'And Telling You a Story': A Note on the Divine Comedy." *Essays Presented to Charles Williams.* Ed. C.S. Lewis. 1947. Grand Rapids, MI: Eerdmans, 1966. 1-37.

—— "The Carpenter's Son." *Catholic Tales and Christian Songs.* Oxford: B.H. Blackwell, 1918.

—— "The Cornice of Sloth," *Further Papers on Dante: His Heirs and His Ancestors.* Volume 2. London: Methuen and Co., 1957. 119-47.

—— *Creed or Chaos.* London: Methuen, 1947.

—— "The Devil to Pay." *Four Sacred Plays.* London: Victor Gollancz, 1948. 105-212.

—— *Dorothy L. Sayers, Spiritual Writings.* Ed. Ann Loades. London: Society for Promoting Christian Knowledge [SPCK], 1993.

—— "The Faust Legend and the idea of the Devil." *Christian Letters to a Post-Christian World.* Grand Rapids, MI: William B. Eerdmans. 1969. 223-36.

—— "Gaudy Night," *Titles to Fame.* Ed. Denys Kilham Roberts. London: Thomas Nelson and Sons, 1937.

—— "The Haunted Policeman." *Lord Peter: A Collection of All the Lord Peter Wimsey Stories*. Ed. and Introduction by James Sandoe. First edition. New York: Harper Paperbacks, 1972. 408-30.

—— *The Letters of Dorothy L. Sayers, 1899–1936: The Making of a Detective Novelist*. Chosen and Edited by Barbara Reynolds. Preface by P.D. James. London: Hodder and Stoughton, 1995.

—— *The Letters of Dorothy L. Sayers, Volume 2, 1937–1943: From Novelist to Playwright*. Ed. Barbara Reynolds. Cambridge: Carol Green Publishing [The Dorothy L. Sayers Society], 1997.

—— *The Letters of Dorothy L. Sayers, Volume 3: 1944–1950: A Noble Daring*. Cambridge: The Dorothy L. Sayers Society, 1998.

—— *The Lost Tools of Learning* (1948). Available online < http://www.gbt.org/text/sayers.html>.

—— *The Man Born to be King: A Play-Cycle on the Life of our Lord and Saviour Jesus Christ*. Written for broadcasting by the BBC Dec. 1941–Oct. 1942. London: Victor Gollancz, 1943.

—— *The Mind of the Maker*. 1941. New York: HarperCollins, 1987. [Reviewed by Patterson in *Mythlore* 17.2 (#64) (1990): 53-54.]

—— *OP. I*. "Adventurers All" Series No. 9: A series of young poets unknown to fame. Oxford: B.H. Blackwell, 1916.

—— "The Other Six Deadly Sins" (1941). *Christian Letters to a Post-Christian World*. Ed. Roderick Jellema. Grand Rapids, MI: William B. Eerdmans. 1969. 138-55.

—— *Poetry of Dorothy L. Sayers* by Dorothy L. Sayers, Ed. Ralph E. Hone. Cambridge, England: The Dorothy L. Sayers Society in association with The Marion E. Wade Center, 1996.

—— "Talboys." *Striding Folly*. 1972. London: New English Library, 1973. 92-123.

—— The Whimsical Christian [18 essays]. Foreword by William Griffin. New York: MacMillan, 1978. [Reviewed by Patterson in *Mythlore* 6.3 (#21) (1979): 14-15.]

—— "The Zeal of Thy House." 1937. *Four Sacred Plays*. London: Victor Gollancz, 1948. 15-103.

Sayers, Dorothy L. and Muriel St. Clare Byrne. *Love All* [by Dorothy L. Sayers] *and Busman's Honeymoon* [by Dorothy L. Sayers and Muriel St. Clare Byrne.] Ed. and Intro. Alzina Stone Dale. Kent, OH: Kent State UP, 1984.

Sayers, Dorothy L. Trans. *The Divine Comedy of Dante Alighieri, The Florentine. Cantica I, Hell*. Harmondsworth, UK: Penguin, 1949.

—— *The Comedy of Dante Alighieri, The Florentine. Cantica II Purgatory*. Harmondsworth, UK: Penguin, 1955.

Sayers, Dorothy L. and Barbara Reynolds. Trans. *The Divine Comedy of Dante Alighieri, The Florentine. Cantica III Paradise*. Harmondsworth, UK: Penguin, 1962.

Scowcroft, Philip L. "Foreigners and Dorothy L Sayers." *Sidelights on Sayers,* 10 (1985): 7-10. Witham, Essex: The Dorothy L. Sayers Society, 1985.

—— "Sayers in Devon." *The Proceedings of the* 1992 *Seminar*. Hurstpierpoint, West Sussex: The Dorothy L. Sayers Society, 1993. 19-29.

—— "Some Bloomsbury Residents." *Sidelights on Sayers* 36 (July 1991): 4-6. Witham, Essex, England: The Dorothy L. Sayers Historical and Literary Society, 1991.

—— "Some Pickings from HAVE HIS CARCASE." Sidelights on Sayers XXX (October 1989): 17-19. Hurstpierpoint, West Sussex: The Dorothy L. Sayers Society.

—— "Wimsey's War." *Sidelights on Sayers*. 1 (July 1981): 16-21. Witham, Essex, England: The Dorothy L. Sayers Historical and Literary Society, 1981.

Sheldrake S.J., Fr. Philip. Quoted in "Religious Life—A Common Language?" St. Paul's Printer (Summer 1993) 4.

Smith, Winifred. *The Commedia dell' Arte*. 1912. New York: Benjamin Blom, 1964.

Speight, George. "The Pantomime Tradition." *The Illustrated London News* (Christmas Number, 1975): 9-13.

Stock, R.D. and Barbara Stock. "The Agents of Evil and Justice in the Novels of Dorothy L. Sayers." *As Her Whimsey Took Her*. Ed. Margaret P. Hannay. Kent, OH: Kent State UP, 1979. 14-22.

Tischler, Nancy M. *Dorothy L. Sayers. A Pilgrim Soul*. Atlanta, GA: John Knox Press, 1980. [Reviewed by Patterson in *Mythlore* 8.1 (#27) (1981): 32-33.]

Tolkien. J.R.R. "On Fairy-Stories." *Tree and Leaf*. London: George Allen and Unwin, 1964. 10-26.

Underhill, Evelyn. *Concerning the Inner Life with The House of the Soul*. London: Methuen, 1959.

Vastokas, Joan M. "Are Artifacts Texts? Lithuanian Woven Sashes as Social and Cosmic Transactions." *The Socialness of Things: Essays on the Socio-Semiotics of Things.* Ed. Stephen Harold Riggins. Berlin: Mouton de Gruyrer, 1994. 337-362.

Virgil's Aeneid. Trans. Michael Oakley. London: Everyman's Library, 1957.

Walsh, Chad. *C.S. Lewis: Apostle to the Skeptics*. New York: Macmillian Co. 1949.

Wand, The Rt. Rev. W.C. *Anglicanism in History and Today*. London: Weidenfeld and Nicholson, 1961.

Ward, Masie. *Gilbert Keith Chesterton*. New edition. Lanham, MD: Rowman & Littlefield Publishers, 2006.

Watts, Alan W. *Easter: Its Story and Meaning*. New York: Henry Scuman, 1950.

Wildhaber, Robert. "Foreword." Venetia Newall's *An Egg at Easter: A Folklore Study*. London: Routledge and Kegan Paul, 1971. xiii-xix.

Williams, Charles. "The Cross." *The Image of the City*. Ed. Anne Ridler. London: Oxford UP, 1958. 131-39.

Woolf, Virginia. "Sex Talk in Bloomsbury." *The Bloomsbury Group: A Collection of Memoirs, Commentary and Criticism*. Ed. S.P. Rosenbaum. Toronto, ON: University of Toronto Press, 1975. 22.

Wynne, Nancy Blue. *An Agatha Christie Chronology*. New York: Ace Books, 1976.

Youngberg, Ruth Tanis. *Dorothy L. Sayers: A Reference Guide*. Boston, MA: G.K. Hall and Co., 1982. [Reviewed by Patterson in *Mythlore* 10.3 (1984): 38.]

Appendix: A Supplemental List of Works By and About Dorothy L. Sayers
by Janet Brennan Croft

This list is designed to supplement the preceding bibliography, as a handy guide to further research and as a selective catalogue of works not cited by Nancy-Lou Patterson (that is, primarily but not exclusively published after 1994).

Bibliographies, reference works, and archives:

There are two major bibliographies of the works of Dorothy L. Sayers, both sadly out of date but complete through the late 1970s. The list maintained on the Dorothy L. Sayers Society website is incomplete, but does include audio and video adaptations of her work.

Gilbert, Colleen B. *A Bibliography of the Works of Dorothy L. Sayers*. Macmillan, 1979.

Harmon, Robert Bartlett, and Margaret A. Burger. *An Annotated Guide to the Works of Dorothy L. Sayers*. Garland Reference Library of the Humanities, 1977.

"Works of Dorothy L. Sayers." The Dorothy L. Sayers Society. https://www.sayers.org.uk/bibliography.html

A more recent bibliography lists all of Sayers's short stories:

Christopher, Joe R. "A Checklist of Dorothy L. Sayers's Short Mystery Fiction." *The Travelling Rug*, by Dorothy L. Sayers, Mythopoeic Press, 2005, pp. 59–78.

There are three main archives of Sayers material:

The Dorothy L. Sayers Society: https://www.sayers.org.uk/society.html, includes Society archives and publications

The Wade Center at Wheaton College: http://www.wheaton.edu/wadecenter/Authors/Dorothy-L-Sayers

The Dorothy L. Sayers Centre, Witham Library, Witham, England: http://www.witham.gov.uk/site/visit-witham/dorothy-sayers/

And a reference work on the Wimsey series (Patterson cites an earlier edition):

Clarke, Stephan P. *The Lord Peter Wimsey Companion*. 2nd ed. Dorothy L. Sayers Society, 2002. (Also available online, updated, for Society members.)

Works by Dorothy L. Sayers:
The Lord Peter Wimsey Series

Whose Body? 1923.

Clouds of Witness. 1926.

Unnatural Death. 1927.

The Unpleasantness at the Bellona Club. 1928.

Strong Poison. 1930.

The Five Red Herrings. 1931.

Have His Carcase. 1932.

Murder Must Advertise. 1933.

The Nine Tailors. 1934.

Gaudy Night. 1935.

Busman's Honeymoon; a Love Story with Detective Interruptions. 1937.

Lord Peter: A Collection of All the Lord Peter Wimsey Stories (Includes *Lord Peter Views the Body* and the Wimsey stories from *Hangman's Holiday* and *In the Teeth of the Evidence*). 1972.

Other Wimsey material

Papers Relating to the Family of Wimsey. 1936.

An Account of Lord Mortimer Wimsey, the Hermit of the Wash. 1937.

"The Wimsey Papers" in *The Spectator* [London], 1939-1940.

The Wimsey Family: A Fragmentary History Compiled from Correspondence with Dorothy L. Sayers. With C. Wilfrid Scott-Giles. 1977.

As continued by Jill Paton Walsh

Thrones, Dominations. 1998.

A Presumption of Death. 2002.

The Attenbury Emeralds. 2010.

The Late Scholar. 2014.

Other Mystery Writing

Introductions to various mystery anthologies, 1928-1935.

Hangman's Holiday (short stories, some Wimsey). 1933.

The Documents in the Case. With Eustace Robert. 1930.

The Floating Admiral. With members of The Detection Club. 1932.

In the Teeth of the Evidence (short stories, some Wimsey). 1939.

Sayers on Holmes: Essays and Fiction on Sherlock Holmes (one Wimsey story). 2001.

The Travelling Rug. 2005.

Plays

The Zeal of Thy House. 1937.

The Devil to Pay. 1939.

He That Should Come: A Nativity Play in One Act. 1939.

Love All: A Comedy of Manners. 1940.

The Man Born to Be King: A Play-Cycle on the Life of Our Lord and Saviour Jesus Christ. 1943.

The Just Vengeance: The Lichfield Festival Play. 1946.

The Emperor Constantine: A Chronicle. 1951

Apologetics

Begin Here; a Statement of Faith. 1940.

The Mind of the Maker. 1941.

Creed or Chaos? And Other Essays in Popular Theology. 1949.

Christian Letters to a Post-Christian World A Selection of Essays. Eerdmans, 1969.

The Whimsical Christian: 18 Essays. 1978.

Spiritual Writings. 1993.

Other writings

Op. I. 1916.

Catholic Tales and Christian Songs. 1918.

Tristan in Brittany. 1929.

Even the Parrot: Exemplary Conversations for Enlightened Children. 1944.

Unpopular Opinions; Twenty-One Essays. 1946.

The Divine Comedy by Dante Alighieri.
—*Volume 1: Hell.* 1949.
—*Volume 2: Purgatory.* 1955.
—*Volume 3: Paradise (completed by Barbara Reynolds).* 1962.

Introductory Papers on Dante. 1955.

Further Papers on Dante. 1957.

The Song of Roland. 1957.

The Poetry of Search and the Poetry of Statement. 1963.

Wilkie Collins: A Critical and Biographical Study. 1977.

Poetry of Dorothy L. Sayers (ed. Ralph Hone). 1996.

Letters of Dorothy L Sayers (ed. Barbara Reynolds)
—*Volume 1: 1899-1936: The Making of a Detective Novelist.* 1996.
—*Volume 2: 1937-1943: From Novelist to Playwright.* 1997.
—*Volume 3: 1944-1950: A Noble Daring.* 1999.
—*Volume 4: 1951-1957: In the Midst of Life.* 2000.
—*Volume 5: Child and Woman of her Time.* 2002.

Selected Secondary Sources: Books

Brown, Janice, *The Seven Deadly Sins in the Work of Dorothy L. Sayers.* Kent State UP, 1998.

Dean, Christopher, ed. *Studies in Sayers: Essays Presented to Barbara Reynolds on the 80th Birthday.* Dorothy L Sayers Society, 1994.

—— *Encounters with Lord Peter.* Dorothy L Sayers Society, 1991.

Downing, Crystal. *Writing Performances: The Stages of Dorothy Sayers.* Palgrave Macmillan, 2004.

McGregor, Robert Kuhn, and Ethan Lewis. *Conundrums for the Long Week-End: England, Dorothy L. Sayers, and Lord Peter Wimsey.* Kent State UP, 2000.

Reynolds, Barbara, ed. *Further Studies in Sayers: Essays Presented to Dr. Barbara Reynolds on Her 90th Birthday, 13th June, 2004.* Dorothy L Sayers Society, 2004.

—— *Studies in Sayers: Essays Presented to Dr. Barbara Reynolds on Her 80th Birthday.* Dorothy L Sayers Society, 1994.

Simmons, Laura K. *Creed without Chaos: Exploring Theology in the Writings of Dorothy L. Sayers.* Baker Academic, 2005.

Selected Secondary Sources: Articles, Chapters, Dissertations, etc.

Beach, Sarah. "Harriet in Rehearsal: Hilary Thorpe in *The Nine Tailors.*" *Mythlore* 19.3 (#73) (1993): 37–39, 65.

Christopher, Joe R. "Dorothy L. Sayers and the Inklings." *Mythlore* 4.1 (1976): 8-9.

Connelly, Kelly C. "From Detective Fiction to Detective Literature: Psychology in the Novels of Dorothy L. Sayers and Margaret Millar." *CLUES: A Journal of Detection* 25.3 (Spring 2007): 35–47.

Doughan, David. "Tolkien, Sayers, Sex and Gender." *Proceedings of the J.R.R. Tolkien Centenary Conference, 1992*. Eds. Reynolds, Patricia and Glen H. GoodKnight. Altadena: Milton Keynes Tolkien Society, 1992. 356-59.

Downing, Crystal. "The Orthodoxology of Dorothy L. Sayers." *Seven: An Anglo-American Literary Review* 22 (2005): 29-44.

Epperson, W.R. "The Repose of a Very Delicate Balance: Postulants and Celebrants of the Sacrament of Marriage in the Detective Fiction of Dorthy L. Sayers." *Mythlore* 6.4 (#22) (1979): 33–36.

Gorman, Anita G., and Leslie R. Mateer. "The Medium Is the Message: *Busman's Honeymoon* as Play, Novel, and Film." *CLUES: A Journal of Detection* 23.4 (Summer 2005): 54–62.

Haack, Susan. "After My Own Heart: Dorothy L. Sayers's Feminism." *New Criterion* (2001): 10-14.

Hannay, Margaret P. "Head Versus Heart in Dorothy L. Sayers' Gaudy Night." *Mythlore* 6.3 (#21) (1979): 33-37.

Heilbrun, Carolyn G. "Sayers, Lord Peter, and Harriet Vane at Oxford." *Hamlet's Mother and Other Women*, Columbia UP, 1990, pp. 252-259.

Lennard, John. "Of Purgatory and Yorkshire: Dorothy L. Sayers and Reginald Hill's Divine Comedy." *Of Modern Dragons and other essays on Genre Fiction.* Humanities-Ebooks, 2007, pp. 33–55.

Loades, Ann. "Dorothy L. Sayers and Dante's Beatrice." *Seven: An Anglo-American Literary Review* 10 (1993): 97-106.

—— "Dorothy L. Sayers: War and Redemption." *C. S. Lewis and Friends: Faith and the Power of Imagination*, edited by David Hein and Edward Henderson, London: SPCK, 2011, pp. 53–70.

Price, M. ""All Shall Love Me and Despair': The Figure of Lilith in Tolkien, Lewis, Williams, and Sayers." *Mythlore* 9.1 (#31) (1982): 3–7, 26.

Ralph, George. "Dorothy L. Sayers and the Proper Work of the Playwright." *Seven: An Anglo-American Literary Review* 7 (1986): 107-16.

Reynolds, Barbara. "Dorothy L. Sayers and War." *Seven: An Anglo-American Literary Review* 20 (2003): 33-47.

Rossen, Janice. "Oxford *in Loco Parentis*: The College as Mother in Dorothy Sayers' *Gaudy Night*." *University Fiction*, edited by David Bevan, Rodopi, 1990, pp. 139-56.

Scowcroft, P. L. "The Detective Fiction of Dorothy L. Sayers: A Source for the Social Historian?" *Seven: An Anglo-American Literary Review* 5 (1984): 70-83.

Siebald, Manfred. "Temptation at Canterbury: T. S. Eliot's Murder in the Cathedral and Dorothy L. Sayers's the Zeal of Thy House." *Seven: An Anglo-American Literary Review* 10 (1993): 107-26.

Sørsdal, Randi, *From Mystery to Manners: A Study of Five Detective Novels by Dorothy L. Sayers*, Masters thesis, University of Bergen, bora.uib.no.

Stein, Thomas Michael. "University Detective Fiction Then and Now: Dorothy L. Sayers's *Gaudy Night* and Amanda Cross's *Death in a Tenured Position*." *Seven: An Anglo-American Literary Review* 10 (1993): 31-42.

Wood, Bethany. "Incorporation of the Incar(Nation): Dorothy L. Sayers's *The Man Born to Be King*." *Ecumenica* 3.2 (2010): 7-30.

Young, Laurel. "Dorothy L. Sayers and the New Woman Detective Novel." *CLUES: A Journal of Detection* 23.4 (Summer 2005): 39–53.

Index

Ezekiel 157; Genesis 34, 53-54; Hebrews 34; Isaiah 4; James 156; Job 46; John 156, 229; Judges 41; Luke 84, 116n26, 156, 226; Mark 156; Matthew 34, 50, 78, 114, 156, 226; II Peter 156; Psalms 41, 104, 131; Revelation 156; Song of Solomon 50, 106; I Timothy 156

Biggs, Sir Impey 16-17

black characters 218; "nigger" as used by Sayers 215, 218

The Black Mask (fictional pulp magazine) 217-218

blackmail 54

blood imagery and symbolism 33-35, 38-39, 53-56, 59, 64-65; *see also* wine imagery and symbolism

Bloomsbury (region of London) 17, 61, 122, 187-211; Bloomsbury Group 189-191, 193-194, 197; Omega Workshop 205

Bluebeard 45

Blundell, Superintendent 94-95, 208

Boiardo, Matteo Maria. *Orlando Innamorato* 186

Bolshevism 205

Book of Common Prayer 33, 157, 179, 209, 228

Booth, Caroline (Lucy) 19

Boyes, Rev. Arthur 14

Boyes, Philip 11, 13, 15-16, 21-22, 166, 171, 204-205, 208

bread and salt imagery and symbolism 38-39

Bredon, Death *see* Wimsey, Lord Peter as Death Bredon

Brighella (*commedia dell' arte* character) 76

British Museum 188, 201, 204

Brown, Father *see* Chesterton, G.K. "The Flying Stars"

Bunter, Meredith 171

Bunter, Mervyn 3, 6, 14-15, 17, 21, 52, 56, 61-62, 90, 100-105, 107, 109-112, 114, 145, 171, 203, 206, 217, 219. Experiences in WWI 6

Burne-Jones, Sir Edward (painter) 131, 133

Burnett, Frances Hodgson. *A Little Princess* 143

Bursar (in *Gaudy Night*) 142

Busman's Honeymoon 4-5, 7, 9, 99-115, 118, 144-146, 150, 152-153, 161-162, 165, 209, 219-220; origin as a play 99, 124, 150; murder weapon (cactus) 99, 102, 105, 112-113; *Prothalamion* 99-100; *Epithalamion* 113-115, 146

Byrne, James (Harlequin actor) 78

Cain (Bible character) 34, 53

Cambridge 190-191, 222

Camelot 134, 136

Campbell, Sandy 132-133, 137

candles 104, 106

264

egg themes, symbolism, and mo-
tifs 16-22, 24; omelette 16-20,
22, 24; folklore of 16, 21,
25n7
Egg, Montague 86n43
ego 174
Einstein, Albert 124
Eliot, T.S. 227, 232; as play-
wright 232. *Murder in the Ca-
thedral* 22; "The Waste Land"
84n3
Elizabeth, Queen 104
"The Enchanted Garden" 186
Endicott, Mr. 40-41, 43
"The Entertaining Episode of the
Article in Question" 203
Envy (*Invidia*) 129
eucatastrophe in Sayers's novels
235
Euripides 80
Eustace, Robert (co-author of
Documents in the Case) 124
evangelicalism 190
Eve 53, 122, 146
*Even the Parrot: Exemplary
Conversations for Enlight-
ened Children* 185-186
extrasensory perception 74

fairy tales 60
farce 28, 48, 53, 58, 65
Farren, Gilda 118, 131-134, 136-
137, 147
Farren, Hugh 131-133, 137
Faust legend 146; Helen in 146
female characters in Sayers's
novels 117-148; "failure of
understanding" 118

female gaze 43
femininity 23
Fenchurch St. Paul 6, 90, 93;
flood at 93-94, 96
Fentiman, Captain George 8
fertility and infertility themes
and symbolism 123, 130, 166-
169, 175, 177, 179
Findlater, Vera 120-123, 147,
217
fish imagery and symbolism 78,
86n33
Five Red Herrings 8, 30-31, 118,
131-137, 153, 200, 219
Fleming, (John) Anthony (Sayers's son by Bill White) 167,
196-199, 210, 228-229, 231
Fleming, Oswald Atherton
"Mac" 167, 196-197, 199-
200, 210, 228-229; alcoholism
167, 207, shell-shock 167
folklore, British 16
Forster, E.M. 189
France and Paris 163, 171, 193,
203
free will 96
Freke, Julian 194, 200, 216
Fry, Roger 189-190
Frye, Northrop. *Anatomy of Criticism* 28-30, 34, 231, 234-235

garden imagery and symbolism
108
Garden, Cremorna (Rosanna
Wrayburn) 13, 19, 21-22
Garland, Leila 29, 44, 49-50, 62-
63

Nancy-Lou Patterson, Illustration for *Mythprint* 154, 30.5-6 (1993).
Further reproduction prohibited.